外教社跨文化交际丛书·外语教育系列

# 跨学段跨文化能力教学

## 从理论到实践

# Teaching Intercultural Competence Across the Age Range

## *From Theory to Practice*

Manuela Wagner　Dorie Conlon Perugini　Michael Byram　编

虞怡达　导读

上海外语教育出版社
外教社 SHANGHAI FOREIGN LANGUAGE EDUCATION PRESS

**图书在版编目（CIP）数据**

跨学段跨文化能力教学：从理论到实践 / (美) 曼
努埃拉·瓦格纳 (Manuela Wagner)，(美) 多里·康伦
·佩鲁吉尼 (Dorie Conlon Perugini)，(英) 迈克尔·
拜拉姆 (Michael Byram) 编；虞怡达导读. —上海：
上海外语教育出版社，2023
（外教社跨文化交际丛书. 外语教育系列）
ISBN 978-7-5446-7813-1

Ⅰ.①跨… Ⅱ.①曼…②多…③迈…④虞… Ⅲ.
①外语教学－教学研究 Ⅳ.①H09

中国国家版本馆CIP数据核字 (2023) 第113815号

图字：09-2022-0465号

出版发行：**上海外语教育出版社**
（上海外国语大学内）邮编：200083
电　　话：021-65425300（总机）
电子邮箱：bookinfo@sflep.com.cn
网　　址：http://www.sflep.com
责任编辑：田慧肖

印　　刷：上海信老印刷厂
开　　本：890×1240　1/32　印张 6.875　字数 300 千字
版　　次：2023 年 10 月第 1 版　2023 年 10 月第 1 次印刷

书　　号：ISBN 978-7-5446-7813-1
定　　价：30.00 元

本版图书如有印装质量问题，可向本社调换
质量服务热线：4008-213-263

# 外教社跨文化交际丛书编委会

# 总　序

　　跨文化交际学是一门在传播学等学科理论的基础上,与人类学、心理学、语言学、文化学以及社会学等相互交叉而发展起来的学科。其实,不同文化间的交流古已有之,但是真正将文化交流进行理论研究进而发展成"跨文化交际学",还只是近四五十年间的事情。想要深入探究这门学科,我们首先要了解它的起源。

　　20 世纪 60 年代是信息技术和交通技术高度发展的年代。随着科技的进步,空间距离大大缩短,各种文化间的交流日益频繁。但是空间距离的缩小并不意味着人们之间的文化距离或是心理距离可以瞬间缩短。与之相反的是,人们不能再用旧有的文化观念和思维方式来理解和解释日新月异的世界里出现的各种新问题。同时,文化差异滋生众多的交际失误、矛盾和冲突,反而使人们的心理距离加大。矛盾和冲突的背后不仅仅是利益或者领土的争夺,也不仅仅是政治和意识形态的分歧,而更多的是文化和价值观念上的巨大隔阂——正是这些隔阂使"地球村"中的人们虽然身在"咫尺"之间,却有如隔天涯之感。

　　美国作为一个多民族、多种族的国家自然而然成为跨文化交际研究的兴起之地,其中以美国人类学家 Edward T. Hall 为代表的一些学者在前人研究成果的基础上提出了跨文化交际的理论,现在学界也一致将他的著作 *The Silent Language*(Anchor Books, 1959)当作是这一学科的奠基之作。

　　到了 20 世纪七八十年代,学者们把研究重点逐渐从对比和分析不同文化交际(Cross-cultural Communication)中的差异转到研究跨文化交际(Intercultural Communication)动态多变的过程中去。以此为基点,William B. Gudykunst 等一批学者建构了动态的跨文化交际理论。理论的突破带来了学科的快速发展,跨文化交际研究所涉及的学科越来越多,研究的内容更加丰富,研究方法日益科学。学科的发展引起了世界各国学者空前广泛的关注,跨文化交际学被引进大学课堂,相关的研究学会和专业学刊相继出现,各种国际学术研讨会也定期举行。现在只要在网上简单查询一下相关书目,我们就会发现此类专著多达几百种,在刊物上发表的论文更是不胜枚举。William B. Gudykunst 曾在其著作 *Cross-cultural and Intercultural Communication*(Sage Publications,2003)一书中总结了 15 种不同的跨文化交际理论。理论研究和探索上的巨大进步标志着跨文化交际学的学科发展日臻成熟。

进入新世纪,"地球村"每个角落的每个公民都不同程度地被卷入了经济一体化和全球化的浪潮。同时,人们清楚地意识到全球化不等于一元化。在多元文化并存的时代中,个人之间、社会全体之间、民族之间乃至国家之间,无不存在着文化差异甚至文化沟壑。培养对文化差异的敏感性,缩短文化距离,发展跨文化交际能力,已经成为新时代的迫切需求。由此,我们不难预见到跨文化交际研究会在 21 世纪被逐步推向高潮。

在关注国际学科发展趋势的同时,让我们把目光转向中国。虽然我国历史上早有注重语言与文化、语言与社会研究的传统,但是现代的跨文化交际研究在我国的起步还要追溯至 20 世纪的 80 年代。当时随着国内学界对于语言学和文化研究的不断重视,在"文化热"和"反思热"的影响下,语言研究人文化成为新的热点,这无疑为跨文化交际研究的兴起奠定了基础。改革开放扩大了国际间的学术交往,外语界的学者和教师成为国内首先接触到跨文化交际研究的一批人,他们理所当然地成为了这一学科的研究主力。我们可以这么说:20 世纪 80 年代是跨文化交际学诞生、成长和发展的关键十年。一方面,海外归来的学者把西方有关跨文化交际理论、研究方法和教学实践介绍和引进到中国;另一方面,国内研究者在学习和借鉴的同时,在继承前人成果的基础上,结合中国实际,多方位、多角度地探索和开发我国跨文化交际的学科外延,开创了初步繁荣的研究局面。

外语教师和对外汉语教师是我国跨文化交际研究领域的主力军。他们在教学的过程中认识到跨文化交际能力的培养应当成为外语教育的重要内容,外语教学必须与文化相结合。在 20 世纪 80 年代末,国内一部分外语院校首先推出了跨文化交际学课程。时至今日,我国已有几十所大学的外语院系开设了这门课程。

1995 年,首届中国跨文化交际国际研讨会在哈尔滨召开,来自世界

20多个国家和地区的几百名学者进行了学术交流与探讨。中国跨文化交际研究会也在这次会议中正式成立——这标志着跨文化交际研究在中国迎来了一个新纪元。自学会成立以来,已定期组织了6次国际研讨会。同时有些院校也多次组织大型研讨会,广泛开展国内不同地区间和国际间的学术交流,跨文化交际研究得到了空前迅速的发展。

广大教师、语言学者们兼收并蓄,著书立说,撰写论文,编写教材。据不完全统计,目前出版的专著和教材多达几十本,发表的论文也有2000篇以上。他们研究和探讨的内容丰富多样,涵盖范围广泛;有些学者和教师的研究更是对西方学者的某些理论提出质疑,提出了自己的视角独特的观点。

由于学科性质所决定,跨文化交际研究比其他学科更需要不同文化间的交流。实际上,中国跨文化交际研究会已成为国际大家庭的一部分,并为推动跨文化交际研究在世界范围上的发展做出了应有的贡献。我们的研究会中有不少教师学者同时也是国际学会会员,他们或在国际学会组织和国际学刊中承担重要工作,或是经常受邀参加在海外举行的学术会议,在会上交流论文。不少论文受到国际学界的好评,并在国际学刊上发表。我国的跨文化交际研究学者也在国外出版他们的专著,传播中国在这一领域的研究成果。

回顾这20余年的学科发展,我们也应清楚地意识到前进路上存在着的诸多问题。首先,在理论研究方面,正如王宗炎先生所指出的,"收集采购之功多,提炼转化之功少",我们还没有形成具有中国文化特点的理论。William B. Gudykunst教授也曾指出亚洲学者需要创建适合自己文化的交际理论。只有学习和借鉴而没有发展和改造,没有结合自己文化特点的理论,是不可能把跨文化交际研究建成一门适合中国国情的学科的。其次,由于理论指导不足,我们的研究多集中在文化对比方面,对动态多变的交际过程的研究和探讨不够,在研究方法和研究内容上尚需要更多的探索和拓展,这些都影响了我们在这一领域的进一步发展。

在新的世纪,我们需要进一步开阔视野,发展我国的跨文化交际研究,推动此领域的学科建设,加强此领域的教学和教材建设,以满足广大教师、研究生以及各方面读者的需要。上海外语教育出版社出于推动我国跨文化交际研究的考虑,决定推出"外教社跨文化交际丛书"。丛书既引进国外权威力作,也出版我国学者的著述,还有中外专家的合力之作。

我国读者可以通过这套丛书学习和借鉴来自不同文化背景的学者的真知灼见，在领略我国学者和专家的新思维和新成果的同时，还可以欣赏各种文化交流的结晶。我们相信"外教社跨文化交际丛书"对于今后我国跨文化交际学的发展将会起到极为重要的作用。在此，我们代表丛书编委会对上海外语教育出版社的大力支持表示诚挚的谢意。

**胡文仲**
北京外国语大学
**贾玉新**
哈尔滨工业大学
2006 年 4 月

# 序　言

　　21世纪的全球化是对教育的挑战,也为教育改革开拓了新的视域。面临这一挑战,外语,作为构建人类社会关系与和谐全球社会的重要人类社会资源,应当发挥其独特的作用。培养世界公民将是21世纪赋予外语教育的重要历史使命。无论我们从事何种语言教学——母语/一语、二语、外语或其他民族/族群语——实质上,无一不是全球化进程中的一部分,其目的无一不是为了培养国家/全球公民。外语教育在(全球)公民教育中有其无与伦比的、其他学科所不具备的人文价值,但目前我们很少意识到这一点。因此,外语教育政策制定者、实践者和学习者在21世纪正面临的挑战的确是前所未有。

　　然而,我们目前的外语教学是否胜任21世纪所赋予的历史使命?综观外语教学现状,我们认识到应该深入发掘外语这一重要的人类社会资源,以使外语教学向全球公民教育的转变成为可能。

　　自20世纪60年代至今的几十年中,随着国内和国际大环境的不断变化,以及语言文化研究的逐步深入,外语教学不断应变,与时俱进,实现了以目标语语言能力为教学目标向以目标语交际能力为目标的跨越。但在21世纪全球化的多元文化时代,学者们开始意识到目标语的交际能力难以确保不同文化之间人们的相互沟通和理解:母语/一语的交际能力是国家价值观的标志,是国家身份(国家公民)的象征,但不同文化的人们对作为共同语的英语或其他语言的交际能力的习得能否说明他们就共享了同一套价值观,从而可使他们的跨文化交际得以顺利进行?以目的语的交际能力为目标的外语教学能否像通过母语教育培养国家公民那样培养世界公民?由于多元文化的存在,价值观、信仰之相对性的存在以及应运而生的文化、语言、社会语言、社会语用、概念相对性的存在、不同文化之间的交际远比我们所预想的复杂得多。仅以概念相对性为例:我国及其他国家英语使用者都用通用的英语单词

"citizenship"表达"公民、国民"的概念,然而,这一概念所内含的核心价值却因文化而异,我国与西方所使用的这同一概念的核心价值便相去甚远。且不谈西方国家对"citizenship"之概念在语义方面的认知差异,他们的"citizenship"价值内核大体上是"民主"框架内的人权和个性自由,而我们这一概念之内核则更加突出道德和社会责任义务,尽管两者是人类尊严的既对立又互补的不可分割的两个侧面。

近年来在交际能力基础上所构建的跨文化交际能力概念会大大促进不同文化间的交际,但促进这一能力之习得仍然难以胜任世界公民教育的重任。我们需要的是既能确保不同文化间的交际得以进行,同时又能保留不同文化之相对差异的一种跨文化交际能力,一种与全球公民概念相匹配的跨文化交际能力。

为达到培养全球公民的目标,当下外语教学所匮乏的至少有以下两个重要方面:一是确立人之作为公民的核心价值为起始点和终极目标的教育观,也就是确立人之作为人的基本道德的人文价值的教育观(the core value of a person as a human being);另一点是由于这一人文价值因时空而异,即不同文化以及不同文化在不同历史(经济、历史、政治等)发展阶段对人之作为人/公民的基本价值有不同的经历、不同的内涵、不同的解读、不同的界定。这意味着在多元文化平等共存的 21世纪,任何文化之价值都有其存在的合理性(reasonableness),这也意味着在多元文化平等共存的 21 世纪,任何文化都不能把自己对这一价值(譬如对人的基本价值)的经历、自己的文化内涵、解读和界定强加给他人。对不同文化、不同价值观(政治或宗教的)、不同生活方式,我们应当持有赞同、欣赏、理解、包容和接受的态度;但当这些方面发生冲突时,我们并不能盲目地理解或接受某些观点,而是要对它们进行理性的思辨和批评。这意味着,我们需要的是一种批判精神,而且,批判之标准有的是普适的,有的是因文化而异的,是多元的。我们所需要的是一种公认的人文价值标准,一种如费孝通先生所说的"各美其美,美人之美,美美与共,世界大同"的平等共处的人文价值观。

为配合这一发展趋势,上海外语教育出版社在"外教社跨文化交际丛书"的基础上,又引进推出一批从跨文化视角进行外语教学的权威力作。这一批以国际著名外语教育家 Michael Byram 教授为首的学者们的著作,是英国多语出版公司(Multilingual Matters LTD)出版的丛书"Languages for Intercultural Communication and Education"(LICE)

中众多专著/文集的一部分。在这些著作中,学者们对以跨文化交际为目标的外语教学进行了开创性探索和实践,对教学理论、课堂实践和成果评估等进行了全方位的论析和阐述。他们所提出的教学目标、教学框架、能力模式、概念、理论、观点、途径、方法以及对整个教学结构的设想,不仅具有挑战性和时代的前瞻性,而且尤其可贵的是,具有很强的可操作性。这些远见卓识无疑引导着当今世界外语教学改革的潮流。

应特别提及的是,Byram 教授在其《从外语教育到跨文化公民教育》(*From Foreign Language Education to Education for Intercultural Citizenship*)一书中,在原有的交际能力以及早期的跨文化交际能力概念的基础上,构建了以"批判性跨文化自觉"为中心的、与世界公民相互补的"跨文化能力"概念。这一概念创新旨在帮助实现外语教学向外语教育的转变,实现以语言能力、目标语的交际能力以及早期界定的跨文化交际能力为目标的外语教学向全球公民教育的跨越。Byram 教授的研究成果不仅在理论上为全球公民教育提供了依据,而且在实际教学实践中也有极强的可操作性,因为他把这一跨文化能力细化为具体的教学目标,使将公民教育变成课堂的教学实践成为可能。

Byram 教授及其他学者的教学经验和研究成果是在欧盟的背景中构建的,如何将他们的经验运用到我国的实际需求,需要深入结合我国特有的外语教学理论和实践框架,但其中所涉及的种种探索对我国外语教育无疑会有重要的指导意义和参考价值,必定会引发新的思考。

感谢上海外语教育出版社,为我们提供这样一套好书,为我们构建了跨文化交际的学习空间。相信本套丛书的出版会促进我国作为世界公民的外语教育的蓬勃发展。


贾玉新
哈尔滨工业大学

# 导　　读

　　随着全球化的发展,人员流动和人文交流增加,语言课程中对跨文化内容的需求越来越大。如何教授文化成为语言课程中的热点,发展学生的跨文化能力也随之成为语言课程的培养目标。但是,由于人们对跨文化能力的本质及其发展规律的认知还不够充分,语言学习和文化沟通之间的联系往往被忽视。在操作层面上,跨文化课程设计支持相对不足,合适的教学材料和活动缺乏,因此如何在语言课程中融入跨文化内容对广大语言教师来说至今依旧是难点。

　　近年来,我国跨文化外语教学的意义、目标和内涵逐步凸显和清晰,但跨文化外语教学实践的相关研究还相对滞后,跨文化外语教学实践与理论研究成果存在脱节的现象。课堂中跨文化教学内容有一定的盲目性和随意性,尤其是不同学段之间的教学内容和衔接比较模糊,教材、教法、测评等各个教学环节都急需提升水平。

　　顺应外语教育发展趋势,上海外语教育出版社引进由Manuela Wagner、Dorie Conlon Perugini和Michael Byram所编的《跨学段跨文化能力教学:从理论到实践》(*Teaching Intercultural Competence Across the Age Range: From Theory to Practice*)一书。美国外语教学委员会(American Council of the Teaching of Foreign Languages, ACTFL)时任主席 Aleidine J. Moeller教授为本书撰写了前言。本书由英国出版社 Multilingual Matters 在2018年出版,是 "Languages for Intercultural Communication and Education" 丛书之一。该系列丛书关注语言和文化之间的关系以及跨文化交际能力的发展。

　　本书收录的教学实践来源于康涅狄格-格拉斯顿伯里-杜伦(UConn-Glastonbury-Durham)合作的教学项目。编者之一 Michael Byram博士是英国杜伦大学荣休教授,是语言教育与跨文化研究领域的国际著名学者。他提出的跨文化交际能力模型(Byram, 1997/2014)在外语界受到广泛关注和应用,该理论框架也为本书中的教学实践提供了理论基础。另一编者 Manuela Wagner 是康涅狄格大学外语教育部副教授,在该校教授名为"(语言)教育中跨文化能力的发展"的研究生课程。她多年来一直与格拉斯顿伯里公立学校外语项目合作,与中小学教师建立了教师实践共同体。第三位编者 Dorie Conlon Perugini 是格拉斯顿伯里公立学校瑙布克小学的西班牙语教师,毕业于康涅狄格大学尼格教育学院,拥有西班牙语教育课程和教学的本科和硕士学位,还获得了中康涅狄格州立大学对小学世界语言教学的交叉认可。

本书展示了一群教育工作者在不同学段的语言课堂中系统应用跨文化能力(Intercultural Competence, IC)理论的尝试。通过整合参与式行动研究,不同学段的外语教育工作者有机会探索应用跨文化能力的概念框架,批判性地反思他们在语言课堂中的跨文化教学实践,并用于促进自己的专业发展。本书的引进将在以下两方面对我国的跨文化外语教学实践产生影响:

一方面,本书为我国跨文化外语教学实践及其研究提供了多学段的借鉴和参考。

外语教学实践研究是外语教育学理论和现实的接口,连接着理论探索和现实问题。外语教育研究与实践领域存在着"外语教育教学理论与实践严重割裂"(王文斌、柳鑫淼,2021:2)这一亟待解决的学科问题。

跨文化外语教学领域中,这一问题也较为凸显。核心问题在于,每个学段适切的跨文化能力教学目标和内容是什么?为了解决这一问题,在2022年7月26日的首届"中国跨文化教育与国际传播能力建设高端论坛"上,《外语教育中的跨文化能力教学参考框架》(后定为《中国外语教育跨文化能力教学参考框架》)正式发布。该框架对大中小学各学段英语教学中的跨文化能力教学的内容、目标进行了界定和描述,旨在为一线英语教师开展跨文化教学实践提供参考。

国内一线外语教师迫切需要通过实践来理解和操作该框架。该参考框架的适切性和有效性验证均在上海的学校完成,实验对象和地区范围不够广泛(张红玲、吴诗沁,2022)。因此通过参考和借鉴本书中的跨文化教学实践,我国各学段一线教师可以结合参考框架,科学、合理地选择和设计外语课堂中的跨文化能力教学内容,精心设计教学过程、实践活动,利用各类资源细化实施要求,并及时对教学过程和效果进行总结和反馈,是以进一步推动跨文化能力教学方法和教学评价研究。

另一方面,本书的实践方式体现了实践共同体(community of practice)的重要性,在提升实践水平的基础上进一步促进教师发展。

教师发展与外语教学实践密切相关,二者相互滋养(张文忠等,2022)。以解决实践性问题为导向,对于解决教师教育中的"知行脱节"问题,提高教师专业发展的实际效果具有很强的启发意义。同时,面向不同学段学生的教师形成实践共同体,"他们对自己所做的事情有共同的关注或热情,并在定期互动的过程中学习如何做得更好"(Wenger,2011)。本书中的教学实践共同体充分体现了"共同的愿景""合作的文化""共享的机制""对话的氛围"等思想精华(张平、朱鹏,2009),对于发展教师跨文化外语教学实践性知识,培育合作性的教师文化,提升教师实践反思和解决问题的能力有着极大的参考价值。书中的教学实践对我国外语教师跨越学段地差异化掌握跨文化外语教学理论、更新课程理念和提高教学能力具有借鉴意义。同时,本书中新手教师、专家教师和指导专家之间的合作可应用于现阶段蓬勃发展的虚拟教研室的建设中。

本书1—7章为教学实践章节。除了六个小学和中学教育项目外,书中还加入大学在线入门德语课程用来扩展所涵盖的学段。章节的排列顺序按照学段展开:其中第1—3章为小学学段,第4章为初中学段,高中学段为第5—6章,大学学段为第7章。收录的教学实践所教授的语言虽然是西班牙语和德语,但是不同语种在跨文化能力教学实践上的经验可以共享,可为国内外语教师带来不同角度的启示。

本书中的教学实践章节(1—7章)围绕以下思路展开:

(1)跨文化能力理论基础

绪论介绍了本书中所有教学实践的理论基础:Michael Byram的跨文化能力框架。它可以被描述为识别跨文化能力主要元素的一种手段,因此也是可行的教学目标。它为教师提供了批判性文化意识的目标,超越了知识和技能的教学,成为实现语言教学关键教育目的的一种手段。

(2)介绍特定教学环境

教学环境包括学生的年龄段和学段要求、外语水平、班级大小、教师背景等。进而以理论为基础选取并结合课程单元关键问题(essential question)进行跨文化教学设计。本书认为跨文化教学活动的设计不应偏离现有课程，也不应妨碍学生实现单元的内容和交流目标，但需要通过重新设计，尽可能多地实现当前课程未达到的跨文化能力相关的目标。

所谓关键问题是不能用一句简短的句子回答的问题，其目的是激发思考和探究，并引出更多问题。关键问题又发展出若干问题，学生可以通过回答和讨论这些问题加深对关键问题的理解。

（3）实施教学，汇报教学结果

教师对教学活动的设计、教学语言的使用、教学技术的使用、课堂评价的选用以及教学成效和研究方法等内容进行汇报描述。

（4）教学反思

教师对有效或是无效的实践进行总结和反思，包括成功的实践、面临的挑战以及未来的努力方向。

除了1—7章的教学实践，本书还回顾了海外学习（study abroad）和跨文化能力教学相关的文献，启发外语教师充分利用海外学习的资源（第8章）。结语主要由Rita Oleksak撰写，她是格拉斯顿伯里公立学区外语和英语学习部主任，正是由于她的支持和鼓励，本书中的教学实践项目才得以顺利完成。下面介绍本书各章的主要内容。

# 第1章　世界各地的住房

本章作者带着4年级学生一起反思不同文化中的住房问题。本章要解决的关键问题是："我们和加勒比海地区的人们有什么联系？"

作者汇报了两轮课程的演进，通过活动设计向学生展现不同的生活空间，并通过这些生活空间可能位于何处的第一印象来引发更深层次的理解，以"促进对目标社会内文化差异的理解，并改进学习者对目标语言和社会的态度"（Abrams, 2002: 144）。学生们还需要描绘出生活空间的家谱图，展现出了住房的多样性和复杂性。针对低年级学生，两位教师在保证学生不过分焦虑的同时尽可能多地用西班牙语授课，确保内容不会因为缺乏高阶词汇而失去跨文化方面的复杂性。

在尝试评估学生的跨文化能力时，教师们给学生布置了反思作业进行自我评估。首先，反思作业是教学计划的一部分，目的是让学生回顾和反思他们的学习经历。其次，这些反思也为教师研究者提供了学生学习的证据，使他们更加直观地了解4年级学生在跨文化认知方面的进步和熟练程度。

学生对其他文化的兴趣和开放性得以激发。学生通过反思自己的先入之见，进而理解并解构现有的刻板印象，这有助于他们持久地理解不同文化中住房的复杂性。同时教师们对家谱图活动指出了未来可以改进的方向，今后会要求学生在完成访谈后确定他们发现了哪些关于他们家庭住房的新信息。两位教师在教学反思中肯定了高度发展的网络技术对项目全程合作的促进作用。合作虽然艰辛，但许多问题变得清晰，可以在未来的实践迭代中得到改进。

## 第2章　发现交通工具

本章作者邀请她的4年级学生进行虚拟实地考察，探索波多黎各的交通。本章的关键问题也是："我们和加勒比海地区的人们有什么联系？"本章的关键问题意味着学生需要有机会比较美国和加勒比地区使用的交通工具之间的相似之处和不同之处。

除了学习与交通相关的新词汇，学生通过Google Earth iPad应用程序导航对波多黎各进行虚拟实地考察。他们所做的不是观看当地美景，而是评估可用的各种交通工具，在使用目标语有限知识的同时，能够运用批判性思维技能完成复杂的真实任务。

教师使用Bennett（2004）跨文化敏感性发展模型（DMIS）来描述学生的态度变化，看他们处在模型中六个阶段的哪个阶段。除此之外，为了评估学生的知识和态度，教师还决定使用日记为学生创造自由和自然地表达自我的机会。由于4年级学生无法用目标语解释他们尚未学习的概念和想法，因此日记可以用英语完成。

本章作者认为撰写反思日记是评估学生IC发展的有力工具，并为教师如何计划后续课程提供了指导。但阅读和回应每个学生的日记耗时巨大，因此需要重新考虑写作频率。作者仍计划使用反思性写作作为衡量学生IC的工具，并考虑在每项活动中加强内容和语言学习的结合，保持使用目标语言教学。

## 第3章　运用五种感官来探索城市

本章作者帮助6年级学生使用他们的五种感官来了解不同的城市。

本章的关键问题是："我看到或做了什么独一无二的事？"

　　两位教师设计了三个活动，循序渐进，目的是不但扩展学生的知识面，提升学生的跨文化交际意识，而且挑战学生原有的对他者文化和自己文化的态度。在第一个活动中，学生们被要求使用西班牙语，用他们的感官来定义"城市"这个词。为了进一步挑战学生对其他文化甚至自己文化的潜在预设的态度和知识，在第二个活动中，两位教师要求学生找出那些他们认为代表城市环境的形象。在最后的活动中，学生被分成几个小组，每组被分配到某个具体的城市和文化环境中。目的是为学生提供机会，批判性地评估他们自己文化以及他者文化中的文化实践和文化产物。

　　三个活动层层推进，将学生在上一次活动中发展起来的不同文化的知识和态度应用于特定的城市和文化环境，从而发展学生的跨文化能力。学生们在了解墨西哥城等城市的同时也解构了他们对美国城市的刻板印象。

　　由于该年级学生的目标语言能力有限，讨论的范围和细节都受限，因此学生还完成了英语的书面反思，匿名回答了相关问题。这一系列活动既是教学手段，也是收集学习证据的手段。本章作者从各个维度寻找学习证据，以此分析学生跨文化能力的变化。

　　本章作者对教学研究方法进行了反思，希望在未来加入量化研究，呈现更多可衡量的结果。他们同时也指出目标语言使用有限，项目难度稍大的困扰，提出可以鼓励在其他学科科目中进行相关讨论的建议，例如社会研究或地理，学生可以用英语讨论该主题。

# 第4章　跨文化能力：反思日常生活

　　本章作者带领8年级的学生将他们与秘鲁农村地区学生的日常活动进行比较，帮助学生从不同的角度看待日常生活。8年级课程的关键问题是："什么是外国？"教师们决定采用daily routine（日常生活）单元的话题进行跨文化教学设计。

　　除了教授日常生活相关的词汇，教学中还使用了批判性思维卡片。卡片上的批判性思维问题为学生提供了一个初步框架来探索自身联系和发现的技能。通过这些问题，教师们能够观察学生的技能、知识、态度以及文化敏感性，甚至存在的偏见。教师们还安排了一系列课堂活动，如观看视频，给一位来访的秘鲁交换生用目标语言写信，与来自秘鲁的人进行真实的互动,并用英语反思写作。

修改后的单元激发了学生的好奇心,并打开了学生发现和理解文化差异的视野。他们开始反思自己的文化信仰,也发展了新的解释和联系的技能,并形成了新的态度,这些都是他们发展批判性文化意识的先决条件。

教师们则在实践中克服了"文化作为一种静态结构"的教学理念和操作方法,和学生一起努力打破了文化作为"可学习的事实"(Philips, 2001:1)的桎梏。学生能够认识到文化群体内行为的可变性,个人在文化创造中的参与作用,以及语言和文化在意义形成中的互动。

本章作者之一接受了教育技术(如Animoti、Adobe Voice、Kahoot、Thinglink)的培训,她意图将教育技术整合进外语教学实践,更创新性地使得学生成为问题解决者,获得在不断变化的全球社会中有效沟通和协作的技能。同时作者们也反思了课程合作安排以及跨学科相关内容给课程设计和实施带来的挑战。

# 第5章　多视角的移民体验

本章两位作者带领10年级和11年级学生体验和思考来自西班牙语不同地区的新移民在美国定居的挑战。参与这个项目的学生在这门课之前已经接受了10年的西班牙语学习,因此语言水平较之前章节的目标学生有了显著提高。本章的关键问题是:"我们是谁? 在多元化的社会中我们是谁?"项目探索将语言和内容融入课程,帮助学生更深入地了解移民经历。

该项目以一份问卷开始,教师们让学生匿名回答了他们对于美国社会中西班牙移民的看法和价值观,并使用结果来描述他们在Bennett(1993)的跨文化敏感性发展模型中所处的立场。该问卷还包括一个开放式的回答,由此获得质性研究数据。作者通过比较学生在项目前和项目后的观点来评估学习本单元对学生的影响。

课堂教学和评价中使用直接评价法(direct assessment),重在表现性评价(performance assessment)。例如设置一个移民家庭刚刚抵达美国的场景,学生需要承担家庭口译员的角色。他们的任务是帮助家庭安顿下来,为家庭的最佳利益行事。课堂教学注重使用DIE(distinguish, interpret, evaluate)的分解步骤。语言活动包括口语和书面语。最后教师要求学生使用《跨文化经历自传》(*Autobiography of Intercultural Encounters*)批判性地反思自己的经历以及其他人如何理解同样的经历。

在这一单元的学习后，学生们开始意识到移民群体在美国遭遇的不平等待遇。这个项目是真正情境化和有意义的，不仅因为学生学有所得，教师自身关于语言学习的信念也受到了挑战。本章还认为在如今日益多元化的社会中，移民主题是社会研究的重要部分，这一主题的学习和讨论可以整合到许多其他相关课程中去。

# 第6章 美与美学

本章两位作者以"美与美学"为主题，帮助11年级和12年级的学生从不同的角度思考美的构成。本章中的西班牙语课程是格拉斯顿伯里高中的大学先修课程（Advanced Placement, AP）和早期大学体验课程（Early College Experience, ECE）。该课程完全用西班牙语授课。所选单元的关键问题是："学习语言和文化如何改变了我们？"

在整个单元中，学生阅读各种关于美的文化意义的课文，并观看相关主题的视频。该单元采取了许多不同的观点，涉及美如何受历史、生物、数学、媒体、技术、经济等因素影响而变化。课程使用反向设计（backward design）来安排。在课程结束时，学生需要完成一个与西班牙语相关的美和美学元素的展示来呈现他们的跨文化能力，这既是一项形成性任务，也是终结性任务。

学生深入研究了他们选择的主题并摆脱了刻板印象。他们使用多样证据和多种视角来评估不同时间和空间现象中的美和与美相关的选择，分享对文化、对美的感知和见解，这是大多数班级以前从未考虑过的。这里要强调的是，相关的展示和讨论都用西班牙语进行。学生能够使用目标语言驾驭这些主题也证明了被跨文化视角学习激发的兴趣能够成为有助于学习目标语言的内在动机。学生们在选择文化元素以及如何表现文化元素方面拥有充分的自主权，得到的指导和要求很少。因此这个过程本身也培养了学生的自主权和对歧义的容忍度，同时整合并鼓励融入协作能力和创造力。在Byram的IC模型的基础上，课程提供评分量规让学生进行跨文化能力发展的自我评估。

本章对如何融入理论模型的其他维度进行了教学反思。同时，作者认为跨文化能力教学不应该局限于外语课堂：它是所有教育分支不可或缺的一部分，深深植根于以学生为中心的批判性教学法中。

## 第7章　跨文化在线：在在线语言课堂中发展跨文化能力

本章两位作者描述了他们在一所大学开设在线德语语言与文化课程时教授和评估跨文化能力的经验和挑战。课程实施混合式教学，包括实时在线互动（synchronous interaction）和线下互动（asynchronous interaction）。两位教师设计了培养非本质主义文化观的活动，同时发展学生相关社会语言和实用技能。

他们对学生跨文化能力发展进行形成性评估，认为教学活动也是评价手段，可以为学生提供各种机会，让他们在学习语言的同时探索跨文化能力。整合表现评估（integrated performance assessment, IPA）是主要使用的评价方法。在这样的评估设计中，单独的语言技能评价不是目标，学生需要综合使用语言来完成表现性评价任务。因此作者在课程设计中同时注重语言交际技能和跨文化内容，而对学生的语言产品（例如日记、网页、项目报告）的分析加深了他们对学生跨文化能力发展的理解，同时也促进了教学反思。

两位教师在反思中提到遇到的大多数挑战都与时间限制有关。虽然是德语课，教师依旧决定在每节课的最后五到十分钟里用英语讨论在线课程中的问题，他们认为这样有助于解构跨文化能力教学中的问题，培养学生对跨文化问题的好奇心。

## 第8章　通过海外学习和经历发展跨文化能力

本章为文献综述，梳理并回答了教师如何通过海外学习和经历培养跨文化能力的问题。本章认为我们不应该假设仅仅有国外生活的经历就能让教师不费吹灰之力地教授跨文化能力。教师应该意识到要发展学习者的跨文化能力，所需要的不仅仅是语言方面的知识和技能，而是需要充分利用各种资源，包括自己的出国留学经历。

因此本章回顾了三方面的文献，研究对象各有不同。一是关于学生出国留学的研究综述；二是关于语言学生的更具体的出国留学经验，因为其中的许多人将成为语言教师；三是关于在职语言教师的海外经历研究。除此之外，本章节还回顾了如何评估海外经历对跨文化能力的影响，以及跨文化能力的提高如何影响语言教师教授语言的能力。本章不论对职前教师还是在职语言教师都有参考价值。

# 结　语

最后本书以 Rita Oleksak 主任关于创建实践共同体整个过程的反思作为结尾，总结了跨机构和跨大西洋合作的原因、成果、乐趣和挑战。对于 Oleksak 工作的学校而言，参与这个合作项目的一大成果是确定了校本跨文化能力定义。她认为 K-16 合作伙伴关系对于培养具有全球视野、准备进一步深造或就业的学生具有无可估量的价值。对教育管理者而言，特定的背景要求他们定制不同的关注和解决方案。本节分享的经验对中国不同学段的教育管理者具有启发意义。

本书开创性地详细描述了知名学者、大中小学教师、研究生的跨学段和跨洋合作，向广大读者展示了他们如何在坚实的理论基础上规划和实施跨文化课程设计、教学和评价，寻找跨越机构和学科界限的合作方式。

虽然学生的年龄段和学段不同，语言水平各异，但是所有课程都在理论的支持下致力于营造真实、有意义的跨文化交流情境，使学生在跨文化体验中去发现、对比、分析、反思、批判乃至实现自我超越。本书将加深和扩展我们在不同学段外语课堂中融入跨文化能力培养的理解和尝试，是有意应用理论助力跨文化外语教学的教师和研究者的必读之物。

通过借鉴和实践，我国跨文化外语教学能够制定符合我国国情以及各学段要求的跨文化能力培养目标、原则和方法，进而逐步形成扎实的实践和研究共同体，促进跨文化外语教育实践的繁荣以及教学理论的发展，满足我国日益增长的对跨文化人才的需求。

虞怡达（上海大学）

## 参考文献

Abrams, Z.I. (2002) Surfing to cross-cultural awareness: Using internet-mediated projects to explore cultural stereotypes. *Foreign Language Annals* 35 (2), 141–160.

Bennett, M.J. (1993) Towards a developmental model of intercultural sensitivity. In R.M.Paige (ed.) *Education for the Intercultural Experience*. Yarmouth, ME: Intercultural Press.

Bennett, M.J. (2004) Becoming interculturally competent. In J.S. Wurzel (ed.) *Toward Multi-culturalism: A Reader in Multicultural Education*. Newton, MA: Intercultural Resource Corporation.

Byram, M. (1997/2014) *Teaching and Assessing Intercultural Communicative Competence*. Clevedon: Multilingual Matters. Reprinted by Shanghai Foreign Language Education Press.

Phillips, E. (2001) IC? I see! Developing learners' intercultural competence. *LOTE CED Communiqué* 3, 1–6.

Wenger, E. (2011) Communities of practice: A brief introduction. Available at: https://www.vpit.ualberta.ca/cop/doc/wenger.doc.

王文斌,柳鑫淼.(2021)关于我国外语教育研究与实践的若干问题[J]. 外语与外语教学(1):1–12+144.

张红玲,吴诗沁.(2022)外语教育中的跨文化能力教学参考框架研制[J]. 外语界(5):2–11.

张平,朱鹏.(2009)教师实践共同体:教师专业发展的新视角[J].教师教育研究21(2):56–60.

张文忠,翟宇,王冬焱,刘浩,徐承萍,冯瑞玲.(2022)外语教育学视域下的"外语教/学实践研究"概述[J].外语教学43(2):10–15+42.

# Teaching Intercultural Competence Across the Age Range

From Theory to Practice

Edited by
**Manuela Wagner, Dorie Conlon Perugini and Michael Byram**

# Contents

# Foreword

The teaching and learning of a world language encompasses more than language acquisition. Language offers us a venue to access the cultural manifestations of another culture, to have a dialogue with others, to negotiate and mediate misunderstandings and to build relationships with those different from and much like ourselves. It is perhaps even more important to develop an understanding of a different culture in order to use language appropriately in social situations, to gain insights into another perspective or world view, and to build connections that promote a deeper understanding of self and other. Scholarly inquiry emphasizes that cultural learning as an instructional goal is equally as important as communication and is essential in the language classroom (Byram, 1989; Kramsch, 1993, 2004; Liddicoat & Scarino, 2013; National Standards Collaborative Board, 2015; Schulz, 2007; Sercu, 2006). With increased globalization, migration and immigration, the need for an intercultural focus in the language curriculum is growing (Kramsch, 2004; Sinecrope et al., 2007; Stewart, 2007).

While language teachers generally believe that language and culture are best acquired together in the foreign language classroom (Han & Song, 2011; Kissau et al., 2013; Moore, 2006; Schulz, 2007), language educators and intercultural scholars acknowledge that addressing culture effectively can be a formidable task (Byram, 1997; Paige et al., 2003; Schulz, 2007). Studies that have reported teachers' beliefs and practices related to teaching culture have underscored how the inclusion of a cultural element in the foreign language curriculum is challenging for teachers (Kissau et al., 2013; Lázár, 2011; Moore, 2006; Schulz, 2007; Social Science Education Consortium, 1999; Young & Sachdev, 2011). Moore (2006) administered a survey to practicing language teachers and reported that 98% of foreign language teachers with a bachelor's degree did not receive coursework related to the teaching of culture. Even when teachers believed that exploring foreign cultures should be an integral component of the curriculum (Han & Song, 2011; Kissau et al., 2013; Moore, 2006; Schulz, 2007; Young & Sachdev, 2011), in practice, teachers expressed a lack of confidence regarding 'how' to teach culture and often overlooked linking communication and culture (Social Science Education Consortium, 1999). Foreign language teachers conceded ignoring cultural studies within the classroom due to a lack of curricular support, suitable materials and a fear of dealing with controversy in class (Han & Song, 2011; Lázár, 2011; Young & Sachdev, 2011). In addition, language teachers who design culture lessons typically do so without the guidance of a conceptual framework, and as a result feel their pedagogical approaches may be ineffective (Schulz, 2007; Social Science Education Consortium, 1999; Young & Sachdev, 2011). In sum, these scholars report a need for more investigation regarding the perspectives of language teachers as they explore incorporating an intercultural approach into the language curriculum (Atkinson, 1999; Lázár, 2011; Paige *et al.*, 2003).

If most teachers believe that culture is an integral component of the foreign language curriculum, yet lack the skills to accomplish this task effectively, then additional guidance in the area of intercultural communicative competence may empower teachers to confidently design lessons in intercultural competence (IC). This book takes up this call to action by scholars and educators by providing examples of classroom-tested learning tasks, approaches and projects designed to build IC in K-20 world language classrooms. This collaboration among language educators in bilingual and foreign language primary, secondary and postsecondary education engaged participants in a targeted conversation about intercultural competence and its integration in language classrooms. Beginning with a symposium on the topic funded by Teachers for a New Era at the University of Connecticut (supported by the Carnegie Corporation of New York, the Annenberg Foundation and the Ford Foundation), followed by a graduate course offering, classroom implementation and action research studies, this project culminated in the publication of this text. Presented are the perspectives of experienced language teachers who have successfully integrated intercultural projects that provide a deeper understanding of the process of moving from traditional culture teaching to incorporating a contemporary intercultural stance within the language curriculum. A variety of levels (elementary through graduate studies), in various language learning settings (immersion, dual language, traditional classrooms) are featured in this volume which illustrate and document the gains in IC by language learners. The perspectives of the teachers provide a rich source of what worked and what was less successful. The 'lessons learned' that describe and analyze bumps in the road that occurred during the implementation process are particularly useful for language educators who wish to explore the integration of an IC curriculum into their own classrooms.

Through the integration of participatory action research, world language teachers were given the opportunity to critically reflect on their current culture teaching practices, explore and study conceptual frameworks for intercultural communicative competence and influence the direction of their own professional learning. Byram's (1997) elements of intercultural competence (knowledge, attitudes, critical cultural awareness, skills of interpreting and relating, and skills of discovery and interaction) provided the theoretical framework for the systematic integration of the IC units in these classrooms. Through the building and support of a community of practice, the teacher participants were able to design intercultural lessons with confidence that impacted student growth in the language classroom. The author teams provide an in-depth, real and authentic portrayal and analysis of classroom implementation at the micro and macro levels.

This book makes a significant contribution to the field of IC by expanding and deepening our understanding of how to create interest and openness towards other cultures at the classroom level while learning about one's own culture. Each chapter provides a greater understanding of the concerns, barriers and strategies associated with developing IC lessons for the world language classroom. Through the IC tasks, the teachers prepared students to communicate beyond the linguistic meaning and use of language to create cultural awareness in the context of their classrooms. Through detailed examination of teachers' perspectives and students' reflections, these studies illuminate elements such as noticing, self-assessment and reflection that foster critical cultural awareness that should be included in foreign language classrooms. The teacher-facilitated dialogues aimed at gaining knowledge of self and other offer a pathway to prepare language students to take on the role of cultural mediators. Kudos to the authors/educators who have provided detailed, diverse case studies for language educators which can serve as models to better understand how to navigate the integration process of IC into K-20 classrooms. This book is a must-read for all language educators in order to prepare and equip our students with the necessary skills to engage in a meaningful and productive intercultural exchange.

*Aleidine J. Moeller, PhD*
University of Nebraska-Lincoln

## References

Atkinson, D. (1999) TESOL and culture. *TESOL Quarterly* 33, 625–654.
Byram, M. (1989) *Cultural Studies in Foreign Language Education.* Clevedon: Multilingual Matters.
Byram, M. (1997) *Teaching and Assessing Intercultural Communicative Competence.* Clevedon: Multilingual Matters.
Han, X. and Song, L. (2011) Teacher cognition of intercultural communicative competence in the Chinese ELT context. *Intercultural Communication Studies* 20 (1), 175–192.
Kissau, S.P., Algozzine, B. and Yon, M. (2013) Similar but different: The beliefs of foreign language teachers. *Foreign Language Annals* 45 (4), 580–598.
Kramsch, C. (1993) *Context and Culture in Language Teaching.* Oxford: Oxford University Press.
Kramsch, C. (2004) The language teacher as go-between. *Utbildning & Demokrati* 13 (3), 37–60.
Lázár, I. (2011) Teachers' beliefs about integrating the development of intercultural communicative competence in language teaching: Case studies of Hungarian pre-service English teachers. *ForumSprache* 5, 113–126.

Liddicoat, A.J. and Scarino, A. (2013) *Intercultural Language Teaching and Learning*. Malden, MA: Wiley-Blackwell.

Moore, Z. (2006) Technology and teaching culture: What Spanish teachers do. *Foreign Language Annals* 39 (4), 579–594.

National Standards Collaborative Board (2015) *World-Readiness Standards for Learning Languages* (4th edn). Alexandria, VA: National Standards Collaborative Board.

Paige, R.M., Jorstad, H.L., Siaya, L., Klein, F. and Colby, J. (2003) Culture learning in language education: A review of the literature. In D.L. Lange and R.M. Paige (eds) *Culture as the Core: Perspectives on Culture in Second Language Learning* (pp. 173–236). Greenwich, CT: Information Age.

Schulz, R.A. (2007) The challenge of assessing cultural understanding in the context of foreign language instruction. *Foreign Language Annals* 40 (1), 9–26.

Sercu, L. (2006) The foreign language and intercultural competence teacher: The acquisition of a new professional identity. *Intercultural Education* 17 (1), 55–72.

Sinecrope, C., Norris, J. and Watanabe, Y. (2007) Understanding and assessing intercultural competence: A summary of theory, research, and practice. *Second Language Studies* 26, 1–58.

Social Science Education Consortium (1999) *Culture in the Foreign Language Classroom: A Survey of High School Teachers' Practices and Needs – Executive Summary*. Boulder, CO: Schulz.

Stewart, V. (2007) Becoming citizens of the world. *Educational Leadership* 64 (7), 8–14.

Young, T.J. and Sachdev, I. (2011) Intercultural communicative competence: Exploring English language teachers' beliefs and practices. *Language Awareness* 20 (2), 81–98.

# Preface

In this book, we share how a group of educators set out to systematically implement theory of Intercultural Competence (IC) in their world (foreign) language classrooms. The projects described here stem from a collaboration between colleagues at universities and in public schools. This started as a small community of practice between the editors and turned into a larger community including graduate students and volunteer teachers.

In retrospect, we realize just how well our stars must have been aligned for this book to materialize. Our stars are, of course, the participants in the projects. The book would not have been possible without the outstanding support of Rita Oleksak, Director of Foreign Languages and English Language Learning at Glastonbury Public Schools, the teachers and graduate students who volunteered for this project, and the students in Glastonbury Public Schools. We are grateful to them all, many of whom must remain anonymous.

We are also indebted to Professor Aleidine Moeller, President-elect of the American Council of the Teaching of Foreign Languages (ACTFL), who generously agreed to write a foreword for us. Her keen observations of current practices and the lack of information about the development of IC epitomize our rationale for embarking on our journey. When we started this project we could not anticipate just how humbled we would be by the commitment, patience, and perseverance of the educators involved in this endeavor. We hope that the materials and experiences from the collaborative projects shared in this book will help language educators to design and implement theory of IC in their own contexts.

*Manuela Wagner, Dorie Perugini and Michael Byram*

# Introduction

## Manuela Wagner, Dorie Conlon Perugini and Michael Byram

Intercultural (communicative) competence, global citizenship, cultural sensitivity and similar terms have become part of our everyday vocabulary when we describe what we want to do in foreign language classrooms. However, when we examine our practice more closely it becomes clear that teaching and assessing intercultural competence (IC) requires much thought and hard work. With the ever-growing demands on teachers, it is understandable that there is not always enough time to integrate IC. This book tells the story of a group of language educators from a variety of backgrounds who made the commitment to design units that integrate IC in a systematic way. In other words, we decided to design together IC units based on a sound theoretical framework, and then teach and assess them in the classroom. In the following chapters we share the products, practices and perspectives – to borrow a phrase from the American Council on the Teaching of Foreign Languages (ACTFL) Guidelines – resulting from that collaboration.

## Project Development as Cooperation

Our experience on this and previous occasions, and in other countries, has shown that curriculum development is most effective when there is collaboration. Theories and ideas for change are modified and improved by classroom implementation, and the novelty of experimentation stimulates teachers' imagination in realizing ideas in practice. This is why we consider it an important part of this book to give an account of our cooperation, in the hope that it will incite others to find ways of working together across institutional and disciplinary boundaries.

Here is how our story began:

**Rita:** Manuela, why don't you ask your students to come to Glastonbury during your graduate course and see what we do? They may be able to help us.

**Manuela:** That's a great idea. Let me think about it.

The current project was a continuation of prior collaborations between a public school in Glastonbury, CT, the University of Connecticut (USA) and the University of Durham (UK). Manuela Wagner, Associate Professor of Foreign Language Education, had been working with Rita Oleksak, the Director of the Foreign Language Programs in Glastonbury Public Schools for many years.

Two years earlier, Manuela had co-organized a Symposium for Language Educators at the University of Connecticut. The event was sponsored by a grant called 'Teachers for a New Era' (TNE). TNE was funded by the Carnegie Corporation of New York and awarded to 11 institutions in the United States with the ultimate goal of improving student learning outcomes in primary and secondary education. Part of the mission of TNE was to foster collaboration between schools of education and schools of liberal arts and sciences in universities. The Symposium for Language Educators brought together language educators from a variety of contexts including teachers in bilingual and foreign language primary, secondary and postsecondary education in order to engage in a targeted conversation about important issues in language education. Manuela suggested Michael (Mike) Byram as one of the keynote speakers. During the symposium Rita mentioned that she would be happy to see more research on how to foster IC in early language learning. This was the basis for an action research project carried out by Mike, Manuela and Dorie Conlon Perugini, Spanish teacher at Naubuc Elementary School in Glastonbury Public Schools. Mike, Manuela and Dorie collaborated over the next several months, planning, implementing and analyzing a unit of Spanish that integrated IC and social justice in a systematic way in 3rd grade Spanish.[1] The collaboration went so well and was so fruitful that we decided to follow up with another project.

Concurrently, Manuela was invited to teach a series of workshops on 'Intercultural Competence in the Language Classroom' to a group of Glastonbury teachers. Manuela knew many of the teachers from previous projects and was also considering future projects with them.

Finally, Manuela taught a graduate course entitled 'The Development of Intercultural Competence in (Language) Education' at the University of Connecticut. Dorie decided to take that course. In a meeting over the summer before the course, Rita suggested a collaboration with the students in the graduate course, an idea which Manuela, Dorie and Mike welcomed, and so the UConn-Glastonbury-Durham IC Project was born.

The plan was to introduce graduate students in literatures, cultures and languages programs to concepts of IC and to foster a community of practice with teachers in primary and secondary schools. The university–school partners then developed their own unit, lesson plans and assessments with the goal of implementing and evaluating theories of IC in a systematic way.

# The Graduate Course

The course was described, in 2013, as follows:

In this course, we will explore the role of culture and intercultural competence in the language classroom from a variety of perspectives, including applied linguistics, education, psychology, neuroscience, philosophy and pragmatics. Through readings, discussions, role-plays, scenarios and presentations students will (a) critically reflect on models of intercultural competence and their relation to student outcomes, (b) examine the role of social justice within the teaching of intercultural competence and (c) investigate and use tools to integrate and assess intercultural competence in the world language classroom.

Students are required to interact with a variety of research methods and complete a final project or paper on a topic of specialization of their choice.

The course was designed to enable students to: (a) plan a 'world language' curriculum – the term now used in the United States for 'foreign language' – which would be focused on the development of IC; (b) create assessments and objectives in the development of IC; (c) compare theories of intercultural communication from a variety of perspectives; and (d) reflect on intercultural communication. The two main readings were *From Foreign Language Education to Education for Intercultural Citizenship* (Byram, 2008) and *Intercultural Communication: An Advanced Resource Book for Students* (Holliday et al., 2010) (see Appendix A of this Introduction for an overview of readings). The participants were three master's students and one doctoral student in German literatures and cultures, one pre-service teacher in the Integrated Bachelor's and Master's program (IB/M) for Spanish education, an elementary school Spanish teacher, and a doctoral student in the pharmacy program who was interested in languages and IC.

After a general introduction to core concepts in intercultural communication, such as 'identity', 'othering' and 'representation' (as presented in Holliday et al., 2010), we discussed categorizations of models of intercultural communication competence (Spitzberg & Changnon, 2009). We then started our conversation about IC in (language) education. We read and discussed Mike's (Byram, 2008) book as well as other articles and some chapters from his 1997 book, *Teaching and Assessing Intercultural Communicative Competence*. Mike joined us via Skype for a session in which we asked questions about the book. The conversation was helpful for students in that it provided context for the theory while it also introduced Mike as a collaborator in the project. Additional readings on the teaching and assessment of IC in language education (e.g. Claire Kramsch, Lies Sercu, Michael Paige, June Philips and Julie Belz) further illustrated the complexity of the topic.

Manuela made the conscious decision to include resources from a variety of contexts in order to provide an introduction to students which pointed to the complexity of the concept of IC in education. Students engaged in several conversations in class and online about key concepts in world language education in the United States, such as social justice (e.g. Paolo Freire, Terry Osborn, Timothy Reagan), emergent bilingualism (e.g. Kris Gutiérrez, Ofelia García), what educators need to know about language (e.g. Catherine Snow), interdisciplinarity and various approaches to IC in different disciplines (e.g. Ron Scollon and Suzanne Wong Scollon, Geert Hofstede, Milton Bennett), and interlanguage pragmatics (e.g. Gabriele Kasper, Kathleen Bardovi-Harlig, Andrew Cohen, Shoshanna Blum-Kulka).

## Project Timeline

At the beginning of the course, the graduate students were informed that they would have the opportunity to participate in a project in which they would apply what they learnt in a primary or secondary school setting. At the same time, teachers in Glastonbury were informed that they could collaborate with a graduate student at UConn. In both settings we made it clear that participation was completely voluntary. In the graduate course, we emphasized that non-participation in the project had absolutely no impact on the course or the students' grades. In Glastonbury, teachers were told that they had the opportunity to participate in the project but that it was by no means part of their teaching or professional development duties.

We shared with everyone that our goal was to integrate IC in our lessons in a systematic way. Our emphasis was on helping the project members become part of a 'community of practice' as we felt that it was important to learn from and with each other, conceptualizing 'communities of practice' as 'groups of people who share a concern or a passion for something they do and learn how to do it better as they interact regularly' (Wenger, 2006: 3). With this definition in mind, it becomes clear that participation needs to be self-motivated. In other words, we wanted to ensure that all members felt they would benefit from participation in the project and that they could contribute equally to it as part of a democratic process of gaining and sharing knowledge and developing practices.

Five graduate students and five teachers of Spanish at different levels (elementary/primary through high school/secondary) volunteered to work together in pairs in order to plan, implement and evaluate a unit in which IC plays a central role and is systematically planned with a foundation in theory. In addition, Dorie, as both course participant and a teacher with the previous project experience behind her, planned her own project with the help of Manuela and Mike, and the group. For everyone, there was a choice of either creating a unit from scratch or modifying an existing unit to implement IC. It is important to note that we had the following reasons for making the decision to work with Mike's model as an example of how theory can be implemented in practice: (1) we had successfully worked with the model in a variety of contexts; and therefore (2) were able to provide examples of units applying Mike's model; (3) we were experienced in using the model ourselves and knew where and how to provide help. However, we also emphasized that we would provide resources for and support to participants for any additional models and theories they wanted to apply to their unit.

Teachers and students were first introduced to one another via email. In addition, one class meeting was held in Glastonbury. Mike joined us for that meeting via Skype. The meeting was held at a time when the partners had already started planning their projects. After Mike had provided a short introduction to his model as a review, partners presented their projects and were able to receive feedback from the group. The meeting was an important step for various reasons. First, the fact that the group met in Glastonbury embodied the beginning link between theory and practice and, for the students, the thought of seeing their co-planned projects become implemented in the schools became realistic. At the same time, teachers felt reinforced in their partners' commitment to the project.

Manuela also created a workspace on pbworks.com – an online social network on which members are able to share ideas and documents and discuss topics. All group members were thereby able to look at all materials, such as readings and discussions, and also to contribute their ideas if they chose to do so.

Over the next weeks the pairs continued to develop their projects and received feedback from each other in class, on PBworks and in meetings. Additionally, Manuela arranged meetings with each pair to ask questions and develop some ideas further. The groups could also email anyone and ask for personal feedback from group members.

Sometime during the fall, Manuela, Dorie and Mike discussed how we could disseminate our findings. This conversation ended with the idea of trying to secure a book contract. Our intention was to reflect the collaborative nature of the project, and therefore every project team was asked if they were interested in writing about their project in the book. Again everyone agreed to participate.

At the end of the semester, in December 2013, the students presented the projects they had worked on with their teacher partner in class. They also wrote a final paper on their co-planned projects focusing on the theoretical framework and on how they envisioned the theory would be implemented. At the same time, Manuela got in touch with the office at her university that determines what kind of permission is required before conducting research involving 'human subjects'. Manuela explained the project and a representative of the office determined in writing that our project did not meet the definition of 'human subjects research' and we were therefore not required to complete additional paperwork. We urge readers to check in with respective representatives in their institutions as it is crucial to abide by standards of ethics in research.

The projects were implemented starting in January 2014. Every project had its own implementation schedule. Some graduate students were able to visit the Glastonbury classes during that time. Others stayed in touch via email, phone or Skype. Conversations about ideas on how to adapt projects to changing situations or implement additional aspects of IC were ongoing during this period.

After the implementation of the projects in the classroom, the partners started writing their chapters. It is important to note that we also considered the writing process as a result of our community of practice.

In addition to the six projects by graduate students and teachers describing collaborations on the primary and secondary education level, we decided to include a report by Manuela and one of her graduate students, Niko, on the integration of IC in an online beginning German course at the university, as an example that extends the age range covered in this book. Finally, we also include a review of literature on the development of IC during study abroad which was the source of interest in the course for some participants, and which raises the question of how we best prepare teachers to develop their own IC.

## Theoretical Background

During this project participants referred to and based their work on 'Byram's model', i.e. the model of intercultural communicative competence which is described in the book entitled *Teaching and Assessing Intercultural Communicative Competence*. It is important to cite the full title of the book in order to emphasize that the model is proposed as a basis for teaching and assessing; it is not a model of learning, as some other models are (notably, and most well-known, Bennett, 1993). It is also important to emphasize that this is a model for teachers of 'foreign' languages in general education systems. 'Foreign language' – or 'world language', the term employed in the United States – is used to allude to the languages taught in compulsory schooling which are considered to be in principle exogenous, even though in practice there are native speakers of the languages living in, and perhaps born in, the country. This is for example very clearly the case for Spanish in the United States, but also for many other situations. While the focus of such language teaching is therefore usually on another country both in terms of the language norms used as a reference in teaching and in terms of any reference to a culture associated with the language, as we shall see in subsequent chapters, it is possible and often desirable to link 'foreign' language teaching with the language(s) used in learners' immediate communities as well.

The term 'model' also requires some explanation. It is used in the original publication (Byram, 1997) without a specific refinement of its meaning, although this has been done subsequently (Byram, 2009a, 2009b). In retrospect, it can be described as a means of identifying the principal elements of IC as they might be useful for foreign language teachers. It explicitly focuses on elements which were considered at the time – and still are today – as feasible teaching objectives for language teachers who had already accepted the principles of 'communicative language teaching'. It deliberately excludes elements of non-verbal communication, not because they are unimportant – for they are very important – but because they would be, and probably still are, beyond what foreign language teachers can envisage within the constraints of ordinary classrooms.

The model describes both 'intercultural competence' and 'intercultural communicative competence'. This is to differentiate between competences required for successful interaction among two or more people where language competence is not a salient problem, i.e. when all speak what is perceived as 'the same' language and, on the other hand, interaction when at least one person is using a language in which they feel they do not have full competence. This distinction is a fuzzy boundary. People who speak 'the same' language sometimes have linguistic misunderstandings, or feel their competence is not adequate to the topic or task around which their interaction with others turns. Similarly, people who are using a 'foreign' language may have high levels of linguistic competence where they do not feel inhibited by using the foreign language for interactions with others. In both cases there may well be cultural misunderstandings, some of which they may not notice whatever their linguistic competence.

Teachers who are planning their lessons might not, however, want to take fuzziness into their planning, except perhaps for more advanced learners. That does not mean that teachers are not aware of the fuzziness of IC. They may also decide to introduce it in some targeted instances, even for beginning learners. However, generally, teachers need to work towards clearly defined objectives for teaching and assessment. The model therefore brackets out some of the fuzziness and offers descriptions of objectives which can guide teachers' planning, and identifies five elements, five clusters of teaching objectives. One of these is 'knowledge' about another country, usually a country where the language is spoken endogenously, i.e. where it is the first and perhaps the official language. The purpose of this element is to provide a focus for teaching and learning and an illustration of how language and culture are related. It also shows how it is important to understand the relationship of language and culture even if the language is used as a lingua franca or used, like Spanish in the United States, to refer to the culture which has grown up in a situation of immigration.

This raises the question of whether referring to 'the' culture of the country is to 'essentialize' or reduce the complexity of the lives of its inhabitants to a representation which borders on stereotyping. In the original text (Byram, 1997), it was argued that countries have 'dominant' cultures. These are transferred from generation to generation by processes of schooling, by the mass media and by other social institutions. Not everyone living in a country subscribes to the dominant culture and some may even reject it as a basis for their lives. All are nonetheless aware of it, and it can therefore, in principle, be the starting point for teaching. All pedagogy begins with simplifications which are complexified as learners progress, as teachers of grammar or of sociolinguistic competence are aware. Adding opportunities for students of all ages and language abilities to tolerate ambiguity throughout the whole process of acquiring IC helps introduce students to some fuzziness throughout.

The model also includes an element which is not, strictly speaking, inherent in IC. This is the element of 'critical cultural awareness'. Because the model was developed to guide teachers working in compulsory schooling, it offers them the objective of critical cultural awareness as a means of identifying and implementing a crucial educational purpose of language teaching which goes beyond instruction in knowledge and skills. In one representation of the model, 'critical cultural awareness' is placed in the center, surrounded by other elements, of skills, knowledge and attitudes. This is a deliberate symbolic representation of the importance of the educational value of foreign language teaching. It emphasizes that language teaching should encourage learners to challenge the accepted, the taken-for-granted norms and practices of dominant cultures in their own country and in others. The model can thus be presented as in Figure 0.1.

SKILLS

interpret and relate

(*savoir comprendre*)

| KNOWLEDGE | EDUCATION | ATTITUDES |
|---|---|---|
| of | | relativising self |
| self and other; | critical cultural awareness | valuing other |
| of | (*savoir s'engager*) | (*savoir être*) |
| interaction: | | |
| individual and societal | | |
| (*savoirs*) | | |

SKILLS

discover and/or interact

(*savoir apprendre/faire*)

**Figure 0.1** Elements of intercultural competence
Source: From Byram (1997).

- **Knowledge** (*savoirs*): of social groups and their products and practices in one's own and in one's interlocutor's country, and of the general processes of societal and individual interaction;
- **Skills of interpreting and relating** (*savoir comprendre*): ability to interpret a document or event from another culture, to explain it and relate it to documents or events from one's own;
- **Skills of discovery and interaction** (*savoir apprendre/faire*): ability to acquire new knowledge of a culture and cultural practices and the ability to operate knowledge, attitudes and skills under the constraints of real-time communication and interaction;
- **Attitudes** (*savoir être*): curiosity and openness, readiness to suspend disbelief about other cultures and belief about one's own;
- **Critical cultural awareness** (*savoir s'engager*): an ability to evaluate, critically and on the basis of explicit criteria, perspectives, practices and products in one's own and other cultures and countries.

A full presentation of the model is provided in Appendix B of this Introductory chapter.

Although we are aware that the American Council on Teaching of Foreign Languages (ACTFL) and the Council of Europe are at the time of writing engaged in work to take further existing documents in which IC is included (*Can-Do Statements for Intercultural Communication* for ACTFL and the *Common European Framework of Reference for Languages* at the Council of Europe), there could be no reference to this work when the projects in this book took place, nor is it possible to make any comparisons at the time of writing this Introduction. We hope that in future there will be potential for associating the work in this book with descriptions and indicators of IC by these two important organizations.

# The Glastonbury Context

## The Glastonbury Public Schools system

In the northeast region of the United States, Glastonbury, CT is a suburban town with a population of over 34,000 located just 7 miles (11 km) outside Hartford, Connecticut's capital city. The Glastonbury Public Schools (GPS) system has approximately 6200 students with over 500 certified teachers. It is comprised of nine schools including one high school, one 7th and 8th grade middle school, one 6th grade school and six kindergarten through 5th grade elementary schools.

The Connecticut State Department of Education uses a classification system known as District Reference Groups (DRGs) in which districts that have public school students with similar socio-economic status (SES) and similar needs are grouped together. In determining a school district's DRG, the State Department of Education uses several variables including income, education, occupation, family structure, poverty, home language and district enrollment. Connecticut DRGs are labeled from A to I, from the very affluent, low-need suburban districts of group A to the seven high-need, low SES urban districts of group I. While DRGs are not indicative of the quality of instruction in a school or district, they do reflect the characteristics of the families with children attending those public schools and present a snapshot of the GPS environment that may be useful to our readers.

The GPS district is assigned to DRG B by the Connecticut Department of Education and is one of 21 districts classified as such, i.e. high SES communities, but less so than DRG A. Their median family income, education level and percentage in managerial or professional occupations are second only to DRG A, and significantly different from all other groups. The group has a similar percentage of children from single-parent families and percentage of children in poverty as adjacent groups. It has the fourth highest percentage of families who do not speak English at home. Its average enrollment is 4741 (Figure 0.2).

| Variable | 2006 DRG | | | | | | | | |
|---|---|---|---|---|---|---|---|---|---|
| | A | B | C | D | E | F | G | H | I |
| Median Family Income | $169,513* | $97,210* | $78,650 | $72,984 | $65,152* | $59,143 | $53,931 | $50,598 | $30,995* |
| Percent with Bachelor's Degree | 79.0%* | 59.5%* | 45.9%* | 35.8%* | 29.9%* | 17.0% | 20.6% | 19.7% | 10.5%* |
| Percent Managerial/ Professional Occupation | 67.5%* | 61.2%* | 52.1%* | 45.3%* | 39.8%* | 31.2% | 33.7% | 28.8% | 21.8%* |
| Percent Children in Single-Parent Families | 9.1% | 10.6% | 12.9% | 17.7% | 16.5% | 21.7%* | 28.3%* | 33.5%* | 54.9%* |
| 2004 Percent Children in Poverty | 0.8% | 3.7% | 4.4% | 9.2% | 9.4% | 17.9%* | 31.0%* | 41.9%* | 65.2%* |
| 2004 Percent Non-English Home Language | 2.1% | 4.6% | 1.5% | 5.0% | 1.1% | 2.6% | 6.1% | 22.3%* | 31.6%* |
| 2004 Average Enrollment | 3,283 | 4,741 | 1,308 | 3,704 | 766 | 1,848 | 4,274 | 7,535* | 14,374* |
| Number of Districts | 9 | 21 | 30 | 24 | 35 | 17 | 17 | 9 | 7 |

* Value is significantly different from every other group.

**Figure 0.2** Characteristics of 2006 District Reference Groups
Notes: *Value is significantly different from every other group.
Source: Connecticut State Department of Education (2006).

## The Glastonbury Public Schools foreign language program

The GPS system provides opportunities for all students to establish the foundations of second language acquisition at an early age. To reach this goal, the GPS foreign language program begins Spanish instruction twice a week for 25-minute classes in 1st grade, when the students are, on average, six years old. In 2nd grade, students increase their studies of Spanish with three

25-minute classes per week and continue learning Spanish in this way until 5th grade.

In 6th grade, when the students are on average 11 years old, students have the option to continue their study of Spanish or switch to French. They may also add the study of Chinese at this age. At this level, and throughout the remainder of their foreign/world language studies, classes are approximately 45 minutes in length and they meet on a daily basis. In 7th grade students have the option to add Russian to their study of French or Spanish. Students continue their language of choice until high school when they have the opportunity to continue studying the same language, add an additional language or switch to a new language. At the time of writing, although not a requirement for graduation, approximately 96% of students study one language at high school level, 15% study two languages and 10% study three. Languages currently offered in the GPS Foreign Language Department include Ancient Greek, French, Latin, Mandarin Chinese, Russian and Spanish.

## Overview of the Book

The chapters have been placed in an order that reflects the age group involved. This is intended to help readers who might want to read what was done with learners of the age they usually teach. The languages taught include Spanish, French and German, but as we believe that the ideas can be transferred from one language classroom to another – with appropriate changes – we have not highlighted specific languages, hoping that, for example, German teachers will find Spanish lessons interesting too. In order to help readers further, each chapter includes a table which provides the essential facts about the learners and the lessons. We also asked the teachers and students to introduce themselves and the particular classroom context in which they worked. All chapters are based on the framework presented in this Introduction. Chapter authors explain additional concepts they applied in their unit development. Finally, we asked authors to tell their story of how they collaborated in their planning and implementation of the unit. We intentionally included lessons learned because we feel that 'bumps in the road' are often not preventable even with impeccable planning. Moreover, we found that these challenges often represented important opportunities for us to learn and grow. After all, work in intercultural communication also involves one's own continuous development in this area.

In Chapter 1 (Houses Around the World), Patty Silvey and Silke Gräfnitz invite 4th grade students to reflect on housing in different parts of the world. In addition, the students explore how their parents and grandparents lived. In the next chapter, also with 4th graders, Dorie Conlon

Perugini invites her students on a virtual field trip to discover transportation in Puerto Rico. Philip Rohrer and Lauren Kagan facilitate 6th grade students' use of their five senses to understand different cities. Here students also deconstruct their preconceptions of cities in the United States while learning about cities such as Mexico City. In Chapter 4 Jean Despoteris and Komo Ananda asked their students in the 8th grade to compare their daily routines with those of students in a rural area of Peru, thus exposing students to a rather different perspective on daily chores and routines. Similarly, Deanne Wallace and Jocelyn Tamborello-Noble provided their 10th and 11th grade students with the challenge of assisting newly arrived immigrants from different parts of the Spanish-speaking world in getting settled in the United States. By comparing students' perspectives before the project with those afterwards they were able to evaluate the impact of their unit. In the following chapter, Chelsea Connery and Sarah Lindstrom used the topic of 'beauty and aesthetics' to help 11th and 12th grade students reflect on diverse perspectives of what constitutes beauty. Manuela Wagner and Niko Tracksdorf describe their experience of and challenges with teaching and assessing IC in an online beginning German language and culture course at the university. Finally, in Chapter 8, Lauren Rommal and Michael Byram synthesize research answering the question of how teachers can become interculturally competent through study and experience abroad.

The book concludes with reflections led by Rita Oleksak on the whole process of the creation of a community of practice, describing the pleasures and challenges of inter-institutional and cross-Atlantic cooperation.

# Appendix A: Reading List for Graduate Course in 'The Development of Intercultural Competence in Language Education'

Please note that not all texts were read in depth by everyone. Some texts were prepared in pairs to be presented to the group. Some texts were recommended and read in excerpts in class.

Bardovi-Harlig, K. (2009) Conventional expressions as a pragmalinguistic resource: Recognition and production of conventional expressions in L2 pragmatics. *Language Learning* 59, 755–795.

Belz, J.A. (2005) Intercultural questioning, discovery, and tension in internet-mediated language learning partnerships. *Language and Intercultural Communication* 5 (1), 3–39.

Bennett, J. (ed.) (2015) *Sage Encyclopedia of Intercultural Competence.* London: Sage.

Bennett, M.J. (2004) Becoming interculturally competent. In J.S. Wurzel (ed.) *Toward Multiculturalism: A Reader in Multicultural Education.* Newton, MA: Intercultural Resource Corporation.

Byram, M. (1997) *Teaching and Assessing Intercultural Communicative Competence.* Clevedon: Multilingual Matters.

Byram, M. (2008) *From Foreign Language Education to Education for Intercultural Citizenship: Essays and Reflections.* Clevedon: Multilingual Matters.

Cohen, A. (2011) Learner strategies for performing intercultural pragmatics. *MinneWITESOL Journal* 28, 13–24.

Cohen, A.D. and Sykes, J.M. (2010) Language learner strategies and their effect on speech act performance. In *Applied Linguistics Forum* (vol. 30; no. 1). Retrieved from http://www.tesol.org/read-and-publish/newsletters-other-publications/interest-section-newsletters/al-forum/2011/11/02/al-forum-news-volume-30-1-(march-2010) (accessed June 28, 2017).

Deardorff, D.K. (ed.) (2009) *Sage Handbook of Intercultural Competence.* London: Sage.

Fillmore, L. and Snow, C.E. (2000) *What Teachers Need to Know about Language.* ERIC Database No. ED444379. See http://files.eric.ed.gov/fulltext/ED444379.pdf. (accessed June 28, 2017).

Freire, P. (1970) *Pedagogy of the Oppressed.* New York: Herder and Herder.

García, O. (2009) *Bilingual Education in the 21st Century: A Global Perspective.* Oxford: Blackwell.

Gutiérrez, K., Baquedano-Lopez, P. and Tejeda, C. (1999) Rethinking diversity: Hybridity and hybrid language practices in the third space. *Mind, Culture, and Activity: An International Journal* 6 (4), 286–303.

Hofstede, G. (2001) *Culture's Consequences: Comparing Values, Behaviors, Institutions, and Organizations Across Nations* (2nd edn). Thousand Oaks, CA: Sage.

Holliday, A., Hyde, M. and Kullman, J. (2010) *Intercultural Communication: An Advanced Resource Book for Students.* London: Routledge.

Kasper, G. (2010) Interlanguage pragmatics. In L. Cummings (ed.) *The Pragmatics Encyclopedia* (pp. 231–234). London: Routledge.

Kramsch, C. (2009) Third culture and language education. In V. Cook and Li Wei (eds) *Contemporary Applied Linguistics, Vol. 1. Language Teaching and Learning* (pp. 233–254). London: Continuum.

Osborn, T.A. (2006) *Teaching World Languages for Social Justice: A Sourcebook of Principles and Practices.* Mahwah, NJ: Lawrence Erlbaum.

Paige, M. (ed.) (1993) *Education for the Intercultural Experience.* Yarmouth, ME: Intercultural Press.

Paige, R.M., Cohen, A.D., Kappler, B., Chi, J.C. and Lassegard, J.P. (2006) *Maximizing Study Abroad: A Student's Guide to Strategies for Language and Culture Learning and Use* (2nd edn). Minneapolis, MN: Center for Advanced Research on Language Acquisition, University of Minnesota.

Phillips, E. (2001) IC? I see! Developing learners' intercultural competence. *LOTE CED Communiqué* 3, 1–6.

Reagan, T. (2006) The explanatory power of critical language studies: Linguistics with an attitude. *Critical Inquiry in Language Studies* 3 (1), 1–22.

Scollon, R. (1995) *Intercultural Communication: A Discourse Approach.* Oxford: Blackwell.

Sercu, L. (2004) Assessing intercultural competence: A framework for systematic test development in foreign language education and beyond. *Intercultural Education* 15 (1), 73–90.

Spitzberg, M. and Changnon, G. (2009) Conceptualizing intercultural competence. In D. Deardorff (ed.) *The Sage Handbook of Intercultural Competence* (pp. 2–52). Thousand Oaks, CA: Sage.

# Appendix B: Objectives of Intercultural Communicative Competence (Byram, 1997)

*Attitudes*: **curiosity and openness, readiness to suspend disbelief about other cultures and belief about one's own**

**Objectives:**

(a) Willingness to seek out or take up opportunities to engage with otherness in a relationship of equality, distinct from seeking out the exotic or the profitable.

The intercultural speaker:

* is interested in the other's experience of daily life in contexts not usually presented to outsiders through the media nor used to develop a commercial relationship with outsiders; is interested in the daily experience of a range of social groups within a society and not only that represented in the dominant culture.

(b) Interest in discovering other perspectives on interpretation of familiar and unfamiliar phenomena both in one's own and in other cultures and cultural practices.

* does not assume that familiar phenomena – cultural practices or products common to themselves and the other – are understood in the same way, or that unfamiliar phenomena can only be understood by assimilating them to their own cultural phenomena; aware that they need to discover the other person's understanding of these, and of phenomena in their own culture which are not familiar to the other person.

(c) Willingness to question the values and presuppositions in cultural practices and products in one's own environment.

* actively seeks the other's perspectives and evaluations of phenomena in the intercultural speaker's environment which are taken for granted, and takes up the other's perspectives in order to contrast and compare with the dominant evaluations in their own society.

(d) Readiness to experience the different stages of adaptation to and interaction with another culture during a period of residence.

* is able to cope with their own different kinds of experience of otherness (e.g. enthusiasm, withdrawal) during residence and place them in a longer term context of phases of acceptance and rejection.

(e)    Readiness to engage with the conventions and rites of verbal and non-verbal communication and interaction.

* notes and adopts the behaviors specific to a social group in a way which they and the members of that group consider to be appropriate for an outsider; the intercultural speaker takes into consideration the expectations the others may have about appropriate behavior from foreigners.

---

*Knowledge*: **of social groups and their products and practices in one's own and in one's interlocutor's country, and of the general processes of societal and individual interaction**

**Objectives** (knowledge of/about):

(a)    Historical and contemporary relationships between one's own and one's interlocutor's countries.

The intercultural speaker:

* knows about events, significant individuals and diverse interpretations of events which have involved both countries and the traces left in the national memory; and about political and economic factors in the contemporary alliances of each country.

(b)    The means of achieving contact with interlocutors from another country (at a distance or in proximity), of travel to and from, and the institutions which facilitate contact or help resolve problems.

* knows about (and how to use) telecommunications, consular and similar services, modes and means of travel, and public and private organizations which facilitate commercial, cultural/leisure and individual partnerships across frontiers.

(c)    The types of cause and process of misunderstanding between interlocutors of different cultural origins.

* knows about conventions of communication and interaction in their own and the foreign cultures, about the unconscious effects of paralinguistic and non-verbal phenomena, about alternative interpretations of shared concepts, gestures, customs and rituals.

(d)    The national memory of one's own country and how its events are related to and seen from the perspective of other countries.

    \* knows the events and their emblems (myths, cultural products, sites of significance to the collective memory) which are markers of national identity in one's own country as they are portrayed in public institutions and transmitted through processes of socialization, particularly those experienced in schools; and is aware of other perspectives on those events.

(e)   The national memory of one's interlocutor's country and the perspective on them from one's own country.

    \* knows about the national memory of the other in the same way as their own (see above).

(f)   The national definitions of geographical space in one's own country, and how these are perceived from the perspective of other countries.

    \* knows about perceptions of regions and regional identities, of linguistic varieties (particularly regional dialects and languages), of landmarks of significance, of markers of internal and external borders and frontiers, and how these are perceived by others.

(g)   The national definitions of geographical space in one's interlocutor's country and the perspective on them from one's own.

    \* knows about perceptions of space in the other country as they do about their own (see above).

(h)   The processes and institutions of socialization in one's own and one's interlocutor's country.

    \* knows about education systems, religious institutions, and similar locations where individuals acquire a national identity, are introduced to the dominant culture in their society, pass through specific rites marking stages in the life-cycle, in both their own and the other country.

(i)   Social distinctions and their principal markers, in one's own country and one's interlocutor's.

    \* knows about the social distinctions dominant in the two countries – e.g. those of social class, ethnicity, gender, profession, religion – and how these are marked by visible phenomena such as clothing or food, and invisible phenomena such as language variety – e.g. minority languages, and socially determined accent – or non-verbal behavior, or modes of socialization and rites of passage.

(j)   Institutions, and perceptions of them, which impinge on daily life within one's own and one's interlocutor's country and which conduct and influence relationships between them.

* knows about public or private institutions which affect the living conditions of the individual in the two countries – e.g. with respect to health, recreation, financial situation, access to information in the media, access to education.

(k)   The processes of social interaction in one's interlocutor's country.

* knows about levels of formality in the language and non-verbal behavior of interaction, about conventions of behavior and beliefs and taboos in routine situations such as meals, different forms of public and private meeting, public behavior such as use of transport etc.

---

*Skills of interpreting and relating*: **ability to interpret a document or event from another culture, to explain it and relate it to documents or events from one's own**

**Objectives** (ability to):

(a)   Identify ethnocentric perspectives in a document or event and explain their origins.

The intercultural speaker:

* can 'read' a document or event, analyzing its origins/sources – e.g. in the media, in political speech or historical writing – and the meanings and values which arise from a national or other ethnocentric perspective (stereotypes, historical connotations in texts) and which are presupposed and implicit, leading to conclusions which can be challenged from a different perspective.

(b)   Identify areas of misunderstanding and dysfunction in an interaction and explain them in terms of each of the cultural systems present.

* can identify causes of misunderstanding (e.g. use of concepts apparently similar but with different meanings or connotations; use of genres in inappropriate situations; introduction of topics inappropriate to a context, etc.) and dysfunctions (e.g. unconscious response to unfamiliar non-verbal behavior, proxemic and paralanguage phenomena; over-generalization from examples; mistaken assumptions about representativeness of views expressed); and can explain the errors and their causes by reference to knowledge of each culture involved.

(c)   Mediate between conflicting interpretations of phenomena.

* can use their explanations of sources of misunderstanding and dysfunction to help interlocutors overcome conflicting perspectives; can explain the perspective of each and the origins of those perspectives in terms accessible to the other; can help interlocutors to identify common ground and unresolvable difference.

---

*Skills of discovery and interaction*: **ability to acquire new knowledge of a culture and cultural practices and the ability to operate knowledge, attitudes and skills under the constraints of real-time communication and interaction**

**Objectives** (ability to):

(a)   Elicit from an interlocutor the concepts and values of documents or events and develop an explanatory system susceptible of application to other phenomena.

The intercultural speaker:

* can use a range of questioning techniques to elicit from informants the allusions, connotations and presuppositions of a document or event and their origins/sources, and can develop and test generalizations about shared meanings and values (by using them to interpret another document; by questioning another informant; by consulting appropriate literature) and establish links and relationships among them (logical relationships of hierarchy, of cause and effect, of conditions and consequence, etc.).

(b)   Identify significant references within and across cultures and elicit their significance and connotations.

* can 'read' a document or event for the implicit references to shared meanings and values (of national memory, of concepts of space, of social distinction, etc.) particular to the culture of their interlocutor, or of international currency (arising for example from the dominance of western satellite television); in the latter case, the intercultural speaker can identify or elicit different interpretations and connotations and establish relationships of similarity and difference between them.

(c)  Identify similar and dissimilar processes of interaction, verbal and non-verbal, and negotiate an appropriate use of them in specific circumstances.

* can use their knowledge of conventions of verbal and non-verbal interaction (of conversational structures; of formal communication such as presentations; of written correspondence; of business meetings; of informal gatherings; etc.) to establish agreed procedures on specific occasions, which may be a combination of conventions from the different cultural systems present in the interaction.

(d)  Use in real-time an appropriate combination of knowledge, skills and attitudes to interact with interlocutors form a different country and culture taking into consideration the degree of one's existing familiarity with the country, culture and language and the extent of difference between one's own and the other.

* is able to estimate their degree of proximity to the language and culture of their interlocutor (closely related cultures; cultures with little or no contact or little or no shared experience of international phenomena; cultures sharing the 'same' language; cultures with unrelated languages) and to draw accordingly on skills of interpreting, discovering, relating different assumptions and presuppositions or connotations in order to ensure understanding and avoid dysfunction.

(e)  Identify contemporary and past relationships between one's own and the other culture and society.

* can use sources (e.g. reference books, newspapers, histories, experts, lay informants) to understand both contemporary and historical political, economic and social relationships between cultures and societies and analyze the differing interpretations involved.

(f)  Identify and make use of public and private institutions which facilitate contact with other countries and cultures.

* can use their general knowledge of institutions facilitating contacts to identify specific institutions (consulates, cultural institutes, etc.) to establish and maintain contacts over a period of time.

(g)  Use in real-time knowledge, skills and attitudes for mediation between interlocutors of one's own and a foreign culture.

* can identify and estimate the significance of misunderstandings and dysfunctions in a particular situation and is able to decide on and carry out appropriate intervention, without disrupting interaction and to the mutual satisfaction of the interlocutors.

*Critical cultural awareness/political education*: **an ability to evaluate, critically and on the basis of explicit criteria, perspectives, practices and products in one's own and other cultures and countries**

**Objectives** (ability to):

(a) Identify and interpret explicit or implicit values in documents and events in one's own and other cultures.

The intercultural speaker:

\* can use a range of analytical approaches to place a document or event in context (of origins/sources, time, place, other documents or events) and to demonstrate the ideology involved.

(b) Make an evaluative analysis of the documents and events which refers to an explicit perspective and criteria

\* is aware of their own ideological perspectives and values ('human rights'; socialist; liberal; Muslim; Christian; etc.) and evaluates documents or events with explicit reference to them.

(c) Interact and mediate in intercultural exchanges in accordance with explicit criteria, negotiating where necessary a degree of acceptance of those exchanges by drawing upon one's knowledge, skills and attitudes.

\* is aware of potential conflict between their own and other ideologies and is able to establish common criteria of evaluation of documents or events, and where this is not possible because of incompatibilities in belief and value systems, is able to negotiate agreement on places of conflict and acceptance of difference.

## Note

(1) The results from this collaboration were published in the journal of the National Network for Early Language Learning: Byram, M., Perugini, D. and Wagner, M. (2013) The development of intercultural citizenship in the elementary Spanish classroom. *Learning Languages* 18 (2), 16–31.

## References

Bennett, J. (ed.) (2015) *Sage Encyclopedia of Intercultural Competence*. London: Sage.
Bennett, M. (1993) Towards a developmental model of intercultural sensitivity. In R.M. Paige (ed.) *Education for the Intercultural Experience*. Yarmouth, ME: Intercultural Press.
Byram, M. (1997) *Teaching and Assessing Intercultural Communicative Competence*. Clevedon: Multilingual Matters.

Byram, M. (2008) *From Foreign Language Education to Education for Intercultural Citizenship: Essays and Reflections*. Clevedon: Multilingual Matters.

Byram, M. (2009a) Intercultural competence in foreign languages: The intercultural speaker and the pedagogy of foreign language education. In D.K. Deardorff (ed.) *The Sage Handbook of Intercultural Competence* (pp. 321–332). Los Angeles, CA: Sage.

Byram, M. (2009b) Evaluation and/or assessment of intercultural competence. In A. Hu and M. Byram (eds) *Interkulturelle Kompetenz Und Fremdsprachliches Lernen: Modelle, Empirie, Evaluation/Intercultural Competence and Foreign Language Learning: Models, Empiricism, Assessment*. Tübingen: Narr.

Byram, M., Perugini, D. and Wagner, M. (2013) The development of intercultural citizenship in the elementary Spanish classroom. *Learning Languages* 18 (2), 16–31.

Connecticut State Department of Education (2006) District Reference Groups, 2006. *Research Bulletin* 1, 3.

Deardorff, D.K. (2009) *Sage Handbook of Intercultural Competence*. London: Sage.

Holliday, A., Hyde, M. and Kullman, J. (2010) *Intercultural Communication: An Advanced Resource Book for Students*. London: Routledge.

Hua, Z. (ed.) (2011) *The Language and Intercultural Communication Reader*. London: Routledge.

Jackson, J. (ed.) (2012) *The Routledge Handbook of Language and Intercultural Communication*. London: Routledge.

Kotthoff, H. and Spencer-Oatey, H. (eds) (2007) *Handbook of Intercultural Communication*. Berlin: de Gruyter.

Kramsch, C. (2009) Third culture and language education. In V. Cook and Li Wei (eds) *Contemporary Applied Linguistics, Vol. 1. Language Teaching and Learning* (pp. 233–254). London: Continuum.

Osborn, T.A. (2006) *Teaching World Languages for Social Justice: A Sourcebook of Principles and Practices*. Mahwah, NJ: Lawrence Erlbaum.

Spitzberg, M. and Changnon, G. (2009) Conceptualizing intercultural competence. In D. Deardorff (ed.) *The Sage Handbook of Intercultural Competence* (pp. 2–52). Thousand Oaks, CA: Sage.

Straub, J., Weidemann, A. and Weidemann, D. (eds) (2007) *Handbuch Interkulturelle Kommunikation Und Kompetenz*. Stuttgart J.B. Metzler.

Wenger, E. (2011) Communities of practice: A brief introduction. Available at: https://www.vpit.ualberta.ca/cop/doc/wenger.doc (accessed June 28, 2017).

Zarate, G., Lévy, D. and Kramsch, C. (eds) (2008) *Précis du plurilinguisme et du pluriculturalisme*. Paris: Éditions des Archives Contemporaines.

# 1  Houses Around the World

## Patty Silvey and Silke Gräfnitz

## Introduction

In this first chapter we will describe our journey to creating and implementing a unit on 'The House' in a 4th grade Spanish lesson in a Glastonbury,
CT school. In Glastonbury schools there is an agreed curriculum, including
the topics taught. Our project fitted into the overall curriculum and was a
modification of an existing unit of study.

### We are Patty and Silke

Patty is a graduate of Assumption College in Worcester, MA, and holds
a master's degree in educational technology from the University of Hartford,
CT. Patty's love of languages was first fostered in meeting her childhood
neighbor and friend whose parents were from Belgium and spoke only French
to their children. She started her 'formal' language education in a nursery
school where she learned to sing, recite and count in French. Language learning in earnest restarted in junior high school and continued in high school
where she was (finally!) able to add her second language, Spanish. She is a
close colleague of Dorie Conlon Perugini, one of the editors of this book who
has been introduced in the Introduction, and has been teaching in the
Glastonbury Foreign Language in the Elementary School (FLES) Department
for the past 15 years. She was intrigued in what intercultural competence
(IC) might look like at the elementary level and wanted to further explore
this idea with both Manuela and Dorie.

Silke Gräfnitz is a PhD candidate at the University of Connecticut where
she has also been teaching classes in German, German literature and human
rights. Previously she studied literature, comparative studies and Japanese studies at the University of Tübingen, where she additionally interned and worked
with the German as a Foreign Language Department. In addition to this she
has been an intern and working student with Mercedes Benz's International
Training Program and International Quality Management, and worked with
Bosch's International Sales Department. Silke is passionate about foreign language acquisition and teaching, and how IC competence can positively affect

us in our everyday lives. To her, fostering early IC is a key ingredient in raising
a future generation of skilled leaders and conflict managers.

## The existing unit in the Glastonbury syllabus

The Glastonbury syllabus provides a detailed approach to the content of
the curriculum for Spanish lessons (see Table 1.1). It consists of statements
about what students are expected to learn, 'enduring understandings', the
use or application of the language learnt, 'essential questions', as well as
the language content. With this as a starting point, and having discussed the
theory and Byram's model in the classroom, we thought:

*Houses around the world. Sounds like an easy enough topic from which to glean
evidence of intercultural competence from our students. Everyone has to live
somewhere and in some sort of dwelling. Houses tell a story and that story can be*

**Table 1.1** Unit on 'The House'

| Unit title | The House |
| --- | --- |
| Unit description | As part of the year-long study of how we are connected to the Caribbean, students will complete the year with a unit that helps them discover and uncover the similarities and differences in various houses across the United States and the Caribbean. This unit spirals the study of 'Structures' from grade 3 as well as the unit of study of Puerto Rico earlier this year. It will give students the vocabulary to speak and write broadly about the structure called a house. |
| Enduring understandings | • Students will be able to describe various houses from the United States and the Caribbean. <br> • Students will be able to describe the similarities and differences between houses from different cultures. |
| Essential questions | • How do I name and describe the outside of a house? <br> • How do I name the rooms and describe the inside of a house? <br> • How can I explain why I like a certain room? <br> • What is a 'patio' and how might it be different in a Hispanic home and Hispanic world? |
| Content | • When prompted 'What's outside your house?' in the target language, students would be able to produce a response using new vocabulary. <br> • When prompted to 'Describe (the outside of) your house', students will be able to produce an oral or written response. <br> • Students will demonstrate correct usage of the verbs *estar*, *ser* and *tener* with regard to describing a house. <br> • Students will demonstrate correct usage of numbers in the hundreds with correct agreement. <br> • Students will demonstrate correct usage of noun/adjective agreement. |

*very personal. Houses reflect the culture of anything from an entire country to a neighborhood community to an individual family. We have all traveled, and read, and know houses can look quite different from one part of town to another, or from one part of the world to another. We know, too, that some of those differences are most certainly based on regional climate and weather patterns as well as personal architectural preferences. These differences may also rely quite heavily on the finances of the people. Hmmm. How far were we willing to tread into this subject matter? After all, I am their Spanish teacher, not a teacher of social anthropology nor of consumer economics and financial planning. What did our students know about houses in other parts of our state or country, much less the world? Would they be able to adjust or suspend their attitudes with the new information presented?*

## Classroom context

The students we chose for this lesson are all in grade 4, roughly aged nine to ten. They attend a public elementary school and, for the most part, have had Spanish instruction since 1st grade. The school itself has approximately 435 students, kindergarten to grade 5. In a January 2014 report to the Glastonbury, CT Board of Education, 28 of these students were reported to come from a home where a language other than English was spoken, with 13 different languages represented. Additionally, 5.4% of this school was eligible for free or reduced lunch services at the time when this project was conducted. Table 1.2 summarizes the situation.

**Table 1.2** Summary of the classroom and students

| Type of school (e.g. primary, middle, high school) | Grade level(s) | Average age of the students | Average number of students per class | Number of classes per week | Number of minutes per class | Number of previous years of language study |
|---|---|---|---|---|---|---|
| Primary | 4th grade | 9–10 | 21 | 3 | 25 | 3 |

# Preparation

In the Glastonbury Spanish curriculum in 4th grade, the students 'travel through the Caribbean' via a year-long, overarching essential question: *How are we connected to the Caribbean?* It is felt that this question, along with the underlying unit essential questions, will, among other things and in the words of Jay McTighe and Grant Wiggins (2013: 17), 'make it more likely that the unit will be intellectually engaging, provide transparency for students, and encourage and model metacognition for students'.

The overarching essential question is revisited over the course of the year, weaving in and out of various other unit themes. It is expected that, on completion of this particular unit on The House, students will have discovered the similarities and differences among various houses across the United States and the Caribbean. The unit as it is written allows for the re-introduction or spiraling of vocabulary from prior grades as well as embedding new vocabulary and grammar structures, through the lens of understanding aspects of life in the Spanish-speaking Caribbean.

The spiraling of vocabulary is done throughout the students' foreign language education in grades 1–12 and is based on Jerome Bruner's (1960: 33) theory that 'any subject can be taught in some intellectually honest form to any child at any stage of development'. Bruner highlights three key features of the spiraled curriculum:

- The student revisits a topic, theme or subject several times throughout their school career.
- The complexity of the topic or theme increases with each revisit.
- New learning has a relationship with old learning and is put in context with the old information.

The unit in question re-introduces elements of a connected unit from grade 3 where students learn about various types of structures, both man-made and natural, albeit in a much broader sense than just housing. Grade 3 thus includes the vocabulary for such man-made edifices as market, church, airport and school as well as lake, beach, mountain and rainforest which represent the natural structures.

Since there were different unit themes from which we could have chosen in the grade 4 curriculum, how did we come to decide on this one? Discussions ensued between us as well as among other colleagues. The outcome was that it all had to do with the timing within the school year for the implementation of the lesson. In our district, and within our elementary foreign language department, we have determined certain units of study to be for mastery and others as supplemental. Mastery units are taught in greater depth over a longer period of time and include more and varied assessments. Supplemental units are shorter, include fewer assessments and support the content and grammar goals of the mastery units. The two aspects of the housing unit, 'Outside of the House' and 'Inside of the House', are both deemed mastery lessons for students in this grade and are taught in the second half of the school year beginning in February and concluding in June.

Patty wanted to bring the modified IC curriculum to all four classes of students in grade 4 to ensure the widest possible sampling of evidence and, additionally, she wanted it to supplement the learning they already received during their regularly scheduled Spanish class. Patty decided, therefore, to do the entire new unit in one additional 75-minute class on Wednesday afternoons, one class at a time, over four Wednesdays. This was possible because the Glastonbury district has built in time on Wednesday afternoons during the months of December through February for special area teachers (art, physical education, Spanish, etc.) to collaborate with classroom teachers and design lessons to supplement the curriculum of both the classroom teacher and the special area teacher, in this case the Spanish teacher. This allowed Patty the flexibility to adjust and to fine-tune each subsequent lesson as needed. You will read later in this chapter about her personal reflections on how this all happened. Although this project was meant to be part of an existing unit and not a new creation, we know, from being experienced teachers, that these things can take on a life of their own and can grow into something much bigger than expected.

In order to accomplish the objectives we had set for ourselves, we worked together to create an outline for the lesson in which we used materials already available for the unit as well as purchasing and making new instructional materials. Ambitious though it was, pieces of the first lesson plan were scrapped before the first class of students even walked into the room. Overplanning was indeed an understatement!

The book usually used in this unit by Lucy Floyd, *Casas en todo el mundo* (Ada & Campoy, 2003), was still used for the modified lesson because it contains vocabulary students already know and introduces new vocabulary at an 'i + 1' model, where students will acquire the new language (input) if it is given at one step beyond their current linguistic competence (Krashen, 1992). Next, because we wanted to use visuals of houses around the world, we needed clear photographs with an explanation of where they are located, i.e. the photos of houses from around the world and the accompanying descriptions should be factual. Furthermore, our plan was to have enough photos for each child to have their own to work with. We were able to purchase from a website (www.shop.montessori-printshop.com/Homes-Around-the-World-GeoF-51.htm) for a small fee the download rights of high-quality photos of 26 unique homes with their accompanying locations as well as what they are called in their specific locale.

The initial plan was for each student to try to identify the country in which they thought the house might be located, but we decided that it would be better for students to work in groups to determine the continent on which they felt the house could be found. Given the varied countries and the number of students in the class, this activity alone might take too much time if done individually. The group activity would, we hoped, bring forth a deeper discussion on their decisions. Additionally, Patty was concerned as to whether these nine and ten year olds would be able to find on a world map the actual country or have any idea that such a country even existed. Without hesitation, students would have been able to locate China, the United States,

Canada and France. Other countries such as Iraq, Kenya, and Turkey would have been much more difficult as the teaching of these geographic locations is neither part of the classroom curriculum nor the Spanish curriculum. It was for these reasons that we decided that the house placement and discussion activity would center on the continent, and not the country, of each house.

Patty's next quandary was that only five of the seven continents were represented in the photographs we had purchased. We were missing Antarctica and Australia and there are homes there too, although some may not be as permanent as others, especially in Antarctica. A much smaller internet search ensued and proved quite fruitful, so that finally all continents would be represented. Since we felt it was important for Patty to be able to show the students on a world map the actual location with the name of the house, she created a presentation inserting the photos into a Prezi®, a cloud-based storytelling and presentation tool, using a world map as the background. In the presentation, she included the name of the country and the region-specific word used for the house.

We also needed something that would demonstrate a growth in 'critical cultural awareness' with respect to the phenomenon of houses and housing and a means for the students to use their new knowledge to create additional knowledge outside the school setting. Our intent was for the lesson to be carried out as much as possible in Spanish without creating anxiety among the students or losing the complexity of the intercultural aspect due to limited or lack of higher order vocabulary. Patty felt, though, that the richness of the new learning and their explanations would be best revealed if they wrote their reflections in English. The reflection sheet became a very personal document where students were asked to 'read the following statements and give personal examples. Your examples can be from this lesson or from any other lesson here in school.'

(1) I am curious and open and understanding to different cultures. Example.
(2) I am interested in other people's way of life, and what other people do on a daily basis. Example.
(3) I have realized that I can understand other cultures by seeing things from a different point of view. Example.
(4) I know some important facts about the dwellings of other cultures. Example.
(5) I can explain and understand why some houses are built in a certain way. Example.

And lastly, we wanted to extend the learning outside the school setting and, after conferring with Manuela, we decided on a final project where students would submit a visual representation of their 'Family Tree/House', as we shall see below.

# Implementation

## First iteration

In the first presentation of this lesson in mid-January, Patty started the discussion by showing students books in Spanish with photos of houses. We used and distinguished between the two words *casas* (houses) and *hogares* (homes) and said that typically people –or as some students said, *familia* (family) – are needed to make a house a home. In Spanish, Patty asked them questions such as: Are all homes equal? Is an apartment a home? Are homes here in Connecticut different from homes in other regions of the US? Continuing in the target language, they were then told they would work in their pre-assigned groups with a photo of a house. Their job was two-fold: they had to decide on which continent they thought one might find that house and explain what evidence they used to make their decision. They also had to decide if one might find this house on another continent and why. They had three minutes in their group with their house.

After the three minutes, each group presented and substantiated their conclusions. Although they wanted and tried to explain in the target language, they found they were lacking crucial vocabulary for this piece of the task. They could repeat the continents in Spanish, but they wanted to expand on their discussion. Therefore, much of what followed was in English. Given that this session was an enhancement and in addition to their regular Spanish class and included many new cultural concepts and vocabulary, Patty was fine with proceeding in English. She can, of course, return to some of these elements using Spanish in future Spanish classes.

Their supporting ideas revolved around the landscape depicted in the photo and their perception or prior knowledge of the continent. For example, the group that had the troglodyte house (Tunisia, Africa) correctly identified the continent. Their reason was 'it looks like sandstone and it looks hot, like in a desert'. They thought you might also be able to find a house like that in either Australia or South America. They also brought up whether people had money for a house. After the six groups placed their respective house on a large, projected map of the continents, and gave their explanation, they received a second more challenging house. It was not until the discussion of the igloo that the idea of weather or climate being a factor in the construction of a house became prominent. It was evident that the students felt that, for the most part, many of the homes could be found somewhere on most continents. It was very interesting that the placement of a castle in the United Kingdom was supported by their statement, 'because a monarchy is still there today'. After this exercise, Patty and the students all sat on a carpet, which was their usual gathering place for reading, and Patty read excerpts from the book *Casas por todo el mundo*. The plan was to read the entire book, but there was also the Prezi to show and we wanted them to complete the reflection sheet too. The book supported two objectives: give them more vocabulary on which to build, and supply them with photos of additional different types of houses. The last activity, viewing the Prezi, allowed us to globe-hop and see in greater detail the houses that were presented for discussion as well as others they had not seen in their groups. Some of the homes elicited 'ooohs' and 'aaahs', and comments like 'I want a house like that one'.

After the Prezi, the students were informed about the project they would be completing. This discussion was in English so as to avoid as much confusion or misinterpretation as possible. Their instructions were to go home and 'interview' their parents and other relatives to discover what their first homes were like using their new knowledge of culture and cultural practices. They were then to create a 'Family Tree House' by illustrating, by hand or with photos or clipart, the houses described to them. We wanted the students to see how the practice of living in a home varies from one generation to another as well as from culture to culture. They had the liberty to include anyone in their Family Tree House who might have lived in a different part of the world and in a different dwelling from what we might have already seen. Students were given one week in which to complete the project at home.

After the project instructions were given, near the end of the 75-minute session, students had still not completed the reflection sheet we presented earlier in this chapter. We wanted to give them ample time to complete the reflection sheet so that they would reflect deeply and thoughtfully on the five questions. So, although it was not planned to give additional work to be done at home, we felt we would get the best responses if they were asked to read and respond to the five statements with personal examples and return the reflection sheet in three days.

## Later iterations

The second time Patty conducted this lesson, with a different class of 4th graders in the following week, it went pretty much as the first iteration with the following exceptions. The students received the same photographs of houses as the first class, but this time while they were supplying their reasoning Patty jotted down their responses. Here are some of their English responses with regard to the particular house they were given:

- Castle (England/Europe): 'Looks like England, it's a house made of stone.'
- Hut (Africa): 'Not a rich mansion, poor, few rooms, dirt, stone; could be in Australia.'
- Apple hut (Antarctica): 'Snow, few other houses, people don't want to live there. Could not be on another continent.' This sentiment was later amended by another group to say that it could be in Canada in North America.
- Single Family House (Australia): 'Big, flat location, hot/warm in Australia. Not cold in Australia. It was very clean and made of stone.'

After this class Patty decided to use a different group of house photos from those she had first used. She wanted to see if she might elicit different responses. Lessons 3 and 4 were very similar and yielded the following responses to the specific houses.

- Tongkonan (Indonesia): It was placed in Africa, 'because there was a lot of open space, not like Hartford (Connecticut)'.
- Stilt House (Cambodia): This, too, was placed in Africa. They said it 'did not look like a wealthy house' and that the houses 'look like sheds' to them. Additionally, they thought it might be found in South America, but South America is 'more wealthy' than Africa. They also thought the murky water made it look like Africa because South America 'has cleaner water'.
- Troglodyte House (Turkey/Asia): This group placed it in Africa 'because there are pyramids in Egypt and Egypt is in Africa'. They said it could also be in Asia.

The group with the yurt (Mongolia, Asia; Figure 1.1) placed it in Africa. They said it was because 'there are very few homes and a lot of land'. They also reasoned, 'It's very hot in Africa and that's why it doesn't have a foundation and it's covered in cloth'. They went on to say that it might also be found in Asia because they are both 'hot'. Finally, the group with the *palafitos* (Chile/South America) placed the photo in Asia with the possibility that it could be in Australia. There is a 'river near the houses with wood holding up the houses, probably so they can't move'. The people living in these houses 'can go fishing from their windows, can drink from the river and can use the river for transportation'. They also thought the river could hold a spiritual or religious connection for these river dwellers.

**Figure 1.1** Yurt (Mongolia)

# Theoretical Foundation

## Lesson planning and methodology

We created the first activity to (1) provide a hands-on task on the housing topic and (2) have students actively working with knowledge or history (Liddicoat & Scarino, 2013; Scollon & Scollon, 1995). The objective of this task is to create awareness of (cultural) similarities and differences between one's own and other cultures, while having students interpret what they see and relate the content to their previous knowledge based on their own cultural context (Byram, 2008). By creating awareness about similarities as well as differences in one's own country/culture and the target countries/culture(s), the students will be provided (and challenged) with the use of intercultural skills, rather than being merely provided with certain knowledge about the target culture (Atay *et al.*, 2009: 132). As Abrams (2002: 143) says, 'culture learning is more effective and motivating if students are first involved in finding out about themselves, their belief system, values, and traditions, and if explicit links are created between their own culture and the foreign cultures and languages'. Our goal was thus to trigger a deeper understanding by questioning the first impression of where these living spaces might be located in order 'to promote understanding of cultural variation within the target society and to improve learners' attitudes toward the target language and society' (Abrams, 2002: 144).

In order to deconstruct stereotypes, we need to make them visible first. The first two activities are working towards this uncovering of existing stereotypes and pre-existing ideas about culture. While the students mainly work with their knowledge (*savoirs*), ideas and interpretations during the first activity, the second activity requires them to put their ideas into words and to dig deeper (Byram, 2008; Byram *et al.*, 2002). They have to argue with what they know and assume based on their individual history (Liddicoat & Scarino, 2013) and then engage in research about their own sociocultural background. To have them go out and explore their own cultural background through exploring their family's history of living spaces means making them aware of the many differences within their own culture. Coperías Aguilar (2007: 62) argues that our own culture is so imminent that we tend to not recognize it in itself and its different facets. Seeing as 'all interpretation is governed by history, meaning the history of a person's experiences' (Liddicoat & Scarino, 2013: 67), we wanted the students to become aware of the multifacetedness of their own culture in order to understand and acknowledge the depth of another culture (Abrams, 2002; Byram, 2008; Philips, 2001).

The next step is to question this knowledge. Here students slowly deconstruct stereotypes and relativize their own cultural knowledge. We agree with Byram *et al.* (2002: 29) that '[w]hat we need is to assess ability to make the strange familiar and the familiar strange (*savoir être*), to step outside [the students'] taken for granted perspectives, and to act on a basis of new perspectives (*savoir s'engager*)'. While we start with the ability to interpret a document, in this case a picture of another culture, we will finish the first activity block by having the students explore differences within and among their personal cultural context and then relate their findings and experiences to the ideas and images of the previous activity (*savoir comprendre*) (Byram, 2008; Byram *et al.*, 2002).

The last part of the housing around the world activities, the essay reflection and the creation of an artistic family tree of living spaces, is meant not only to create awareness about the multifacetedness of one's own culture, but also to learn about similarities and differences between one's own and the other culture(s). Understanding gained through reflections on the students' own concepts and preconceptions helped them deconstruct their existing stereotypes, thus contributing to their enduring understanding of the complexity of representations of housing in different cultures.

Another anticipated outcome in combination with all previous activities, is to create interest and openness towards other cultures. To be prepared to rethink or dismiss one's own knowledge and assumptions (*savoir être*). 'This means a willingness to relativise one's own values, beliefs and behaviours, not to assume that they are the only possible and naturally correct ones, and to be able to see how they might look from an outsider's perspective who has a different set of values, beliefs and behaviours. This can be called the ability to "decentre"' (Byram *et al.*, 2002: 12).

Through these activities we aim to prepare students to communicate beyond the linguistic meaning and use of language and to create cultural awareness and equip students with the necessary skills to engage in a meaningful and productive intercultural exchange (Atay *et al.*, 2009; Byram, 2008; Byram *et al.*, 2002; Aguilar, 2007; Liddicoat & Scarino, 2013; Scollon & Scollon, 1995). In some multicultural environments, classrooms also become more and more diverse (Condon & Nam, 2009). The tendency in the teaching of culture has moved away from presenting mere knowledge and stereotypes to the students. With our activities we aimed to have the students explore culture and acquire important skills to think and rethink culture as they encounter it, and to question their own knowledge of a foreign culture as well as their knowledge about their own culture (Abrams, 2002). By using those skills, students engage in a meaningful cross-cultural dialogue, while being aware of their role as cultural mediators (Aguilar, 2007). In the following part we take a closer look on how we built and structured the activities around Byram's model.

## Skills and critical cultural awareness

While trying to think of a way to assess our students' IC we came to the conclusion that we would like to implement an experimental self-assessment to see how well our young students could reflect about their own progress and proficiency in intercultural awareness.

Working with Byram's model, we had the students first make comparisons between the photos of several living locations, in an attempt to let them try and figure out where those living spaces might be located. To make these assumptions, students would need to use what Byram (2008) defines as **skills of interpreting and relating**, which are presented in detail in the Introduction to this book and its Appendix B. This became evident during the group presentations and discussions on where they, as a group, determined the placement for the living space. Students had to come to a consensus first, in order to give their rationale.

To take it a step further we asked the students to interview their parents and find out about their family living history. We thus created a safe environment for our students to become cultural anthropologists themselves, having to use **skills of discovery** to gather new knowledge and ideas and relate them to their previous experience. In this task students were to depart from the school setting and use their new knowledge, cultural awareness and interviewing skills to derive a new understanding of what family homes were like one, two or three generations ago.

In order to supplement the student's own discoveries and experiences, the teacher provided some further **knowledge** through her Prezi presentation and the students also helped and informed each other. Of course this knowledge is then subject to a re-evaluation and reinterpretation through the students. Although the first plan was to have each student individually work with a single house, the ensuing group plan worked better given all the material Patty wanted to cover. By creating the Prezi using a wider selection of photos she was able to globe-hop, thus allowing the students the chance to view all the houses and locations.

One of the most crucial skills of Byram's model is that of **attitudes**. Engaging in intercultural work and research requires a certain openness to relativize the beliefs and assumptions of one's own culture. In this step, the students were encouraged to suspend their usual assumptions about houses and homes by showing them a multiplicity of constructions and locations where 'other' people live; the 'ooohs' and 'aaahs' referred to above were a good indication that this was working. There were also comments such as, 'Awww, I'd like to live in that [yurt] house!', 'A floating house! – Cool!'

Finally, the students were asked to take all their previous experiences and skills into account and write a reflection paper. This step was not just meant to be an indicator of their **critical cultural awareness**, but also a stimulus to bring this awareness to the front of their minds. In our next part, we would like to take a closer look at their texts.

## Student Reflections and Critical Cultural Awareness

The reflection papers were the first part of their homework to be completed. As is the case with many homework assignments, some students put in the time and effort, and wrote quality, reflective statements; others not so much. These papers served two purposes. First, they were part of the teaching plans and had the purpose of making students think and, literally and figuratively, look back and reflect on their learning experiences. Secondly, they also provided evidence, for us as teacher-researchers, of the success of our planning.

The first statement is closely tied to that part of the model which emphasizes attitudes, but students were invited to use examples not only from their work in the unit but from anywhere in school; in fact, they went beyond this. The statement had two elements: attitudes in the phrase 'curious and open' and cognition in the word 'understanding':

(1)  *I am curious and open and understanding to different cultures. Example.*

Some responses refer immediately to students' own experiences, including their experiences in other countries. Please note that the students' names are pseudonyms and do not reflect their real names. In the first example, the 'friends' are probably in the home environment, but the second refers to travel abroad:

> 'I have friends of different cultures. I'm open to hearing them talk about their cultures.' (Soledad)

> 'This summer I went to Egypt, I got to understand the culture. One way I got to eat different food and traditional cookies. I went to historical places. One was pyramids.' (Nora)

Open attitudes are exemplified by the willingness to listen. Understanding is exemplified by the experience of eating others' food and seeing their historical icons, the pyramids. The next example has a hypothetical reasoning but also grounds the student's openness in willingness to engage with otherness in the notion of hearing about other places and cultures:

> 'In Africa a lot of people live in the desert. If a kid from Africa came to my class I would ask a lot of questions.' (Mateo)

In two other cases, curiosity and openness are exemplified in an interest in language learning. In the first case the student has a view of language learning which is evident in Byram's theory too, that language and culture are integrated:

'I am open to different cultures because I think it should be a goal to know another language and if you want to know another language then you should know the culture around it.' (Josué)

In the second case, the relationship of language and culture is perhaps not seen in the same way since it is implied that one first learns the language and then satisfies one's curiosity by going to the country, in this case France.

'Yes I am curious to different cultures. For example, I would like to learn French so I can one day go to France.' (Sara)

The second statement in the list was focused on the notion of 'way of life':

(2) *I am interested in other people's way of life, and what other people do on a daily basis. Example.*

Here are some of the responses we found particularly interesting:

'My friend is Muslim and he has a different schedule than Americans. He prays five times a day.' (José)

'When I went to Mexico I wanted to learn how a kid's life works and what they study.' (Estela)

'I have a friend who is part of another culture, and I am interested in what she does that relates to her culture. I like trying new foods that are part of her culture.' (Natalia)

'I liked learning about the Chinese culture. Some Chinese people live in very small houses or apartments in big cities. They have very small families because so many people like to live in cities.' (Marisol)

In the third reflection statement, many students not quoted here wrote about learning about the Spanish culture in class. Others remarked on having seen cultural performances that made them aware of the importance of that art form to the presenters. Still others remarked on lessons learned from their classroom teachers that helped in their understanding of other cultures:

(3) *I have realized that I can understand other cultures by seeing things from a different point of view. Example.*

'When learning about other cultures, looking at pictures helps me understand the culture by showing me how other people live since I can't be there to experience it.' (Benjamín)

'I understand that people have different religions and that can affect how they eat and what they do during the day.' (Corina)

'When I sleep over at Emma's house I get to see and eat Albanian breakfast food.' (Alana)

'When I was in the Dominican Republic I saw different types of homes and different meals and I did not think that was weird because it is their culture.' (Lucas)

'I can pretend that I am from a different culture and realize how they might feel.' (Miguel)

One response was particularly interesting in that it showed an ability to change perspective and make the link between language and perspective very clear:

'Meeting Mariana (a recently-arrived student from Colombia) because she sees everything in Spanish and I see everything in English. I now realize how hard it is for her in this new school. We are learning from each other.' (Mercedes)

The fourth and fifth statements focused on the knowledge acquired through the lesson. The fourth was as open as possible:

(4)   *I know some important facts about the dwellings of other cultures. Example.*

'The houses in Mexico are made of stucco so the cool will stay in.' (Andrés)

'In Greece in the summer the houses have shutters that open up for air because it is so hot they need shutters because some people do not have air conditioning.' (Carla)

'In Haiti, houses are made of tin because wood is hard to find and they don't have the money to buy a house.' (Mateo)

'Some homes have roofs that collect rain or get rid of it by having the roof on a different angle.' (Nicolás)

'People in Alaska live in igloos for temporary times. Some people in Africa live in mud houses and I live in a two-story house.' (Carlos)

'I know ways other houses have been made based on the climate in which they live.' (Perla)

'Some important facts about the dwellings of other cultures are that dwellings are built in a certain way because of their surroundings!' (Ema)

The fifth statement also gave students the opportunity to record their deeper understanding of housing and its link with the environment:

(5)  *I can explain and understand why some houses are built in a certain way. Example.*

> 'Some houses built near rivers are built on stilts to protect the house from rising waters and to keep the people inside dry.' (Benjamín)

> 'Some houses are built a certain way because of where they live it might be very cold or very warm. Maybe the lifestyle they live in, or they have a big or small family. Sometimes they have to build their houses out of nature.' (Francesca)

> 'Some houses are built a certain way to go with their climate or area.' (Rebeca)

> 'The land in Japan is very scarce because it is very small and that's why the houses are very small.' (Miguel)

> 'I know that houses are built to protect people from rain and snow and the coldness or the hotness outside. They are also built because we need places to sleep and outside is <u>no</u> place to sleep (unless you are going camping).' (Catalina)

> 'Everyone needs a home. Some houses are built differently because of the weather.' (Marisa)

## Student Projects: The Outcomes

The students' culminating project – an interview about their first homes with members of their own family – yielded a lot of variety and complexity in the product.

Some students decided to write, in English, a description of their interviews. In one particular family the student wrote that grandpa lived in a fourth floor brick apartment with no elevator in the Bronx while grandma came from a two-bedroom apartment in New York City with a doorman. Another student wrote that his Memère/grandmother lived in a two-story house that had a hair salon above and Pepère/grandfather lived in a small ranch-style house with farm animals and a big yard. Other examples referred to a grandmother's house that had no refrigerator, just an icebox; mom's beautiful apartment in Mumbai, India that had a huge mango tree that she and her friends would throw rocks at until the mangos dropped; and grandpa's boring rented house that he hated because 'it was not something a child should live in'.

When we come to the pictures students created after their interviews, many wrote the caption below the photo or drawing in Spanish, although this was not required. Figures 1.2–1.5 show four examples of projects, originally in color. Some of the other projects not pictured here included such

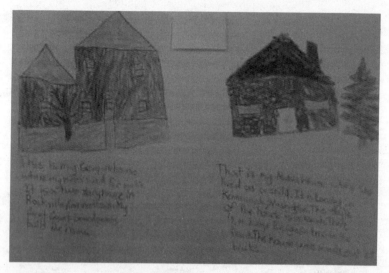

**Figure 1.2** Student's drawing and description of grandparents' childhood home

**Figure 1.3** Here, for example, 'Great-grandparents (G.G.) lived in a white barn house (with) two floors and had a chicken coop located in Texas'.

**Figure 1.4** In this 'Family Tree House' Grandpa Lin's house in Taichung, China was a traditional Chinese courtyard house.

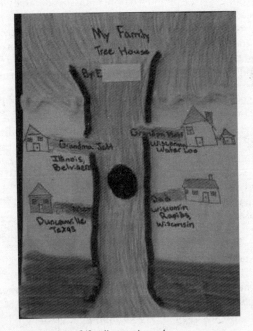

**Figure 1.5** Student's drawing of 'family tree house'

comments as, 'Mi tio (my uncle) lived in a trailer', 'My mom's house had 2 stories. It was tight, especially when you had to fit 9 people in it.' and 'This is my grandma's first house. It was at a GI barracks at Southern Illinois University.' Finally, a student whose mother was born in Giza, Egypt described her home in a long, descriptive narrative:

The flat was on the 6th floor of a 10 floor apartment building. It had a nice balcony but my grandfather did not allow anyone to use it that much because of his fear of heights. It had no elevator, so they had to go up 6 flights of stairs all the time. My grandma and mom were born in the same flat/apartment which was 3 miles from the pyramids. My grandmother's mother owned the whole building that had 3 apartments and some separate small barn rooms to raise chickens, pigeons, rabbits, and goats. These rooms were located between the second and third level. All the kids loved playing with the animals. Standing from the top of the apartment building you could see the pyramids.

## Lessons Learned

This was our experiment and a number of issues became clear and could be in some cases corrected in future iterations. In retrospect, the Family Tree House project could have benefited from one additional task. We should have asked students to identify what new learning and information about their family homes they discovered after completing the interviews. Was it exciting and interesting to learn about first homes? Was there anything that really surprised you? Additionally, pre-printed directions for the project should have been distributed to the students as that would have greatly reduced the number of questions they had. Even a veteran teacher can sometimes overlook the fact that what we assume are clear directions may not be seen that way by eight-and nine-year-olds. However, there are some indications in the texts and pictures that the students did indeed discover new things about their own families and we can often infer that they had not previously talked to older people, particularly their grandparents, about the life they had led. These young people began to realize that it is not just in other countries and locations that life is different but also in previous times.

With respect to the cooperation in the project, we realize that we are most fortunate to live in such an electronic and technologically connected world as it facilitated our collaboration throughout the course of this project. Notes, thoughts and ideas, first drafts, convention presentations and edits were accomplished through face-to-face meetings, Skype calls, multiple emails and shared documents. We Glastonbury teachers were also given privileges to share documents through the UConn departmental site for the course in which the graduate students were enrolled.

We both look back together and feel the one component of collaboration that we both missed out on was for Silke to have been able to see first-hand one of the lessons. This comes with the understanding that elementary public schools and university academic calendars vary and cannot always accommodate all needs. Not only do the calendars vary, but the days and times of classes vary at the university level, too. We both agree, however, that this is not a reason not to collaborate and that there are most certainly a variety of ways to create a partnership of teaching and learning cultural practice across any and all academic environments.

## References

Abrams, Z.I. (2002) Surfing to cross-cultural awareness: Using internet-mediated projects to explore cultural stereotypes. *Foreign Language Annals* 35 (2), 141–160.

Ada, A.F. and Campoy, F.I. (2003) *Acerquense!* Orlando, FL: Harcourt.

Aguilar, M. (2007) Dealing with intercultural communicative competence in the foreign language classroom. *Intercultural Language Use and Language Learning* (pp. 59–78). Dordrecht: Springer.

Atay, D., Kurt, G., Çamlibel, Z., Ersin, P. and Kaslioglu, Ö. (2009) The role of intercultural competence in foreign language teaching. *Inonu University Journal of the Faculty of Education* 10 (3), 123–135.

Bruner, J.S. (1960) *The Process of Education*. Cambridge, MA: Harvard University Press.

Byram, M. (2008) *From Foreign Language Education to Education for Intercultural Citizenship*. Clevedon: Multilingual Matters.

Byram, M. and Feng, A. (2004) Culture and language learning: Teaching, research and scholarship. *Language Teaching* 37 (3), 149–168.

Byram, M., Gribkova, B. and Starkey, H. (2002) Developing the intercultural dimension in language teaching. Strasbourg: Council of Europe. See www.coe.int/t/dg4/linguistic/source/guide_dimintercult_en.pdf (accessed June 28, 2017).

Condon, J. and Nam, K.-A. (2009) The DIE is cast: The continuing evolution of intercultural communication's favorite classroom exercise. *International Journal of Intercultural Relations* 34 (2010), 81–87.

Krashen, S.D. (1992) *The Input Hypothesis: Issues and Implications*. Torrance, CA: Laredo.

Liddicoat, A. and Scarino, A. (2013) Designing classroom interactions and experiences. *Intercultural Language Teaching and Learning* (pp. 63–82). Somerset, NJ: John Wiley.

McTighe, J. and Wiggins, G. (2013) *Essential Questions: Opening Doors to Student Understanding*. ASCD.

Osborn, T. (2007) Teaching world languages for social justice. *Journal of Christianity and Foreign Languages* 9 (8), 11–23.

Scollon, R. and Scollon, S.W. (1995) *Intercultural Communication: A Discourse Approach*. Oxford: Blackwell.

# 2 Discovering Modes of Transportation

## Dorie Conlon Perugini

## Classroom Snapshot

During a classroom virtual field trip to Puerto Rico, I can't help but smile as I watch the varied reactions my 4th grade students have when I suggest we hop into a *carro público* (a type of shared taxi) on our way to Viejo San Juan. Some students are wide-eyed with excitement while others look completely terrified. The simple fact that they understand and react so strongly to the concept of using a *carro público* shows how far they have come in their learning, and how much I have evolved in my teaching of the 4th grade Modes of Transportation unit. During this particular lesson, my students are using the Google Earth iPad app to independently navigate their way through a virtual field trip of Puerto Rico. But they are doing more than just viewing photographs of San Juan's sandy beaches and El Yunque's lush jungle. They are discussing with their partner whether they should hop on the back seat of a moto-taxi or flag down a *gua* (a local bus) to get from the airport to their hotel in Old San Juan. It was a real pleasure hearing them evaluate the different types of transportation available to them and watching them work through complex authentic tasks using critical thinking skills, all while using their limited knowledge of the language they are learning.

## As for me...

I am a graduate of UConn's Neag School of Education with undergraduate and master's degrees in curriculum and instruction for Spanish education. I also received a cross-endorsement for the teaching of world languages for elementary/primary school from Central Connecticut State University. At the time of this project I have been teaching Spanish in elementary school for eight years, and for the past few years I have been using Byram's (2008) model of intercultural competence (IC) as a guideline for incorporating a more systematic way of guiding my students' development of IC. I was first introduced to Byram's model by Manuela Wagner in 2011 during a Glasport

(CT) task force meeting. The Glasport task force, funded by a federal Foreign Language Assistance Program grant from the US Department of Education, met to discuss alternative assessments for world language instruction. During the course of the meeting, Manuela and I began discussing the idea of assessing IC using elements of Byram's model. After this meeting, Manuela and I decided to work together with Mike Byram to see if we could systematically implement IC-building skills into the elementary foreign language curriculum. Manuela, Mike and I met regularly to discuss IC and practical ways to apply Byram's model in the classroom. The results of this collaboration were published in the National Network for Early Language Learning's journal, *Learning Languages* (Byram *et al.*, 2013). The following year, I enrolled on the UConn graduate course so I could expand my knowledge of IC and deepen my understanding of the research available. It was my goal to use this as a professional development opportunity with the objective of implementing what I learned in my classroom.

## Context

The students participating in the lesson described above are in 4th grade, nine and ten years old, and have been studying Spanish in school for approximately 75 minutes a week since they were six years old (Table 2.1). This year, students have Spanish class three times a week, each session lasting 25 minutes. Having foreign language instruction in this format means I teach between seven and ten classes each day, am responsible for instruction at four different grade levels and have a total of around 250 students each year. This presents many unique challenges that will be discussed throughout this chapter.

For this project I decided to work with my 4th grade students. This is the same cohort of students who participated in the project discussed in the *Learning Languages* journal article previously mentioned (Byram *et al.*, 2013). By 4th grade, students are in their fourth year of language study and receive approximately 75 minutes of Spanish instruction each week. A majority of the students in this grade are at the Novice Mid to Novice High levels of proficiency as defined by American Council on the Teaching of Foreign Languages (ACTFL)'s (2012) Proficiency Guidelines. This means that students

**Table 2.1** Summary of the classroom and students

| Type of school | Grade level(s) | Average age of the students | Average number of students per class | Number of classes per week | Number of minutes per class | Number of previous years of language study |
|---|---|---|---|---|---|---|
| Primary | 4 | 9–10 | 20 | 3 | 25 | 3 |

can communicate using a number of isolated words and memorized phrases, and can sometimes communicate using complete sentences. Students at the Novice level thrive when communicating in the particular context in which the language has been learned, but students at this level struggle to create new language which has not been directly taught or memorized.

The 4th grade curriculum in Glastonbury, as also explained in Chapter 1, is centered on the 'essential question': *How are we connected to the Caribbean?* To answer this question, students participate in units of study which include lessons designed to help them gain enduring understandings, such as 'there is a relationship between culture and leisure activities' and 'there is a unique relationship between Puerto Rico and the United States'. In theory, each unit of study should help students gain a better understanding of the essential question guiding their learning. While some units of study, such as the 'Geography of the Caribbean', have a strong connection to the year-long essential question, other units, like the 'Modes of Transportation' unit, only have a loose connection. It is each individual teacher's responsibility to find meaningful and authentic ways to make strong connections between each unit of study and the year-long essential question. Since the essential question is culturally based, I see this as an opportunity to incorporate lessons and activities that help students develop skills of intercultural competence. Table 2.2 provides an overview of the existing unit and its purposes.

## Implementing the Project

Using the 'Understanding by Design' model of the curriculum embraced by Glastonbury Public Schools, the first step in planning a unit which helps students develop IC is to identify the desired results. For this project, I decided to continue to work with Byram's (2008) model of IC as a guideline for desired results. For the unit to allow for student IC growth, it must give students opportunities to develop each of the competencies Byram identifies as aspects of IC: knowledge, skills of interpreting and relating, skills of discovery and interaction, attitudes, and critical and cultural awareness. Byram also argues the importance of an 'action in the community' component – something I personally embrace in my own philosophy of education. I decided I would plan for some type of action opportunity as part of this project.

In order to adjust the curriculum to include Byram's aspects of IC and therefore provide students with the activities needed to develop their IC, I had first to examine the current curriculum to see where natural opportunities to include such activities exist. I believe that inclusion of IC-building activities should not be a departure from the existing curriculum, nor should it hinder students from reaching the unit's content and communication goals. Instead, the students' development of IC should complement the curriculum in natural and authentic ways.

**Table 2.2** Unit on 'Modes of Transportation'

| Unit title | Modes of Transportation |
|---|---|
| Unit description | As part of the year-long study of how we are connected to the Caribbean, students will discover the different types of transportation used throughout the Caribbean and the United States. Students will explore transportation used in the past at the time of the Spanish explorers as well as contemporary transportation. The unit provides the vocabulary in the target language for students to write and speak about the various modes (land, air, sea) and types of transportation. |
| Enduring understandings | • Students will understand that there are many types of transportation.<br>• Students will know the modes of transportation: air, land, sea.<br>• Students will understand that transportation serves as a vehicle for exploration.<br>• Students will understand the evolution of the many types of transportation over time, from the time of the explorers to the present and into the future. |
| Essential questions | • How do people explore/travel?<br>• What are the different types of transportation?<br>• How do I name and describe the different types of transportation?<br>• What was transportation like in the past?<br>• What is transportation like now?<br>• How is transportation similar and/or different in the Caribbean and the United States? |
| Content | • When prompted, students will be able to name and group, by air, land and sea, the different modes of transportation.<br>• When prompted to describe a type of transportation, students will be able to produce an oral or written response using new and spiraled vocabulary, including size, shape, color and speed.<br>• Students will know the common transportation used in the past and the common transportation used today.<br>• Spanish explorers sailed in ships across oceans.<br>• The Taínos indigenous people of Puerto Rico used canoes.<br>• Students will know the types of transportation common to certain parts of the world and the impact of geography on modes of transportation.<br>• Students will understand that transportation makes exploration possible.<br>• Students demonstrate correct usage of the verb ser (to be) with regard to describing a type of transportation.<br>• Students demonstrate correct usage of the verb ir (to go) to indicate how one gets somewhere.<br>• Students will demonstrate correct noun/adjective agreement. |

In analyzing the existing units and reflecting on how I have taught those units in previous years, I found one unit that seemed to have a very weak connection with the essential question, the 4th grade 'Modes of Transportation' unit (see Table 2.2 above). The unit summary states: 'as part of the year-long study of the essential question: *How are we connected to the Caribbean?*, students will discover the different types of transportation used throughout the Caribbean and the United States.' This description of the unit, along with the unit's essential questions, implies that students will be given an opportunity to compare and contrast the similarities and differences between transportation used in the United States and the Caribbean, but a closer look at the contents of the unit showed that this may not actually be realized in practice.

While exploring the 'Content' and 'Key Vocabulary' sections of the unit plan, it is evident that cultural information, corresponding to the knowledge competence in the Byram (2008) model, is presented as undisputed facts, such as 'Spanish explorers sailed in ships across oceans' or 'the Taínos (the indigenous people of Puerto Rico) used canoes'. While Byram's model does include a knowledge component, in order for students to develop IC they must have opportunities to go beyond activities of rote memorization. Phillips (2001: 1) states that 'the presentation of culture as a set of learnable "facts" may promote the notion of culture as a static construct'. Furthermore, overgeneralized statements such as these, although easily understood by novice-level speakers, can easily lead to students forming stereotypes or essentialism (e.g. Holliday, 1999) because they ignore the multifacetdness of the Spanish explorer or Taíno cultures. Holliday et al. (2010) argue that stereotypes, which are often infected by prejudice, can lead to 'othering', reducing people to less than they are. To avoid this overgeneralization of culture and help students develop skills of IC, the newly designed unit must give students opportunities to discover and interact with the target cultures rather than digesting the cultures by consuming cultural factoids presented by the teacher.

Another aspect of the Modes of Transportation unit that I had to consider in order to give students the opportunity to develop IC is the content itself. In the 'Content' and 'Key Vocabulary' sections, there is a glaring absence of modern-day means of transportation used in the Caribbean. The vocabulary list contains only the types of transportation already familiar to the average student in Glastonbury: car, bus, plane, boat, train, metro, etc. What are not present in the unit vocabulary are the types of transportation *unfamiliar* to the Glastonbury students but commonplace in the Caribbean. For example, many people living in the Caribbean rely on a *gua gua* (the minibus used as a shared taxi we saw in the introduction) to meet their daily transportation needs. Unfortunately, this type of transportation is not seen anywhere in the unit description. To allow students to develop their skills of IC and move towards an ethno-relative point of view, I would have to design new unit activities which would expose students to products, and even concepts (such as a shared taxi), that are unfamiliar to them.

Now that I had identified a few end results for the modified unit, the next step of 'Understanding by Design' was to determine the acceptable evidence of learning. In other words, how will I know if my students have met my desired outcomes? Some of the competences in Byram's model can be demonstrated explicitly in the classroom through participation in certain activities included in the lesson plan. For example, students can show a growth in knowledge by articulating the new information they learned during classroom conversations. Development of other competencies – attitudes, for example – cannot be assessed in the same manner.

To evaluate student growth in some of these other areas I decided to use Bennett's (2004) Developmental Model of Intercultural Sensitivity (DMIS). This framework can be used to describe how a student's reaction to a specific cultural situation can fall into one of six stages of sensitivity to difference, moving from an ethnocentric to an ethno-relative point of view. To assess students' knowledge and attitudes of the content being studied, I decided to use journaling to create opportunities for them to express themselves freely and naturally. In order for them to do this, I realized they must be allowed to express themselves in English since 4th grade students using novice and intermediate levels of Spanish are unable to explain concepts and ideas they have not yet learned in the target language. Communicating in English for a substantial amount of Spanish class time, however, goes against ACTFL's recommendation of 90% use of the target language (ACTFL, 2012) and my personal goal of 100% use of the target language. To solve this problem, I decided to collaborate with the 'classroom teacher', i.e. the person who is responsible for teaching all of the other subjects (e.g. mathematics, social studies, writing) in the curriculum. After explaining the project to her, we together decided that the students could write in English in a journal for ten minutes after Spanish class ended. The time they spent journaling in English would be part of their regular classroom writing time and, as a result, they would not have to spend any of their Spanish class time using English.

These reaction journals proved to be a powerful tool in assessing how students were developing their IC skills, and in providing me with guidance as to how to plan subsequent lessons. For the 10 minutes after Spanish class, students could choose either to free-write their reactions to that day's lesson or to answer a prompt I had written on the board. The prompts I wrote were often very general, with questions ranging from 'What were three new things you learned today?' to more specific prompts such as 'Would you feel safer using public transportation in the United States or in the Caribbean? Why?'. Some days, rather than asking the students a question, I would ask them to write any questions they had or anything they were curious about. I enjoyed reading their candid responses and questions and would often find myself adjusting, or even completely changing, the next day's lesson plan based on their writings. I believe this helped me create lessons that were interesting and engaging for my students and, in turn, as they realized what they wrote in their journals had importance, the quality of their writing and questions increased as the unit progressed.

## Lesson Planning and Lessons

Now that I had identified my desired results and acceptable evidence, it was time to plan the lessons for my modified Modes of Transportation unit. Before beginning the unit, I decided to use the student journals to assess my students' a priori knowledge of the Caribbean and of transportation in the Caribbean. Not only did I want to know what knowledge they already had, I also wanted to gain a better understanding of where they possibly fell on Bennett's Scale of Intercultural Sensitivity. For example, did they understand that there might be differences between modes of transportation around the world or did they assume, ethnocentrically, that transportation in the Caribbean would be the same as in the United States? Once I understood where they stood, I could get a better handle on the kinds of activities they would need in order to develop skills of IC. For their first journaling activity I gave them two questions: *What do you know about transportation in the Caribbean?* and *What questions do you have about transportation in the Caribbean?* Reading through their responses, I could see the varied levels of knowledge and attitudes regarding the Caribbean and transportation beginning to emerge.

In analyzing the journal entries, it was important for me to remember that a single statement made in reaction to a lesson cannot give me a full picture of their knowledge and attitudes. Nevertheless, these entries combined with classroom observation of student behavior and responses gave me a starting point in understanding their current level of ethnocentricity or ethnorelativity. While the responses certainly fell across Bennett's scale, I would place most students' responses in the 'denial of difference' stage. Most students expressed in their journal that they did not believe there would be any difference in transportation between the United States and the Caribbean. Many responses echoed the sentiment that the Caribbean must have cars and buses 'just like we do'. One student, for example, stated 'I think they all look the same. Like the same cars and trucks in the Caribbean and in the US.', while another wrote 'I think transportation in the Caribbean is kind of similar because the U.S. has cars and so does the Caribbean'. Other students, despite not having much, if any, experience with the Caribbean, knew they would encounter some differences: 'I think that the transportation in the Caribbean is different. Like, maybe the engines are different or the brands or style or how they could have set up the inside steering wheel might be different.' and 'I think maybe the transportation is different because maybe they ride bikes and motorcycles more because the weather is warmer and there is no snow. But it might be the same too because of cars and busses.' Although these responses are a step towards an ethnorelative point of view, journal entries of this type were few and not well developed. For these reasons, I decided to focus on Bennett's recommendations for moving students out of the denial of difference stage towards the next stage – 'defense of difference'.

Bennett (2004) says that the developmental task for students in the denial of difference stage is to 'recognize the existence of cultural differences' through the 'facilitation of structured contact with other cultures through films, slides, panel presentations, etc.'. In my lesson planning stages, I used Bennett's suggestions on how to support learners at this stage:

- illustrate ideas with user-friendly activities;
- embed differences in non-threatening contexts;
- promote an inclusive, non-blaming climate;
- address learner anxieties in existing categories, but limit time;
- build on what they already know.

After reading my students' journals, I thought the most productive way to introduce them to new and unfamiliar types of transportation used in the Caribbean would be to build on what they already knew. I began the Modes of Transportation unit the same way I had done in years past: using the Total Physical Response (TPR) (Asher, 1969) method to introduce vocabulary for the types of common transportation used in Glastonbury. In using the TPR method the teacher encourages students to use physical movements to represent each of the vocabulary words they learn. On Day 1 of the unit, I brought pictures of the common modes of transportation students are familiar with: car, truck, airplane, boat, motorcycle, bike, etc. Rather than choosing physical movements to represent these types of transportation for my students, I asked them to use their imaginations to invent gestures we could use as a class for each of the vocabulary terms (e.g. they decided to gesture using their hands moving a steering wheel to represent a car). Once the students mastered the new vocabulary, we continued the unit in the traditional way, using their knowledge of already-mastered vocabulary and sentence structures to describe and state opinions about the different modes of transportation. In this way, students could produce sentences to describe the modes of transportation familiar to them:

- *El carro es azul.* (The car is blue.)
- *El avión es muy grande.* (The airplane is very big.)
- *La motocicleta tiene dos ruedas.* (The motorcycle has two wheels.)
- *Me gusta el tren. No me gusta el barco.* (I like the train. I don't like the boat.)

After I had gathered evidence that they had acquired the knowledge of the types of transportation already familiar to them, I decided it was time to introduce modes of transportation used in the Caribbean. I began this lesson by showing a short video of a typical ride in a *carro público* (a shared taxi). Here, the students can see the inside of a *carro público* with passengers entering and exiting, as well as different types of transportation viewed through the eyes of a *carro público* passenger: cars, trucks, *gua guas* (local taxi buses), motorcycle taxis, people walking, etc. It was quite obvious to the students that transportation in the Caribbean was quite different from what they expected, i.e. that Caribbean and US transportation would be the same. Through watching this video, they realized that not only were different types of transportation available, but they also made other interesting observations which were recorded in their journals.

After reading the responses, I could see the majority of students no longer believed that transportation in the United States and Caribbean are essentially the same. One student summed up this sentiment quite clearly, 'Everything in the Caribbean looks so different!' Other students noticed that comparing the United States and the Caribbean was a bit more nuanced and even talked about things related to transportation outside of the vehicles themselves, 'Some things were the same that we have in Connecticut like cars, trucks, motorcycles, tiny trucks and buses. Other things were the same too like radios, steering wheels and police officers. Some things are different like *mototaxis* and *carro publicos* and *gua-guas*.' While reading through each journal entry, it seemed as if by simply exposing my students to authentic resources, they were able to move beyond the denial of difference stage of the Bennett scale. What I still couldn't tell from their responses is what attitudes or opinions they had about the difference they discovered. To help elicit this type of response, after the second day of using authentic photos and videos to reinforce the vocabulary for the types of transportation commonly used in the Caribbean, I asked them to journal about some of their opinions about what they had learned so far.

A few students had positive responses in their reactions, mentioning that it is a good thing that the Caribbean seems to have more public transportation than is available in Glastonbury, and that it is better for the environment and cost effective for passengers: 'I think we should use *carro publicos* because they run on less gas and in the video I noticed many people can ride together' and 'I think that Glastonbury should have public cars, because it costs less and people without much money might pay less for transportation'.

However, most students seemed to express more negative opinions about Caribbean transportation. Many students commented on the safety issues, ranging from the lack of seatbelts and helmets: 'The *mototaxis* are very unsafe. People ride without a helmet and they can get injured', to sitting next to a stranger: 'I don't like the *carros publicos* because they look uncomfortable, small and hot. You could also be squished next to a bad person whom you don't know. I'd rather take a bus. They have more room.' They even noted the absence of traffic lights: 'I think it is very unsafe to drive in the Caribbean. There are no traffic lights and cars can hit each other. The cars looked very beat up.' Some students took it a step further and addressed the attitudes they had assumed about Caribbean drivers: 'It looks like Caribbean people have road rage because they honk their horn more than enough! I also notice a couple of people jay walked in the middle of traffic.' These observations, combined with the reactions students displayed in the classroom, showed me that most of the student responses were now falling into the defense of difference stage 'characterized by dualistic us/them thinking and frequently accompanied by overt negative stereotyping' (Bennett, 2004).

At first, it was difficult for me to read my students' journal entries. I thought their reactions were quite judgmental and negative, and as someone who emphasizes open-mindedness in my classroom I felt I had failed. I had to remind myself that moving from denial of difference to defense of difference on the Bennett scale is a natural progression and, despite seeming to be the opposite, my students were actually growing their IC skills. I also took comfort in knowing that they were gaining the IC skills identified in Byram's model. Evidence showed the students were gaining more knowledge of the target culture, but they were also demonstrating curiosity and a real desire to use their skills of discovery and interaction to learn more.

Now that my students had shown knowledge of the new vocabulary and ability to use their new language skills in basic sentences, I thought it was time to apply this knowledge in some activities that required critical thinking skills. Since students were already familiar with the geography of Puerto Rico and how to use the Google Earth iPad app from previous units, I created a lesson in which the students would plan their own virtual trips to Puerto Rico, an excerpt from which began this chapter. For this activity, students were told they would start their journeys at Naubuc School in Glastonbury, CT and continue to San Juan, Puerto Rico where they would be given a list of places they would visit (the beach, el Moro, Viejo San Juan, etc.). They were asked to work with an assigned partner to create an itinerary that would outline which modes of transportation they would use to get from place to place.

For example, one group decided they would use a car to get from Glastonbury to the airport in Connecticut's capital city, Hartford. They would then use an airplane to get from Hartford to San Juan. Once in San Juan, they chose to use several different types of local transportation to get from one location to the next, all dependent on how long the trip would take and what they might be carrying with them at the time. This culminating activity not only allowed me to assess whether or not the students had acquired new vocabulary, but it also demonstrated their skills of discovery and interaction and critical cultural awareness.

At the end of the virtual trip to Puerto Rico, I was able to assess the students' progress towards my initial goals. They had met my expectations of growth in knowledge of Caribbean transportation and demonstrated growth in IC in each of the competences outlined by Byram. It was also important to me that the inclusion of these new IC-building activities did not hinder their ability to master the content of the traditional Modes of Transportation unit; it was evident that it did not. They were still able to discuss modes of transportation at the same level as students from previous years, with the added ability of being able to discuss transportation in the Caribbean. In my opinion, the addition of the Caribbean modes of transportation not only reinforced the vocabulary from the traditional unit, but also had a stronger connection to the 4th grade essential question: *How are we connected to the Caribbean?* The students' comparisons and contrasts were one kind of evidence of this, at a cognitive level, but their expressions of attitudes, of likes and dislikes, were also an important indicator of their personal engagement with the notion of 'connection' at the heart of the essential question.

Even though I had finished my curricular goals for the unit, I still felt there was something missing. My students were still expressing excitement in the topic through their journals and still had some interesting unanswered questions. I also had hoped to incorporate an action component to the lesson to allow the students to bring their learning outside the classroom. Unfortunately, we ran into two problems: (1) we ran out of time for this unit and needed to move on to the next unit of study; and (2) the students did not possess a sufficient control of the language to continue researching these topics in the target language. With these two concerns in mind, I made the decision to once again partner with the classroom teacher.

In 4th grade, students focus on 'persuasive writing' in their language arts time with their classroom teacher, where they focus on developing their competences in English. They learn the elements of a good argument and practice writing persuasive letters on various topics of interest to the students. One classroom teacher and I decided to use 'persuasive writing' as a way to expand the Modes of Transportation unit. We worked together to create a lesson in which the students would choose one topic related to transportation (either in the US or in the Caribbean) and create a persuasive argument related to this topic. Rather than asking the students to write a persuasive letter, which is what they practice in their language arts time, we used this lesson as an opportunity to introduce students to other methods of persuasion: commercials, billboards, songs/jingles, poetry, posters, radio broadcasts, podcasts, etc. The teacher and I paired the students up and allowed them to work independently on their persuasive project.

We were quite pleased with the projects students created. The topics included increasing public transportation in Glastonbury, asking motorcyclists in the Caribbean to wear helmets, and limiting the number of passengers in a *carro público* to the number of seatbelts available. The persuasive products the students created to convey their messages varied from songs to commercials to poster campaigns.

# Project Strengths

## Community of practice

Since, at the time of this project, I was both a teacher in Glastonbury Public Schools and a graduate student at the University of Connecticut (UConn), I completed this project without an assigned partnership from the UConn course. This is not to say, however, that I was able to modify the unit on my own. A community of practice, despite being different from the other partnerships in this book, was a necessary element for success.

My community of practice consisted of Manuela, Mike, the students in the UConn graduate course, the foreign language director, other foreign language teachers in my department, and the classroom teachers at Naubuc School. It was critical for me to have people work alongside me to accomplish the goals of this project. Each person listened to my ideas, provided valuable feedback and support, helped implement the project and helped me overcome some of the challenges presented. At times when I thought the project might be too difficult to implement, or the required time or materials weren't available, I worked together with my community of practice to brainstorm ways to go forward. For example, when I first thought of asking students to journal their thoughts and experiences throughout the project, but was worried about the amount of classroom time the students would spend communicating in English, it was a classroom teacher who suggested they use the classroom block of writing time to write in their journals.

## Use of target language during classroom instruction

Since many of the competences of Byram's model of IC require higher order thinking skills to develop, it is tempting to conduct some lessons in English, especially since students at the elementary level often communicate at the novice or intermediate level. Considering the short length of classes, at just 25 minutes each, it would be much easier to present the cultural concepts in English, since introducing foreign concepts and nuances of culture is challenging enough without the added burden of a linguistic barrier. However, as mentioned earlier in this chapter, I follow ACTFL's recommendation of 90% or more target language use in my classroom.

In my experience, I have found that if the activity I am asking my students to do requires higher order thinking, then the language I am asking them to produce must be simple, otherwise the students will just resort to speaking English. In contrast, if the task I am asking them to complete is relatively simple, then students can use more of their energy to focus on language use and the linguistic task can be more complex. For example, in this unit students were asked to describe modes of transportation used in the

Caribbean, a task that uses lower order thinking skills. As such, students could focus more on language use and incorporate various sentence structures as well as richer vocabulary. During this lesson students used the new vocabulary words in complete sentences using details: '*La moto es pequeña y rapida. Tiene dos ruedas redondas. La moto es peligrosa. No me gusta la moto.* (The motorcycle is small and fast. It has two round wheels. The motorcycle is dangerous. I don't like the motorcycle.)' In contrast, when students were asked to do a cognitively complex task, such as evaluating the types of transportation available and deciding which one to use to get from point A to point B, the linguistic task I asked them to do was relatively simple: list the transportation used. In other words, deciding what transportation to use is cognitively complex, but saying '*la moto*' is linguistically simple. Deciding in advance what aspect I wanted students to focus on for each activity, the content or the language, allowed me to keep instruction in the target language without frustrating my students.

## Challenges

### Time

It is no surprise to teachers that time is always a challenge when implementing new elements into existing curriculum. While I was able to overcome some time constraints by working with the classroom teacher to provide additional time for Spanish class activities that connected to the classroom curriculum, at other times I had to change plans outright or forego my original intent. As mentioned earlier in the chapter, I would have liked to develop the action component in more depth and provide students with a way to connect their learning to our community in some way. Unfortunately, I had to move on to the next unit in our curriculum or risk my students falling behind district expectations. There were also other competences of Byram's model that I thought could have been developed further before starting the next unit. Ultimately, I decided that those components could be developed in other units through the course of the year.

The 25-minute class structure also posed challenges. There were times I felt as if my students had just warmed up to an idea, or we were in the middle of an engaging activity or conversation, when the class had to come to an abrupt end. At many times I would ask the students to continue their thoughts in their journals, but by the time we began the next class session the momentum was lost. While I am not in a position to change the structure of our instructional schedule, I would like to seek additional ways, beyond the student journals, to preserve the excitement and enthusiasm of a lesson from one class to the next.

Lastly on the topic of time, there is the challenge presented by the number of students I teach. Mentioned in the context section of this chapter,

I teach up to ten classes each day and have a total of approximately 250 students. While reading my students' journals provided me with a lot of insight into their thinking and evidence of growth in IC skills, reading and responding to each student's writing took a significant amount of time. While the concept of journaling is one I would like to continue in the future, the practicality of it needs to be considered. The costs of journaling, i.e. the time used in class to write and the teacher's time used to read and respond, must be weighed against the benefits. Although I will not be asking my students to continue journaling at the same frequency for the remainder of the year, I do plan on using reflective writing as a tool for gauging student growth in IC in the future.

### Student autonomy

When working in conjunction with the classroom teacher to create the guidelines for the students' final project (i.e. the persuasive writing piece), we wanted to give the students as much autonomy as possible. We did not want to give them a prescribed list of possible projects such as 'Create a TV commercial, billboard or podcast', but rather allow them to use their imagination, as well as their knowledge of the world around them, to design a creative persuasive product. We led the students in a group brainstorming activity so that they would have some examples of possible products. Despite listing well over 20 different ways persuasion is used within society and giving students the option to create whatever they desired, students seemed to be unable to start their project without more concrete guidance. They wanted to be told what exactly they were expected to make, rather than working independently using their problem-solving and critical thinking skills to develop an innovative persuasive argument. With much emphasis in education placed on having the 'right answer', they were afraid to take risks and practice creativity. While the final products were interesting and creative in their own right, I admit I was disappointed that all groups, save one that created a new type of helmet and wrote a song to be used in a commercial to advertise the helmet, created a traditional poster. I believe the more I give students opportunities to practice autonomy in the classroom, the more they will be able to develop the 21st century skills of taking initiative and being self-directed learners.

# Final Reflections

Looking back on my original goal of designing lessons to help my students gain skills of IC, I can see many ways in which this took place. To identify these areas, and help plan for future lessons, I created a table to reflect on each competency of Byram's model and identify how these areas were addressed throughout the traditional and IC-modified unit:

| Goals | Traditional unit | IC modified unit |
|---|---|---|
| Knowledge | Vocabulary of transportation focuses on transportation commonly used in the United States. | Include vocabulary for the types of transportation commonly used in the Caribbean (unfamiliar to students). Other knowledge (to be discussed through journaling): cost of transportation, concepts of public versus private transportation, what is considered 'safe'. |
| Skills of interpreting and relating | Students categorize transportation into different groups: land, air, water. Students view examples of bus schedules used in our community. | Relating transportation used in the United States to transportation used in the Caribbean. Interpreting videos of common types of transportation in the Caribbean (e.g. after students view a video of a motorcycle taxi, the teacher asks, 'What is happening in this video? Does it remind you of anything you have ever seen before?'. These questions are asked in the target language using novice-level language). Students also respond to these questions through journaling activities. |
| Skills of discovery and interaction | Students ask each other questions about how they get around (e.g. Student A asks Student B, 'How do you get to school in the morning?') addressed only to 'us' and 'our' way of life. | Discovery: Students discover unfamiliar types of transportation through pictures and video. Students also discover new concepts (e.g. the concept of shared taxis). Interaction: Students interact with the Caribbean culture using the Google iPad app. Students discover photos uploaded in real time that are geotagged by users in certain locations along their virtual trip to Puerto Rico. |
| Attitudes | Traditional unit does not address attitudes. | Students express their attitudes through their journaling experience. Students have opportunities to reflect on essential questions in English through an action project completed in partnership with the classroom teacher. |
| Critical, cultural awareness | Traditional unit addresses culture in a surface way. It briefly mentions that transportation varies worldwide but does not provide many examples. | Through discovering unfamiliar types of transportation, students question what types of transportation we use and why: Why do we use the types of transportation we do? What types of transportation do other countries have that we do not? etc. Secondly, students reflect on the grounds for their initial reactions to other types of transport, its advantages and disadvantages. |

(Continued)

| Goals | Traditional unit | IC modified unit |
|---|---|---|
| Concern about social justice | Traditional unit does not provide opportunities to discuss concerns about social justice. | Through journaling, students are encouraged to consider questions of social justice: Can all people afford private transportation? Which types of transportation are safer than others? Students are also encouraged to write their own questions to help guide their learning. |
| Action component | Not present. | At the end of the unit, students complete an action project in collaboration with the classroom teacher. Students are given the opportunity to create a persuasive argument to change something about US or Caribbean transportation with which they did not agree. |
| Cross-curricular teaching | Not present. | Students journal their questions and comments during a special journal time. Journal time takes place with the classroom teacher and is done in English. Students also participate in an action project in collaboration with the classroom teacher connecting to their persuasive writing language arts unit. |

This table helps reinforce the idea that IC must be implemented through careful planning. It is not enough to simply have intentions of helping create globally minded students, but rather I as a foreign language teacher have the responsibility to take a systematic approach to including IC in my curriculum. Throughout the course of this project, I realized that to meet this goal it was crucial to develop a community of practice, to take time to reflect on each day's lesson, and to have avenues for open and honest communication with my students. This project has given me knowledge and experience I can use to replicate this approach of incorporating IC in future units of study.

# Appendix: Unit Timeline

Each day represents one 25-minute session.

| Day | Activity | Aspect of Byram's model addressed |
|---|---|---|
| Before starting unit | Assess students' prior knowledge of transportation in the Caribbean through journaling. | Pre-assessment of knowledge<br>Attitudes |
| Day 1 | Introduce vocabulary for types of transportation commonly used in Glastonbury using TPR methods. | Knowledge |
| Days 2–3 | Review transportation vocabulary and describe types of transportation using vocabulary and sentence structures already familiar to students. | Knowledge |
| Days 4–5 | Introduce vocabulary for types of transportation commonly used in the Caribbean using authentic photos and videos.<br>Students journal their reactions to the different types of transportation. | Knowledge<br>Interpreting and relating<br>Discovery and interaction<br>Attitudes |
| Day 6 | Review Caribbean transportation vocabulary and describe types of transportation using vocabulary and sentence structures already familiar to students.<br>Students are asked to analyze and evaluate different types of transportation in the US and the Caribbean in their journals. | Knowledge<br>Critical cultural awareness |
| Days 7–8 | Students use Google Earth iPad app for a virtual trip to Puerto Rico.<br>Students journal about what they saw on their virtual trip and the decisions they made along the way. | Discovery and interaction<br>Critical cultural awareness<br>Attitudes |
| After unit is completed | Students create a persuasive argument related to either US or Caribbean transportation. | Knowledge<br>Discovery and interaction<br>Critical cultural awareness<br>Action component |

# References

ACTFL (2012) ACTFL *Proficiency Guidelines 2012*. Alexandria, VA: American Council on the Teaching of Foreign Languages.

Asher, J.J. (1969) The total physical response approach to second language learning. *Modern Language Journal* 53, 3–17.

Bennett, M.J. (2004) Becoming interculturally competent. In J.S. Wurzel (ed.) *Toward Multiculturalism: A Reader in Multicultural Education*. Newton, MA: Intercultural Resource Corporation.

Byram, M. (2008) *From Foreign Language Education to Education for Intercultural Citizenship*. Clevedon: Multilingual Matters.

Byram, M., Perugini, D. and Wagner, M. (2013) The development of intercultural citizenship in the elementary Spanish classroom. *Learning Languages* 18 (2), 16–31.

Holliday, A. (1999) Small cultures. *Applied Linguistics* 20 (2), 237–264.

Holliday, A., Hyde, M. and Kullman, J. (2010) *Intercultural Communication: An Advanced Resource Book for Students*. New York: Routledge.

Phillips, E. (2001) IC¿ I see! Developing learners' intercultural competence. *LOTE CED Communiqué* 3, 1–6.

# 3   Using the Five Senses to Explore Cities

Philip Rohrer and Lauren Kagan

## Introduction

The primary goals of this project were to examine theoretical models of intercultural competence (IC) and put the theory into practice by revising an existing 6th grade world language classroom curriculum to include activities that would enhance students' IC. These activities would aim to expand students' knowledge and awareness and challenge their attitudes about other cultures and their own. The following question thus guided our project:

*How can the theoretical underpinnings of intercultural competence be applied practically and systematically in a 6th grade Spanish classroom?*

To answer this question, we modified an existing unit of teaching in a 6th grade Spanish classroom (see Table 3.2 below) in order to include objectives associated with IC, as defined in Byram's (1997) model of IC, described in the Introduction to this book. Current classroom activities were modified or new activities were created to address as many objectives as possible related to IC not being met by the current curriculum. The remainder of this chapter details the implementation of these activities, the outcomes observed, challenges faced, and how these activities align with objectives associated with IC in theory. The activities are presented in the order in which they were implemented in the classroom.

### The students

The study took place in five 6th-grade Spanish classes at Glastonbury Middle School with an average of 25–27 students per class. The students were between 10 and 12 years of age and had studied Spanish from grade 1. Each of the five classes per week lasted about 40 minutes. Table 3.1 gives an overview of the participants and their courses.

**Table 3.1** Summary of the classroom and students

| Type of school | Grade level(s) | Average age of the students | Average number of students per class | Number of classes per week | Number of minutes per class | Number of previous years of language study |
|---|---|---|---|---|---|---|
| Middle | 6th | 10–12 | 25–27 | 5 | 40 | 5 |

## And we are Philip and Lauren

Prior to and following his graduate studies at the University of Connecticut, Philip has been employed as a health actuary. It was during his graduate career that he met Manuela. Having always had a love and interest for languages, he asked Manuela if he could join her graduate course on the development of IC in language education.

Lauren graduated from the Neag School of Education at the University of Connecticut. One of Lauren's most memorable semesters was the one she spent abroad in Granada, Spain, in spring 2006. This experience truly affirmed her love for Spanish language and culture. Lauren completed her student teaching and master's internship in Glastonbury, CT, but on completion of her degrees from UConn she taught 6th, 7th and 8th grade Spanish in another Connecticut school district before returning to Glastonbury to teach 6th grade Spanish for the 2013–2014 school year. She was excited by the opportunity to work with Manuela, one of her UConn professors, and collaborate with Philip to explore ways to incorporate IC in her 6th grade foreign language classroom. What we clearly had in common and made for a rewarding collaborative relationship was a passion for teaching and learning.

## The Existing Unit

Table 3.2 provides an overview of the classroom environment in which our project was implemented. Having received 75 instructional minutes of Spanish per week for the past five years, at the 6th grade level students increase their studies of Spanish to 40 instructional minutes, five days per week, with a total of 200 minutes per week. These students are generally able to engage in simple conversations about familiar topics in the present tense, such as their school schedule and their likes and dislikes. They can also describe their appearance and personality traits as well as those of others. At the time of this project, Lauren was teaching five Spanish classes at the 6th grade level throughout the day, with 25–27 students in each class.

**Table 3.2** Overview of existing unit 'Exploring Mexico'

| Unit title | Exploring Mexico |
| --- | --- |
| Unit description | Students will learn about Mexico City, exploring the city center, Teotihuacán, Chapultepec Park and beyond, including the state of Michoacán, site of the wintering-over sanctuaries for Monarch butterflies. Students will also practice their ability to ask questions and describe what they do and eat. |
| Enduring understandings | • Mexico is a culturally rich and ethnically diverse country.<br>• Mexico has a fusion of traditional and modern cuisine. |
| Essential questions | • What kind of a place is Mexico City?<br>• What would I see and do in Mexico that is unique?<br>• How do I order food in a restaurant?<br>• How are we alike and different as a people, a culture, a country?<br>• How can I write long, interesting descriptions of what I do as a traveler, in Spanish? |
| Content | • Food and Mexican cuisine.<br>• Regular verbs in the present tense.<br>• Stem changing verbs (food related): *querer, preferir, server, pedir*.<br>• Places in the city. |

The Glastonbury syllabus provides a detailed approach to the content of the curriculum for Spanish lessons. It consists of statements of what students are expected to learn, 'enduring understandings' and the use or application of the language learnt, 'essential questions', as well as the language content. The existing unit of teaching on which we focused was entitled 'Exploring Mexico'. Taught over the course of three days, students are introduced to new vocabulary related to city locations, including markets, shops, restaurants and other tourist attractions such as museums and amusement parks. Because the focus of the existing unit is Mexico, the essential questions, as can be seen above, target Mexico City specifically.

The existing unit involves students receiving the vocabulary worksheet shown in Figure 3.1 at the start of the unit. The American English translation for the Spanish vocabulary seen on the worksheet is provided to students as well. Students are first instructed to highlight words with which they are familiar. Vocabulary is then enhanced through the use of visual aids: images of the words are shown to students to increase their understanding of the language. Students then discuss, in Spanish, different methods of transportation in a city environment and also learn about Chapultepec Park, a central attraction of Mexico City. Although the principal focus of the existing unit and essential questions is not necessarily to enhance IC, some of the questions such as the question that provokes an examination of the similarities and differences between Mexican culture and one's own culture can aid in this purpose.

## Lugares
(Places)

**el pueblo** – the town
**la ciudad** – the city
**el lugar** – the place
**el centro** – the center of town
**el ayuntamiento** – the town hall
**la agencia de viajes** – travel agency
**el aeropuerto** – the airport
**el campo** – the countryside
**el jardín** – the garden
**el parque** – the park
**la fuente** – the fountain
**la estatua** – the statue
**la playa** – the beach
**la escuela** – the school
**el gimnasio** – the gym
**el estadio** – the stadium
**la piscina** – the swimming pool
**el acuario** – the aquarium
**el hospital** – the hospital
**la farmacia** – the pharmacy
**el banco** – the bank
**la oficina** – the office
**el rascacielos** – the skyscraper
**el correo** – the post office
**la biblioteca** – the library
**el museo** – the museum
**el teatro** – the theater
**el cine** – the cinema
**el mercado** – the market
**el supermercado** – the supermarket

**la tienda** – the store
**la bodega** – small neighborhood store
**el almacén** – the department store
**el centro comercial** - the shopping center
**el restaurante** – the restaurant
**el café** – the coffee shop
**la gasolinera** – the gas station
**la estación de tren** – the train station
**la estación de metro** – subway
**la estación de autobús** – bus station
**la estación de policía** – the police station
**la estación de bomberos** – the fire station
**la iglesia** – the church
**la sinagoga** – the synagogue
**la catedral** – the cathedral

### En México:

**la taquería** – the taco shop
**el tianguis** – the flea market
**la pirámide** – the pyramid
**el quiosco** – the newsstand

### Métodos de transporte:

**el coche/ carro / automóvil** – the car
**el tren** – the train
**el taxi** – the taxi
**la motocicleta** – the motorcycle
**la bicicleta** – the bicycle
**la camioneta** – the small truck or van
**el camión** – the truck
**el barco / el bote** – the boat
**el avión** – the airplane
**el metro** – the subway
**el autobús** – the bus
**el helicóptero** – the helicopter

**Figure 3.1** Vocabulary sheet

## The Modified Unit

To better align classroom activities with the objectives associated with IC, the following activities were implemented through the modified unit. Total student responses for each activity are not always equal since students may have been absent on one or more days over the course of the unit being taught.

## Pre-assessment activity

Our senses are used on a daily basis to discover and understand what is around us. We use sight to see where we are going, taste to discover our dislikes and likes particularly when trying new foods, hearing to understand the words and sounds around us, and smell to recognize the air that we breathe. It is these senses that communicate to us the world in which we live. In the first activity, students were asked in Spanish to define the term 'city' using their senses. We reviewed the vocabulary for each of the senses – *Yo veo* (I see), *Yo oigo* (I hear), *Yo huelo* (I smell), *Yo como* (I eat), *Yo bebo* (I drink). Using prior knowledge, teacher assistance and dictionaries, students then listed words and phrases that describe a city and are representative of one of the senses. Students then shared their responses with their classmates. This activity provided a baseline against which responses to future activities could be compared. For example, many students might associate sight with towering skyscrapers and yellow taxi cabs. One of the goals of attaining IC is to set aside preconceived stereotypical beliefs about other cultures as well as one's own culture and challenge one's attitudes and knowledge of products and practices found in other cultures compared to those found in one's own culture. Sight, for example, might also include a more atypical city image of a vast recreational park occupied by the presence of wildlife. The following two activities aimed to broaden students' understanding of the term 'city', challenging their preconceived beliefs of the term.

## A City in Pictures activity

A popular saying is 'a picture is worth a thousand words'. Images can greatly increase our understanding of the unfamiliar. The existing unit of teaching involves presenting students with photos and other pictorial images to enhance their understanding of the unit vocabulary. Generally, students most often think of skyscrapers or noisy, bustling crowds when they hear the word 'city'. To further challenge the attitudes and knowledge of our students with regard to their potential presuppositions about other cultures and even their own culture, we presented to the students, in the modified unit, both stereotypical urban images of skyscrapers and busy streets as well as more atypical urban images of public markets and parades and asked them to identify those images they believed were representative of a city environment (see Table 3.7 for images presented). Students were also asked about the location in which they believed the photograph was taken. For example, New York City hosts a Hispanic Day Parade each year in October to celebrate Hispanic Heritage Month. Although held in the United States, photos from such an event would be reminiscent of Mexican culture, suggesting Mexico as the location of the photo. We exposed students to ambiguities such as this one to challenge any preconceived notions of what might be considered American or Mexican. This helped Lauren identify her students' prior presuppositions based on the pictures shown. This also enabled her to create awareness in her students that we have a biased view of certain events and situations.

## A Day in the City activity

In the final activity, students were divided into small groups and each group was assigned one of the following cities: New York City (NYC), Mexico City, Madrid, Boston or Glastonbury. Although Glastonbury is a town rather than a city, it was included to provide students with the opportunity to critically evaluate the cultural practices and products of their own culture as well as others. Boston and NYC were included for ease of research and because most students were familiar with these cities. Madrid, Spain, was included to provide students with an opportunity to further investigate the culture of Spain since Madrid was studied as part of the 3rd grade Spanish curriculum and Spain is the cultural context of the 7th grade Spanish curriculum. Using websites preselected by the teacher, each group conducted research over two days during class time to design an itinerary in Spanish that highlighted popular foods, places of interest and modes of transportation in their assigned city. Each student within each group was assigned a specific topic to research for their city as follows: traditional cuisine, cultural celebrations, museum or historical buildings, park or outdoor spaces and main modes of transportation. Because our students have minimal prior research experience at this grade level, assigning each a specific topic provided them with a more focused task. Acting as tour guides for their city, students then presented their results to their peers in Spanish. This activity met two objectives. First, it addressed the essential questions for this unit – mainly: *What would I see and do that is unique?* Secondly, it developed students' IC by broadening their knowledge of the practices and products of various cultures and applying students' knowledge of and attitudes towards different cultures developed during the previous activity to a specific urban and cultural environment.

Following the presentations and building on the essential questions, students engaged in in-classroom discussions in the target language to discuss similarities and differences between the cultures of the different cities presented. Students were asked, for example, whether anything about the culture of their city surprised them and why differences between the various cultures might exist. For example, buses provide a means of public transportation in Glastonbury, but in NYC, in addition to buses, there are trains, taxis, and other modes of public transportation because the population of NYC far exceeds that of Glastonbury, providing justification for these additional modes of transportation in NYC.

These discussions, in Spanish, were limited in scope and detail due to the limited linguistic capabilities of the students at this grade level, and students also completed an in-class written reflection in English. The written reflection allowed them to provide feedback that may have otherwise gone unheard due to their limited proficiency in the target language or timidity in speaking in front of their peers. It also served as a means for tangible data collection. To encourage students to provide candid responses, they were asked to respond anonymously to the following questions:

(1)  What is something that surprised you during your research or during the presentations?
(2)  Why is this surprising to you?
(3)  Identify something similar between two of the cultures/places presented.
(4)  Identify something unique or special about the culture/place you researched or about a culture/place presented in class.

## Student Response

### Pre-assessment activity

Tables 3.3–3.6 reflect student responses in the pre-assessment activity (a complete list of student answers is found in the Appendix to this chapter). Students were asked to define the term 'city' in the target language using four of their senses (sight, sound, smell and taste). On the day it was completed in the classroom 125 students participated in this activity. Students were given the opportunity to write as much as they could for each of the given senses. While most were able to come up with three to four responses for each category, others came up with fewer or even with more. This explains why the response numbers may be higher than the number of students present on the day of the activity. Below are the top five responses in each sense category.

### Yo veo ... (I see ...)

**Table 3.3** Results of 'Yo veo ... (I see ...)' activity

| Responses | Number of students |
| --- | --- |
| Transportation | 100 (taxis – 58) |
| Skyscrapers and buildings | 74 |
| Statues and sculptures | 39 |
| Banks | 26 |
| Parks and gardens | 24 |

## Yo oigo ... (I hear ...)

**Table 3.4** Results of 'Yo oigo ... (I hear ...)' activity

| Responses | Number of students |
|---|---|
| Transportation (cars, trucks, buses, planes, trains, motorcycles, helicopters, taxis) | 351 |
| People | 45 |
| Fountains | 9 |
| Religious buildings | 6 |
| Beach/ocean | 5 |

## Yo huelo ... (I smell ...)

**Table 3.5** Results of 'Yo huelo ... (I smell ...)' activity

| Responses | Number of students |
|---|---|
| Cafes/restaurants/food | 179 |
| Gasoline | 94 |
| Gardens/parks/flowers | 83 |
| Smoke/smog | 19 |
| Markets/stores | 16 |

## Yo como .../Yo bebo ... (I eat .../I drink ...)

**Table 3.6** Results of 'Yo como/yo bebo ... (I eat/I drink ...)' activity

| Responses | Number of students |
|---|---|
| Water | 101 |
| Fruits | 94 |
| Soda | 89 |
| Hamburgers | 84 |
| Pizza | 43 |

Lauren observed that many students responded with words they knew, even if that particular item was not something typically seen, heard, smelled or tasted in a city. Further, many students used responses they had heard or seen from their classmates. In the taste category, many students used cognates (e.g. *hamburguesa, pizza, fruta*). Additionally, students utilized dictionaries to find words as needed and Lauren observed that students tended to use vocabulary learned in previous years of Spanish. Fruit, for instance, is a unit taught as part of Glastonbury's 3rd grade Spanish curriculum, so many students responded with fruit for the taste category despite the fact that many could not say whether they truly ate fruit in a city.

## A City in Pictures activity

Table 3.7 shows the 15 images students were shown, what each image is depicting, the location of each image, and the percentage of students who believed the image was or was not representative of an urban environment. In other words, the two left-hand columns describe the pictures, whereas the two right-hand columns reflect student responses. Students were only shown the image without knowledge of where it had been photographed or what was being depicted in it, unless this information was provided directly in the image. The question posed to students, in Spanish, was: *¿Es una ciudad? Decide si las fotos representan una ciudad.* Translated into American English, the question reads: *Is this a city? Decide whether the photos represent a city.*

We might be tempted to describe an urban environment with phrases such as large crowds, towering skyscrapers or bustling streets filled with yellow taxi cabs and buses. Images 8, 9 and 10 depict these mainstream stereotypical features of a city, and over 97% of students agreed that such images are representative of a city. On the other hand, those such as Images 2, 11 and 12, depicting more atypical urban locales, were not easily identified by students as images representative of a city environment. Many were surprised to learn that all of the pictures were taken in cities, and particularly that many well-known cities (e.g. New York City) were represented by some of the parks, outdoor spaces and cultural celebrations seen in the photos. In the pre-assessment, while only a few students mentioned hearing music in a city, no students identified seeing parades or celebrations in a city. Images 5 and 14 depict cultural celebrations being held in a city. Few students identified Image 14 as being representative of a city, but most students did identify Image 5 as representative of a city, primarily due to the presence of large buildings in the background, as many students pointed out during discussions about the images. Also, the absence of the words 'parades' and 'celebrations' from the pre-assessment may be a result of students' limited linguistic skills, but the *surprise* element Lauren observed in the students is a first step toward greater IC because students are learning to challenge their preconceived beliefs and attitudes about what represents a city.

## A Day in the City activity

A number of interesting comments were received from students in their written reflections following this activity. When asked to identify something that surprised them during their research or during the classroom presentations, the presence of parks, museums and an abundance of transportation

**Table 3.7** Student responses for A City in Pictures activity

| Image | Depiction | City environment | Not a city environment |
|-------|-----------|------------------|------------------------|
| 1 | Central Park in New York City | 49.6% | 50.4% |
| 2 | Chinese Tower in the English Gardens in Munich, Germany | 50.4% | 49.6% |
| 3 | English Gardens in Munich, Germany | 90.4% | 9.6% |
| 4 | Quincy Market in Boston, Massachusetts | 90.4% | 9.6% |
| 5 | Hispanic Day Parade in New York City | 96.0% | 4.0% |
| 6 | Louvre in Paris, France | 86.4% | 13.6% |
| 7 | Charging Bull statue in New York City along Wall Street | 96.0% | 4.0% |
| 8 | Twin Towers in New York City | 100.0% | 0.0% |
| 9 | New York City taxis | 99.2% | 0.8% |
| 10 | New York City transit | 99.2% | 0.8% |
| 11 | Public market in Pittsburgh, Pennsylvania | 61.6% | 38.4% |
| 12 | Public market in Vancouver, Canada | 56.8% | 43.2% |
| 13 | San Diego Zoo in San Diego, California | 36.0% | 64.0% |

(Continued)

**Table 3.7** (*Continued*)

| Image | Depiction | City environment | Not a city environment |
|---|---|---|---|
| 14 | Scottish groomsmen in New York City | 52.0% | 48.0% |
| 15 | World's busiest pedestrian crossway in Tokyo, Japan | 97.6% | 2.4% |

modes were the most frequently mentioned. Interestingly, in the A City in Pictures activity, over 85% of students recognized that Images 3 and 6, depicting a park and museum, respectively, represented a city. Students did note, however, during classroom discussions about these photos, that the tallness of the buildings in the images heightened their inclination to record the image as representing a city.

In responding to the question that asked students to identify something that surprised them during their research or during the classroom presentations, one student commented that they were surprised 'the taxis in Mexico City were green'. Many adults and children alike would most often associate a taxi with the color yellow, perhaps due to media portrayal, but this statement by the student is a challenge to set aside any preconceived beliefs or attitudes about what color a taxi should be and accept that not all taxis are yellow. This observation thus demonstrates growth in IC.

Nearly 10% of students who completed the written reflection noted commonalities between their own town of Glastonbury and the other cities, including the presence of parks, museums, and buses as a means of public transportation. Of these students, many remarked that one usually associates tall buildings and busy streets with a city environment, but they were intrigued to discover that local parks and museums are also common features of a city and not only of a small town like their own. Through their research, many students acquired new knowledge about various locations and events in the cities they were assigned. Students' use of the internet during class time led them to discover, for example, parks other than Central Park in New York City and various historical buildings, unknown to the students, in Glastonbury. Many students also learned about cultural events involving art and local history in nearby Boston that they did not know existed. This is evidence of their ability to compare and contrast and acquire new knowledge about other cultures and their own and is also an example of students revising their preconceived beliefs or attitudes about what is and what is not representative of an urban environment.

In the next section we further explain the connections between the theoretical approach and the practice of IC.

# Analysis of Intercultural Competence

Following the suggestion made by Byram *et al.* (2013), Table 3.8 outlines the five overarching components of Byram's (1997) model of IC. Within each component are various objectives, and the table highlights whether these objectives were present in the existing unit or became present following implementation of the modified unit. In the following sections we discuss how the modified unit addressed each of the components of Byram's model of IC shown in Table 3.8.

## Attitudes

The A City in Pictures activity pushes students to broaden their perspectives on what a city really is and challenges the students to suspend any preconceived beliefs about their own culture and others. For example, almost 51% of the students, when shown the first picture of the park, believed that this was not representative of a city environment. When they discovered that this was in fact an image taken from Central Park in NYC, many students expressed their surprise and said that in their experience parks are usually found in suburban communities like their own and not in cities. Yet another example can be seen with the image of the San Diego Zoo in San Diego, CA, where 64% of the students did not feel that this image was representative of a city. Once they learned the true city location, many of the students who had traveled to the zoo shared that they 'forgot' that the zoo was in a city because it did not look that way in the picture.

Under the existing unit, as stated in the chart above, objectives relating to cultural attitudes are present in the classroom but more informally as 'teachable moments'. These teachable moments would not, however, be the primary objective of the existing unit's lesson. On the other hand, in the modified unit, the A City in Pictures activity directly aimed to turn these teachable moments into a main objective of the lesson, challenging students to begin to change their earlier interpretations of city environments, to 'suspend belief' about what is normal and open their minds to new ideas and concepts.

## Knowledge

The knowledge component of Byram's model of IC was most notably addressed in the A Day in the City activity. In the process of researching different aspects of a particular city (e.g. modes of transportation), students became knowledgeable about different social groups and their products and practices. Through their research, students discovered parks other than Central Park in New York like the Emerald Necklace chain, cultural events like the Boston Arts Festival in Boston and the Puerto Rican Pride Parade in

**Table 3.8** Components of intercultural competence present in the existing unit versus modified unit

| | | Present in existing unit | Present in modified unit |
|---|---|---|---|
| Attitudes: | A1: curious and open; receptive to cultural differences | X | X |
| | A2: readiness/willingness to suspend disbelief(s) about other culture(s)/country | X | X |
| | A3: readiness/willingness to suspend own belief about own culture(s)/country | X | X |
| Knowledge: | K1: of social groups and their products and practices in one's own culture(s)/country | X | X |
| | K2: of social groups and their products and practices in country culture being studied | X | X |
| | K3: of the general processes of societal and individual interaction | | X |
| Skills of interpreting and relating: | IR1: ability to interpret a document or event from another culture, to explain it and relate it to documents from one's own | | X |
| Skills of discovery and interaction: | DR1: ability to acquire new knowledge of a culture and cultural practices | X | X |
| | DR2: ability to operate knowledge, attitudes and skills under the constraints of real-time communication and interaction | | X |
| Critical cultural awareness/ political education: | CA1: ability to evaluate critically and on the basis of explicit criteria perspectives, practices and products in one's own culture(s)/country | | X |
| | CA2: ability to evaluate critically and on the basis of explicit criteria perspectives, practices and products of other cultures and countries | | X |

Source: Based on Byram (2008).

New York, and historical buildings like the Welles Shipman Ward House in Glastonbury. Furthermore, and in alignment with the essential questions for the unit, students were encouraged to think critically about and understand some cultural practices. This happened, as we saw previously, when students discussed in the classroom differences in the modes of transportation between Glastonbury and New York City and why these differences might exist.

## Skills of interpreting and relating

The existing unit focused primarily on utilizing the internet to explore Chapultepec Park in Mexico City. In the modified unit, however, the A Day in the City activity encouraged students to utilize multiple preselected internet-based resources, thereby exposing students to web-based documents and publications (e.g. transit maps, restaurant menus) from other cultures and in the target language. Students were encouraged to use these documents during their presentations, although it was difficult for most students at this grade level to speak about these documents in the target language. The students' exposure, however, to these varied documents during their research sparked curiosity, as similarities and differences between other cultures and their own were discussed. As an example, transit lines, bus lines and trains are in abundance in NYC. In Glastonbury, however, only bus lines, and far fewer of them, can be found as a means of public transportation. Reflections such as these were made during informal conversations following the presentations. The teacher prompted the students to reflect – both verbally and in their written reflections – on questions such as 'What similarities did you recognize between Glastonbury and the cities presented?' and 'What differences did you observe between Glastonbury and the cities presented?' Due to the students' limited linguistic ability in the target language at their age and grade level, these discussions and reflections took place in English.

## Skills of discovery and interaction

Skills of discovery and interaction were developed continuously throughout the unit. The attainment of new knowledge about other cultures and the students' own was most evident in the students' responses on the final written reflection, discussed earlier in this chapter, and when students were also able to express their newly acquired knowledge and their attitudinal changes about other cultures through classroom presentations. While the existing unit provided many opportunities for communication in the target language, it did not always guarantee discussions in the target language regarding the comparison of different national and international cities. Classroom presentations, incorporated in the modified unit, ensure students the opportunity to enhance target language communication skills.

## Critical cultural awareness

In the A Day in the City activity, students were very much engaged in critically evaluating the practices and products of other cultures as well as their own. This was particularly evident in the written reflections, completed in English, where many students remarked on the numerous modes of transportation present in many of the cities. While buses are the only means of public transportation in Glastonbury, numerous additional modes of public transport (e.g. trains, taxis, buses) are present in the other cities. Students discussed these variances across different cultures and societies and explanations for them in in-classroom discussions held in Spanish. Providing students with the opportunity to investigate multiple cities, rather than Mexico City alone, greatly enhanced their curiosity and awareness of the ambiguity that can exist within and across various cultures, including their own. For example, one student shared, 'Something that surprised me was how a small town like Glastonbury could have so much in common with a large city like New York, Boston, etc. [This] is surprising [to me] because a suburban town like Glastonbury has many of the same features as a big city like New York.' Another student wrote, 'I was surprised that all of the pictures in the slides were cities. Some of them looked like anything that could be found in a town ...'. Relating to that comment, another student shared, 'Not all cities have to have lots of busy streets and tall buildings. So many pictures of cities include tall buildings and not a lot of space to play, but when I saw the pictures of cities, [it] was very surprising.'

Comments and reflections such as these illustrate the students' growing ability to critically reconsider their preconceived notions.

# Challenges and Recommendations

The research component of this unit proved to be challenging for the 6th grade students. Once divided into groups and assigned a city, each student was given a specific topic to research for their city. Knowing the age and research experience of the students, we felt that having a specific topic to research would provide for a more focused task. As mentioned earlier in this chapter, the specific topics for each city were as follows: traditional cuisine, cultural celebration, museum or historical building, park or outdoor space, and main modes of transportation. However, we had not anticipated that many students believed they had to search for 'one right answer'. It was difficult for many to come to terms with the fact that there were multiple possibilities for each of their topics. At the conclusion of their presentations, Lauren discussed, in English, with the students how this assignment could have been completed multiple times, with different findings likely each time. In fact, because these activities were incorporated into five different Spanish classes held throughout the day, the examples students presented for the various topics varied from one class to the next for the same city. For example, one group in one Spanish class identified Boston Commons as an outdoor public park in Boston. However, another group in a different Spanish class identified the Emerald Necklace chain of parks in Boston. Students learned in the end that cities have multiple cuisines, multiple cultural celebrations, multiple museums and historical buildings, multiple parks and outdoor spaces and multiple means of transportation. Coming to this conclusion, however, was not easy, as many students needed guidance and affirmation along the way. While we highlight this as a challenge, it is also a major accomplishment. In the teaching of IC, we aim to increase our students' awareness of the variation that can exist within a single and across different cultures. This is a great achievement because students' minds are opened and curiosity abounds as preconceived beliefs about another culture or even one's own are challenged. Although time did not permit, we would have liked to review the findings from all the presentations collectively with each of the classes or to have allocated some time for interaction between the students in all the classes combined. This would hopefully create an awareness that even among their peers, variation in the responses to the same questions across different classes existed. The extent to which these conversations would be in Spanish may be limited due to the students' linguistic capabilities at this grade level, but the conversations nonetheless would enhance the students' IC. It may even be possible to encourage these discussions in other disciplinary subjects, such as social studies or geography, where the students could discuss the topic in English.

Another challenge we faced was the limited use of Spanish, although the student presentations in the modified unit were an enhancement in this regard over the existing unit. If logistics and technology allow, incorporating conversations with native speakers or other Spanish language learners as a source for the students' research, for example, is one idea we suggest other teachers explore if they wish to implement similar activities to those presented in this chapter in their classrooms. These conversations, in Spanish, would further provide students with an opportunity to simultaneously enhance their real-time communication skills and inquire about and explore cultural practices different from their own. Additionally, these conversations might generate other areas of research focus for the students in preparation for their final presentations. In the modified unit, students completed both the pre-assessment and final itinerary presentations in Spanish, and much of their research included sources in the target language. Conversations with native speakers, however, would add an additional growth element to the students' current levels of IC, especially to the linguistic components of intercultural communicative competence. Also, while it would have been meaningful to complete the reflection questions and post-unit discussions in Spanish, it was decided that doing so in English would be beneficial so that students would have less difficulty in expressing their feelings and opinions regarding the work they completed.

A final recommendation we make is to have the students complete a pre- and post-assessment activity that would provide a more reliable measure of their development of IC. Doing so would allow for a statistical analysis of any change in student viewpoints. Identifying key words and recognizing the number of times these words appear in students' responses, for example, would provide a quantitative measure with which to evaluate student growth towards greater IC. This type of analysis may be desirable among teachers and educational institutions interested in turning student responses into measurable results. While the activities presented in this chapter demonstrate, qualitatively, growth in IC among students, conducting a study that additionally incorporates some quantitative measures to demonstrate the statistical significance of these qualitative results would provide additional confirmation of the growth in IC among students.

We share these challenges and suggested recommendations in the hope that they aid teachers in implementing and measuring the outcomes of these activities in their own classrooms.

## Conclusion

At the onset of this project, we formed a question: *How can the theoretical underpinnings of IC be applied practically in a 6th grade Spanish classroom?* We answered this question by revising a current classroom curriculum to include activities that would meet the objectives associated with IC. Although the purpose of this project was to increase the IC of students in a world language classroom, we feel it would be disingenuous on our part not to mention that growth in IC does not need to happen only in the classroom. Interactions between a company executive and overseas clientele or communications between distant Facebook friends each create opportunities to enhance one's IC. Increasing IC occurs along a continuum from birth through, and including, adulthood. As Byram (1997) points out, there are classroom locations and 'field' locations, and there are moments when learners develop independently, and there are moments when the teacher has an important role as guide, particularly when encouraging the emergence of critical cultural awareness. We believe, that striving to implement activities within the classroom in which IC is a primary focus will encourage students' curiosity about other societies as well as their own and will broaden students' knowledge and critical thinking skills, indubitably benefiting them in the classroom and beyond.

# Appendix

*Yo veo ... (I see ...)*

| Category | Number of students responses |
| --- | --- |
| Transportation | 100 (taxis = 58) |
| Skyscrapers and buildings | 74 |
| Statues and sculptures | 39 |
| Banks | 26 |
| Parks and gardens | 24 |
| Cafes and restaurants | 19 |
| Stores and kiosks | 16 |
| Museums | 15 |
| Theaters/movie theaters | 13 |
| Hospitals | 11 |
| Supermarkets/markets | 10 |
| Stations(bus, train, police, fireman) | 9 |
| Malls | 8 |
| Beach/pool | 7 |
| Fountains | 7 |
| Schools | 7 |
| Stadiums (sports) | 7 |
| Airports | 6 |
| People | 6 |
| Town hall | 5 |
| Libraries | 5 |
| Offices | 4 |
| Clocks | 4 |
| Pharmacies | 3 |
| Religious buildings (synagogues, churches, cathedrals) | 2 |
| Post offices | 2 |
| Pyramids | 2 |
| Gyms | 1 |
| Maps | 1 |
| Streets | 1 |

## *Yo oigo ...* (I hear ...)

| Category | Number of students responses |
|---|---|
| Transportation (cars, trucks, busses, planes, trains, motorcycles, helicopters, taxis) | 351 |
| People | 45 |
| Fountains | 9 |
| Religious buildings | 6 |
| Beach/ocean | 5 |
| Stadium (sports) | 4 |
| Movie theater/concert/music | 3 |
| Cell phone | 1 |
| Birds | 1 |
| Mall | 1 |
| Lightning | 1 |
| Rain | 1 |
| Wind | 1 |

## *Yo huelo ...* (I smell ...)

| Category | Number of students responses |
|---|---|
| Cafes/restaurants/food | 179 (hot dog = 1) |
| Gasoline | 94 |
| Gardens/parks/flowers | 83 |
| Smoke/smog | 19 |
| Markets/stores | 16 |
| Pools/beaches/salt water from ocean | 6 |
| Transportation | 6 |
| Movie theaters (popcorn) | 3 |
| Trash | 2 |
| Stadiums (sports) | 1 |
| Factories | 1 |
| Bathrooms | 1 |
| Hospitals | 1 |
| Rubber | 1 |

## *Yo como .../Yo bebo ...* (I eat .../I drink ...)

| Category | Number of students responses |
|---|---|
| Water | 101 |
| Fruits | 94 |
| Soda | 89 |
| Hamburgers | 84 |
| Pizza | 43 |
| Milk | 31 |
| Tacos | 27 |
| Vegetables | 10 |
| Lemonade | 9 |
| Hot dog | 6 |
| Coffee | 6 |
| French fries | 5 |
| Gatorade/fruit juice | 4 |
| Sandwiches | 3 |
| Bacon | 3 |
| Chocolate/sweets/dessert | 3 |
| Bread | 2 |
| Enchiladas | 2 |
| Milkshake | 1 |
| Eggs | 1 |
| Nachos | 1 |
| Salt | 1 |
| Popcorn | 1 |
| Hot chocolate | 1 |
| Quesadilla | 1 |
| Gum | 1 |
| Fast food | 1 |
| Spaghetti | 1 |
| Meat | 1 |
| Scallops | 1 |

## References

Byram, M. (1997) *Teaching and Assessing Intercultural Communicative Competence.* Clevedon: Multilingual Matters.

Byram, M. (2008) *From Foreign Language Education to Education for Intercultural Citizenship.* Clevedon: Multilingual Matters.

Byram, M., Perugini, D.C. and Wagner, M. (2013) The development of intercultural citizenship in the elementary school Spanish classroom. *Learning Languages* 18 (2), 16–31.

Wiggins, G. and McTighe, J. (2005) *Understanding by Design* (expanded 2nd edn). Alexandria, VA: Association for Supervision and Curriculum Development.

# 4 Intercultural Competence: Reflecting on Daily Routines

## Jean Despoteris and Komo Ananda

## Introduction

We are a Spanish teacher and a graduate student in German studies brought together by the project described in the Introduction to this book. Jean is a Spanish language teacher in the Glastonbury Public Schools system. She has a bachelor's degree in Spanish, two master's degrees, one in secondary education and the other in educational leadership, and 32 years of experience as an educator. She has taught at the elementary, middle and high school levels in the Glastonbury School District and she had recently participated in a workshop on intercultural competence (IC) taught by Manuela and, having a strong interest in educational technology, had attended a number of workshops in this area. Komo was at the time of the project a graduate student in German studies at UConn. He had a prior interest in languages and cultures and in IC. When he heard about the opportunity to participate in a project in which he could co-design a unit that would later be taught in a public school, he immediately volunteered.

Now let us introduce our students. We decided to plan our unit for 8th grade students in classes with an average of 22 students per class (Table 4.1). The students in this grade are about 13 years old with an average of seven years of prior language study. They have five Spanish class meetings per week, each consisting of 44 minutes of instruction. In language competence the students ranged from Novice High to Intermediate Mid according to the American Council on the Teaching of Foreign Languages (ACTFL) ratings from the Assessment of Performance toward Proficiency in Language (AAPPL). Learners in the Intermediate range can maintain a conversation about themselves and their life. They can also use language to express their thoughts and get the things they need. They can use more than one sentence at a time. They can ask and answer questions and do all this in a way such that the teacher and others who are used to language learners can understand what they are saying. Some learners are ready to express their feelings entirely in the target language (ACTFL, 2012).

**Table 4.1** Summary of the classroom and students

| Type of school | Grade level(s) | Average age of the students | Average number of students per class | Number of classes per week | Number of minutes per class | Number of previous years of language study |
|---|---|---|---|---|---|---|
| Middle | 8th | 13 | 22 | 5 | 44 | 7 |

# Our Project

Like many foreign language teachers, we faced the challenge of implementing constructive and practical dimensions of culture in the classroom and in the foreign language. We also realized that even the best educators frequently find themselves in the conventional mode teaching the target culture through a one-way transmission of facts – providing information about the people, products and customs of a country or countries where the target language is spoken (Philips, 2001). We thought that, if teaching culture remained a set of learnable 'facts' as the norm, educators risked presenting 'culture as a static construct [and may] fail to recognize the variability of behavior within the cultural community, the participative role of the individual in the creation of culture, or the interaction of language and culture in the making of meaning' (Philips, 2001: 1). In other words, teachers and second language learners would maintain a recycled and superficial knowledge of culture. Therefore, we strived to reach beyond learnable facts to cultivate curiosity, self-awareness and the ability to mediate, and to raise learners' consciousness of their own cultural misconceptions. We were helped in this perspective and in locating it in a theoretical framework by the course described in the Introduction to this book.

## Planning and implementation

During our initial meeting we sorted through many of the curricular themes taught in the school district while keeping in mind the overarching 'essential question' which is at the focus of the 8th grade curriculum: *What is foreign?* Among the many themes discussed, we considered the most pertinent to be daily routines, transportation, dining out, preparing to travel abroad and childhood activities. After much discussion and reflection, we decided to try to develop learners' IC in the unit of 'daily routine'. There was an existing unit that had been in the curriculum for many years. We decided to take this unit and modify it to implement IC in a more systematic way. For an overview of the existing unit see Table 4.2.

The existing unit provided the students with reflexive verbs, e.g. to brush your hair, to take a shower, to dress yourself, to wake up and to eat breakfast (*despertarse, levantarse, desayunarse, cepillarse, ducharse, secarse, cepillarse, afeitarse,*

**Table 4.2** Overview of existing unit 'My Daily Routine'

| Unit title | My Daily Routine (Mi Rutina Diaria) |
| --- | --- |
| Unit description | Students will be able to describe their daily routine on a typical school day in both the present and past tenses. Students will use the appropriate vocabulary for daily routines among their peers and adults. |
| Enduring understandings | Students will learn about the differences of daily routines in both the United States and another Spanish-speaking country. |
| Essential questions | How do I describe my daily routine? How is it different from the routine of students in a Latin American country? |
| Content | Students will learn the reflexive verbs in both the present and past tenses and the vocabulary necessary to describe their daily routines and household chores. They will also learn transitional words, adverbs and the vocabulary for toiletries. They will utilize vocabulary from previous years of learning Spanish in the elementary schools (clothing, body parts, school subjects and adjectives). |

*peinarse, cepillarse, ponerse la ropa, vestirse*) and, in addition, vocabulary reflecting personal hygiene care, such as comb, hairbrush, soap, shampoo, toothpaste, etc. (*el peine, el cepillo, el jabón, el cepillo dental, champú, pasta de dientes*). The unit focused on mastering the vocabulary and grammar necessary or helpful for describing daily routines. Many assessments were given to check for understanding. The culminating activity of this unit consisted of projects in which the learners had the option of completing a booklet, poster, PowerPoint presentation, video or iMovie describing their daily routine. In whichever they chose of these media, learners described specific actions of their daily routine, using both the past and present verb tenses. They also included in their projects the foods they ate, what types of clothing they wore, the school subjects they studied and the obligatory chores for which they were responsible. Although there were many ways in which the unit could be implemented, when we examined the content of the unit we realized that the cultural component was not a major part of the project in the existing unit. For example, the learners' booklets, posters or PowerPoint presentations, videos or iMovies of the daily routine did not present opportunities for learners to consider the routine of a student from a culture different from their own.

In contrast, we intended for our modified unit to include many opportunities for students to develop skills and attitudes required to develop IC. After our initial meeting in which we also presented our ideas to the other project participants and received feedback and further ideas, we spent many hours emailing, calling and texting each other in order to plan the unit. We also had conference calls with Manuela when we needed further clarification and direction. We Skyped on several occasions. Komo also came to Jean's school and observed her Spanish classes so he could obtain a better under-standing of middle school students in her school district. Jean provided Komo with a textbook and examples of the curriculum. We uploaded our notes and ideas onto a wiki page that Manuela had created and received feedback and comments from other project members. Their advice and comments were valuable and provided suggestions, direction and insight into the project. In addition, after implementing the project Jean went to the Storrs campus at UConn after the teaching was finished in May, to go over the students' work and to discuss how the project had progressed.

In order to avoid repetition, we now report on our implementation while also linking what we did to our theoretical background. With the intention of moving away from a fact-based method of teaching culture in this unit, we turned to Byram's (1997) model of IC.

The unit consisted of the following steps: (1) introduction to the Spanish vocabulary in relation to 'daily routine'; (2) presenting the 'critical thinking cards' in English in the class so that they would understand them and then respond to them by writing in their journals; (3) viewing two short video clips of some Peruvian students' daily routines; (4) completing various post-viewing activities focused on answering questions to observe growth in IC; and (5) discussing responses from an interview with a Peruvian teacher.

The modified unit was introduced in December 2013 in five 8th grade Spanish classrooms. Implementation took four days. In congruence with the existing unit, we first activated the students' prior knowledge followed by an introduction of new vocabulary students would need to describe daily routines. However, in contrast to the existing unit in which it was custom-ary to introduce mainly vocabulary related to the students' own daily rou-tines, we included more extensive vocabulary that they would need to describe the routine of students in a different country, such as different foods, geographic features, animals and housing structures. They also learned words related to poverty, hardships and different living conditions.

In the next step we asked students to respond to questions on critical thinking cards. These questions were based on the concepts of knowledge, attitudes, skills of interpreting and relating, and skills of discovery and inter-action in Byram's (1997) model. Komo had read about the critical thinking cards in von Munchow (2012). The critical thinking cards were planned to determine the current knowledge and attitudes of the 8th grade middle school students around their daily routine as well as the daily routine of a Peruvian student in rural Peru, prior to viewing the video.

The questions we developed and asked the students to respond to were:

(1)  What does the word 'routine' mean to you?
(2)  When you talk about your daily routine, what does that include?

(3)   What do you think routine means to a Peruvian student?
(4)   What would that include?

The students wrote their answers in their daily journals. We asked them to reflect and write in English in order to allow them to think about the questions more deeply. Here are some examples of students' answers:

(1)   *What does 'routine' mean to you?*
Most students thought the word 'routine' meant tasks and chores that they do and repeat in their everyday life. The following are a few quotes taken from students as examples when asked 'what does routine mean to you':
'A sequence of events you do every day to get ready.'
'The term means to me a specific list of things that you normally do in your daily life.'
'Steps of responsibility you do daily/weekly.'
(2)   *When you talk about your daily routine, what does that include?*
Students felt that their daily routine consisted of getting up, eating, brushing their teeth, putting on make-up, combing their hair, getting dressed and preparing for school. Some students had chores or tasks to do before they left for school:
'I wake up, eat breakfast, brush my teeth, get dressed, brush my hair, ride the bus to school.'
'My daily routine includes getting ready for school, going to school, finishing my homework, playing soccer, doing chores, and going to sleep.'
(3)   *What do you think routine means/includes for a student in rural Peru?*
Most students thought that routine was the same for a student in Peru, but some students thought that there would be more hardship and more chores to complete:
'I think they probably have more chores and they eat different foods than we do.'
'It includes walking to school. raising the flag. going to school coming home. herding the sheep/chores. studying.'

Although many students' responses to the first question were quite similar, it is clear that the questions challenged the students' knowledge and attitudes, making them more aware of their understanding of their routines. They thought that a daily routine was daily or weekly tasks and responsibilities, something that was repetitive, a scheduled task, activities consisting of your day and things you do before you start your day. What we want to point out is that, while for the majority of Jean's students, routine was a 'repetitive task', five of the students went further and described routine as 'responsibility'. Already there are varying attitudes to and degrees of understanding of what exactly routine might mean to a middle school student in the United States.

For an overview of the students' responses regarding their own daily routines and the ones they thought a student from Peru might have, see Table 4.3. The results shown in bold present the activities described by middle school students as representative of their daily routine. The results shown in italics present their perception of the activities performed by students in rural Peru. By analyzing the chart, we deduced that the majority of students include eating breakfast, brushing teeth, doing hair, getting dressed and getting ready as major activities or tasks in their daily routine. In reporting their initial knowledge about Peruvian routine, the majority of students assumed rural Peruvian students took part in activities such as chores, getting ready, waking up at a different time and walking to school. Responses show that the Glastonbury middle school students do not walk to school at all, and fewer US students do chores as part of their daily routine.

We speculated that the students' prior exposure to different countries might have enabled them to think that a student in rural Peru might have to walk to school even if none of the students walked to school themselves. In addition, there were some responses by students that showed that they made judgments about the life of students in Peru without basing them on facts or data. For example, some students had expressed that Peruvians must eat tacos and guavas because they had learned in previous units of study that people from other Spanish-speaking cultures eat these foods.

It is clear that the students were challenged to think about their prior knowledge as well as attitudes towards daily routines in another country. What is important about the critical thinking cards is their ability to show where students are located in and through their assumptions. Although not directly linked to our project, an example of one student's observation can illustrate this further. In the beginning of the year, Jean had provided a short excerpt from 'When I was a Puerto Rican' by Esmeralda Santiago which depicted Puerto Ricans eating guavas. Albeit our study focuses on the daily routine of students in Peru, one student transferred the assumption that people in all Spanish-speaking countries eat guavas, when responding to the critical thinking cards. This anecdote is important because it shows what we are attempting to accomplish through IC. The modified unit aims to bring these assumptions to the conscious forefront of the minds of our learners.

In addition to insight into students' sub-competences of *knowledge* and *attitude*, the critical thinking cards provide an initial framework for students to explore skills of *relating* and *discovering*. Question 2 of the critical thinking cards help students to discover the routines of their own, and Questions 3 and 4 provoke students to think about their assumptions or stereotypes of rural Peruvian young people. What we hoped would occur was for the students to begin to think about their daily routine and possible characteristics of Peruvian young people and begin to think and relate notions of daily routine to each other.

**Table 4.3** Students' perceptions of daily routines

| Written student answer | Number of students indicating answer is part of US routine | Number of students indicating answer is part of Peruvian routine |
|---|---|---|
| *Watering plants* | | 1 |
| **Watch TV** | 1 | |
| **Washing face** | 1 | |
| *Walking long distance* | | 1 |
| *Walking to school* | | 4 |
| *Waking up at a different time* | | 6 |
| *Waking up early* | | 1 |
| **Video games** | 2 | |
| *Uniform* | | 2 |
| **Sports/hobbies** | 4 | 2 |
| *Singing* | | 1 |
| **Showering nightly** | 2 | |
| **Showering** | 4 | |
| **Riding the bus** | 1 | |
| **Riding bike to/from school** | 1 | |
| **Prepare clothes (nightly)** | 1 | |
| **Make-up** | 5 | |
| **Make lunch** | 1 | |
| *Holidays/culture* | | 1 |
| *Hike mountains* | | 1 |
| *Herding* | | 3 |
| **Homework** | 4 | 1 |
| **Go to bed** | 4 | |
| **Going to bus stop** | 2 | |
| **Go to school** | 5 | |
| **Getting ready** | 15 | 4 |
| **Getting dressed** | 13 | |
| *Flag raising* | | 1 |
| *Fetch water* | | 2 |
| *Feed animals* | | 2 |
| *Farming* | | 1 |
| *Eat guava* | | 1 |
| **Doing hair** | 11 | |
| *Different meal times* | | 1 |
| *Different chores* | | 1 |

(Continued)

**Table 4.3** (*Continued*)

| Written student answer | Number of students indicating answer is part of US routine | Number of students indicating answer is part of Peruvian routine |
|---|---|---|
| Cooking | | 1 |
| Chores | 4 | 7 |
| Care for pets | 1 | |
| Brushing teeth twice | 1 | |
| Brushing teeth night | 1 | |
| Brushing teeth | 12 | 1 |
| Breakfast | 16 | 1 |

To summarize, these results of the initial and single implementation of the critical thinking cards provided us with an insight into the students' perceptions of their own daily routine compared to that of a student in rural Peru while also creating a starting point for further analysis of how, if at all, students changed in their knowledge and attitudes to daily routines and their first assumptions about Peruvian students.

In the third part of the unit, we provided the students with a six-minute video clip of a morning routine of rural Peruvian children. The suggestion to use an authentic video clip came from Manuela and students in the graduate course. We then searched the internet to look for videos that would depict the daily routine of a young person from another country in South America. With the help of one of Jean's colleagues we found an appropriate video which we then shared with the students. It is important to mention here that the enthusiasm of teaching IC was shared by Jean's colleagues and they too were giving us suggestions and ideas to use in the classroom. This shows the different levels of collaboration on planning IC in our program.

This video clip, taken from the short documentary *Camino a la escuela* (Saco, 2004), begins with the silhouette of a young boy walking outside in the early morning. He then joins his family inside their rural home for a hot breakfast before heading out to the hills of Peru to begin his trek to school alongside his cousins. The documentary follows these boys as they hike through the mountains and talk about the dangers they face along the way, including the time one of his cousins almost died after he fell into the river. The video then continues to introduce the audience to the schoolteacher and her daily routine of preparing the classroom.

After we had showed the video clip of the Peruvian student's typical school day and daily routine, we asked students to fill out the answers to the following IC questions which were developed in Glastonbury as part of the Glasport Project:

(1) What is your reaction to what you have seen?
(2) What in this video challenged your own beliefs or assumptions about the culture represented?
(3) Was there anything that made you feel uncomfortable or seemed inappropriate in regard to your own views of how things should be done? Explain what and why.
(4) Name one thing that contrasts with your own culture that you observed in this video?

As mentioned in the Introduction to this book, in Glastonbury we use the foreign language in class most of the time and require our students to do the same. However, we were concerned that we might limit our students' depth of reflection. Therefore, we decided to present the critical thinking cards and the post-viewing questions in English so that all students would understand the questions and their reflections would be deeper and more nuanced than their current language level would permit.

The six-minute video activity addresses one of the components of Byram's model: interpreting and relating. The short clip was a 'document or event' which had to be interpreted from the perspective of the other person – the Peruvian boy in this case – and then had to be related to the learners' own way of life. The desire was to use the video to help students arrive at a different view of (a small part of) another culture. The video clip is an authentic document which stimulated our students to identify and recognize their stereotypical perspectives and preconceived ideas about a Peruvian student's daily routine. After viewing the video clip, our students had the opportunity to write in their journal about their experience, and the journal entries aided in their ability to reflect more deeply about what they had observed in the video. Furthermore, learners recognized 'areas of misunderstanding', i.e. what had they assumed to be true about a Peruvian student's daily routine in contrast to what they found.

Students had many reactions to the video. The answers obtained from the questions after the video showed that in one class, for example, seven out of 24 students were responsible for doing chores in their households, and at least five students said their chores were not difficult compared to the chores of the Peruvian students. The students who did chores or tasks in their households had minor ones, such as making their beds, setting or clearing the table or taking out the trash. In addition, we found that in many cases their parents did the chores or they had maids or nannies to help with these tasks.

By asking these types of critical thinking questions, we were able to observe students' skills, knowledge and attitudes, and their cultural sensitivity. The post-viewing questions afforded the students the opportunity to reflect on their assumptions and beliefs about cultural routines in Peru and the United States. Comparing their responses to the critical thinking card questions and their reflections after the video, we observed a shift from a point of view that was mostly related to their own experience to a point of view which also included questions and different perspectives. Many students demonstrated growth in their knowledge about Peruvian culture, stating they did not know that many families lived without heat, or that kids performed many more chores. Many students assumed the only difference between the two cultures had to do with diet and education. They reacted with surprise to the distance which Peruvian students had to walk to school as well as their relationship to their teacher.

The students were also surprised to learn of the unsafe conditions in which some Peruvian young people live and travel. They could not believe that some Peruvians risked their lives every day just to get to school. One of the students found it unbearable that one of the Peruvian students almost died on the journey to school. Furthermore, the students were astonished to learn that many people in rural Peru do not have running water. One student 'thought it was bizarre how such a young child fixed roofs, cooked, and herded animals'. Another student expressed sympathy and said 'it was very sad that kids have to walk almost 3 hours to get to school'. A third student was surprised they have so few resources compared to the United States. Many more were saddened and surprised that students had to fetch water and struggled as much as they did.

While reading their comments written in English, we learned a great deal about the thoughts, attitudes and sensitivities of our students. We were able to see how they think critically. We also learned about the different attitudes and prejudices by viewing the responses that the students had written. It is, however, often difficult to gauge if the comments made by the students are assumptions, reactions or judgments. For example, one student said, 'she felt bad' because the Peruvian students lived in such poor conditions. Another student made the remark that their way of living would 'make them stronger', and a third student said she felt sad, yet she discovered and realized how lucky she was 'to have what [she] has and [she] should help others'. The difference between these three statements shows the progression we are looking to reach with the implementation of IC in the classroom. The remark made by the first student is a basic feeling of empathy. This is a positive remark, yet it does not result in the student's further gain of competence. There may be a shift in knowledge, but the student does not interact nor further interpret what she has seen. The student who made the second observation demonstrates cultural competence in an ethnocentric and limited way because they are judging another culture based on their own values. However, the last comment goes further. We see the student discovering the inherent hardships of the rural students in the video, and she stops and interprets what she has learned so far, and remarks that 'I am lucky' to have the life she has by relating what she has seen in the video clip to her experiences of daily routine; she is starting to develop the 'critical cultural awareness' of Byram's model. Thus we observed our students' progress from the 'knowledge' sub-competence of Byram's model to 'interpreting and relating' and finally, some students showed beginnings of 'critical cultural awareness'. Jean also felt that she saw a deeper level of thinking in the students' writing than she had ever before seen in 8th grade.

As part of the post-viewing activities and assessments we then asked learners to write a paragraph comparing and contrasting their routine with that of young people from Peru. We hoped that this activity would help them delve more deeply into areas of 'interpreting and relating' and 'discovery and interaction' as we asked them to complete this task in the target language. They were also assessed in a speaking activity about daily routines in which one student portrayed the student living in Glastonbury and the other student represented a student living in rural Peru. These conversations were recorded in the language laboratory and graded as an interpersonal speaking assessment.

Later, the learners viewed another video clip of young people going to a suburban school in Lima, Peru, so they could see the difference between the rural and suburban areas of a country. They discussed and answered more IC questions similar to the post-viewing questions from the first video. They were surprised by the differences between the two types of schools in Peru, and remarked that they did not know there was so much poverty and affluence in the same country. They then commented on the fact that these students' lives in the second video were very similar to their own. They realized that there were both urban and rural parts in every country and that you could not make assumptions about any country in general. This activity brought several of the students to a heightened sensitivity.

In order to observe the growth of knowledge and critical cultural awareness, we decided to add an intercultural element to the student's mid-year summative writing assessment. We asked our learners to write an imaginary letter to a Peruvian exchange student who was coming for a visit. They were given the instructions for the writing prompt in English, but were told to write the letter entirely in the target language. In addition to the context of the imaginary letter, the instructions also included tips for formatting a letter as well as what information Jean was looking for in each paragraph. She also gave students a graphic organizer visualizing the letter format which they could choose to use to help plan their letter. Students had one whole class period, totaling 44 minutes, to plan, write and edit their letter. Given that the purpose of this assignment was to assess the students' independent writing skills, they were not allowed to use their textbooks or other resources in the process of writing. Also, when grading the letters, Jean assigned a grade based on the students' writing performance and not on any evidence in growth of IC, but although the assessment was not graded for knowledge of content or growth in IC, the letters did provide valuable insight into the students' minds for this project.

One element of the letter-writing task which was based on the 'discovery' component in Byram's model, was to ask questions about the Peruvian student's daily routine. The students demonstrated growth by asking some very thoughtful questions about life in Peru and demonstrating authentic curiosity. Some examples are: 'What is your daily routine like in Peru?' 'How long does it take you to get to school?' 'How is your life in Peru different than the daily life in the United States?' 'What is a typical breakfast and lunch in Peru?' 'Do you shower or bathe in the morning or the evening? 'What time do you get up in the morning?' They were able to do this in the target language and we noticed that many of the students demonstrated growing cultural awareness in their writing.

After the completion of this writing assignment, we thought it would be beneficial for the learners to move beyond the imaginary letter and have an authentic interaction with someone from Peru. We put in place a plan to interview a student who had moved to Glastonbury from Peru and attended our local high school. We invited her to come to Jean's class to be interviewed by the students in Spanish. Due to a number of practical difficulties, this did not work out. Not wanting to abandon the idea of allowing the students to interact with someone from Peru, Jean changed the plan and interviewed a teacher in her school district who is Peruvian and moved to the United States as a young student. Jean and Komo worked together to write questions they thought would be of interest to the students based on their reflections on the critical thinking cards as well as their imaginary letter-writing assessment. Ideally, Jean and Komo would have preferred to have this colleague visit the class in person, but it was not possible due to scheduling conflicts. Instead, they compiled a list of questions and emailed them to her for answers.

Here are the interview questions Jean asked her colleague:

(1) What part of Peru are you from? Is it a rural or urban area?
(2) What was your morning routine like on a school day?
(3) Did you shower in the morning or the night before?
(4) What did you eat or drink for breakfast?
(5) Did you have any chores in the morning?
(6) What was your family's routine like?
(7) How did you get to school? (Walk, transportation by bus, parent?)
(8) What did you do after school?
(9) Did you have any chores after school?
(10) What was your expectation about moving to America?
(11) Were these expectations met or has your opinion changed?
(12) If it has changed, how has it changed?

Before sharing the colleague's answers with the students, Jean asked them to predict what her routine might have been like based on where in Peru she was living. After a rich discussion of predictions, in Spanish, Jean shared the email response from her colleague with the students. This activity also provided a good opportunity for the students to be exposed to the opinions that somebody from a different country might have about America, and this began the process of critical reflection on their own culture which is part of the concept of 'critical cultural awareness'. The students were interested in hearing about another person's point of view and asked some thought-provoking questions.

# Challenges and Recommendations

## Language of instruction

We were very interested to learn how students felt during the activities in the unit. We wanted to hear about their deep thoughts, opinions and sensitivities but felt uneasy as we are required to teach the class predominantly in the target language. Therefore, we decided to include some activities (written responses to the critical thinking cards and reflections on IC questions after viewing the video) in English while maintaining the use of Spanish in their oral work. We considered this to be useful as the students responded both inside the class in discussions and question and answer and outside the class in their journals. When we implement this project again we would like to create an interdisciplinary unit with either the English teacher or the history teacher on our team core. A team core in our school is a team of teachers from different content areas (mathematics, science, history, English, world language education, special education) serving the same approximately 100 students. This would enable us to conduct the Spanish class in Spanish, and have the students complete their journal entries and writings in another class. The grades earned on the assessment of 'interpreting and relating' could count for both classes. Another strategy would be for the students to reflect in their journals for a homework assignment rather than using class time.

## Logistics

Some of the challenges of our collaboration were related to finding time to connect when the college and school district had different vacations and different work schedule expectations (e.g. mid-terms, final exams, formal assessments in schools, papers). Another challenge was the interruption of the flow of the unit due to the harsh winter weather with many snow days, and school district delayed openings due to icy conditions, SBAC (Smarter Balanced Assessment Consortium) state mandatory practice sessions and CMT (Connecticut Mastery Testing) and departmental mid-year assessments. It was also difficult to coordinate schedules to bring a Peruvian student, teacher or community member into the classroom for an interview session. We had to reschedule the interview several times due to the many interruptions during the school year. We look forward to implementing the project again and would start planning early to add the component of the students interviewing a person from Peru, such as a teacher, student or community member for an additional cultural viewpoint. We would identify a Peruvian at the start of the project and start the process of interviewing them earlier. We want to repeat the other parts of the project in the future and would continue to keep IC journals in the classroom and have the students write about what they learned about culture during the school year. In addition, viewing an additional film or two, depicting various routines not only in rural Peru but also in urban neighborhoods, alongside examples of routines for middle school students in the United States, would provide students with additional information they could compare and analyze critically.

Jean was also recently trained to use additional educational technology (e.g. Animoti, Adobe Voice, Kahoot, Thinglink, and various other formats for digital storytelling). She would use this technology to enable her students to become creative, innovative problem solvers with effective communication and collaborative skills in a changing global society.

## Conclusion

In conclusion, we feel that the modified unit, based on Byram's model, enabled the students to examine events and documents from a point of view other than their own. This modified IC unit triggered curiosity and opened the students' eyes to cultural differences. They problematized their own beliefs about cultures, one where the target language is spoken and their own, and were exposed to different perspectives. Some students clearly became more empathetic to another way of life, and they also developed new skills of interpreting and relating, and developed new attitudes which are all prerequisites for their development of critical cultural awareness.

## References

ACTFL (2012) ACTFL *Proficiency Guidelines 2012*. Alexandria, VA: American Council on the Teaching of Foreign Languages.

Byram, M. (1997) *Teaching and Assessing Intercultural Communicative Competence*. Clevedon: Multilingual Matters.

Phillips, E. (2001) IC? I see! Developing learners' intercultural competence. *LOTE CED Communiqué* 3, 1–6.

Saco, H. (2004) *Camino a la escuela*. Peru: País. See https://vimeo.com/21228993.

von Munchow, P. (2012) Cross-cultural discourse analysis and intercultural education in foreign language teaching and learning. *Journal of Intercultural Communication* 29. See https://www.immi.se/intercultural/nr29/munchow.html (accessed 28 June 2017).

# 5 Diverse Perspectives of the Immigrant Experience

Deanne Wallace and
Jocelyn Tamborello-Noble

## Introduction

The ultimate quest for a language teacher is two-fold: linguistic competence and increasing skill in the target language, and the integration of culture and (inter)cultural competence as the language is being taught. The aim of this project is to have students improve their intercultural competence (IC) while at the same time improving their linguistic competence. This project was designed to increase the awareness that our students have of the struggles that immigrants may face so that they might understand what it is like to be an immigrant in the United States. The project begins with the connection to our 'essential questions' from the Glastonbury curriculum for this class: *Who are we? Who are we in a diverse society?* We look at answering these questions through the creation of a new project about immigration.

## Who we are

Deanne attended the University of Connecticut from 2009 to 2013 and graduated with a BA in German studies and political science, and continued with an MA in German studies. She graduated in 2015 and currently works as a project manager for a software company. During her studies she worked on several projects related to IC in education, including the one presented here.

Jocelyn was born in Santiago, Chile and received her BSc degree in Spanish education, an MA in foreign language education, and a 6th year degree in education administration from the University of Connecticut. During the course of this project, Jocelyn was teaching Spanish in Glastonbury Public Schools and has also taught English as a second language in the district. At the time of writing, Jocelyn is a District Coach for English Learner Services at Hartford Public Schools, and at the district level, she is a District Cohort Lead with Hartford Public School's Literacy Curriculum as well as District Coordinator for LASErS (Literacy and Academic Success for English Learners Through Science) with the Educational Development Center.

## Our students

In this chapter you will read about the collaboration between Deanne and Jocelyn on the creation of a new project to help Jocelyn's students grow in IC. Working together, through the use of email, Skype, Google Drive and face-to-face meetings, Deanne and Jocelyn designed this project to fit within the current curriculum of the Spanish 5 class which Jocelyn was teaching at that time in Glastonbury.

The students that participated in this project were mostly in grade 11, with two being in grade 10. The language program in Glastonbury is a well-articulated program, where students have received 10 years of sequential Spanish before this class (Table 5.1). The school has approximately 2,000 students and this class is one of five Spanish 5 Level 1 classes taught in the year of the project. In the Glastonbury foreign language context, Level 1 language courses are designed for students who achieve an A- average or above in their previous year's language study and can be equated to honors level classes in other districts.

**Table 5.1** Summary of the classroom and students

| Type of school | Grade level | Average age of students | Average number of students in class | Number of classes per week | Number of minutes per class | Number of years of language study |
|---|---|---|---|---|---|---|
| High school | 11th grade | 17 | 25 | 5 | 45 | 10 |

# Project Outline

Our project was especially relevant to the continuing idea in the Glastonbury schools' curriculum of *Who are we?* and *Who are the groups that make up our diverse society?* This type of project is one that can be integrated into many curricula due to the topic of immigration being aligned to units in social studies.

## Preparation

In accordance with the agreed Glastonbury Spanish curriculum in Spanish 5, the students discover and learn regarding the immigrant experience, with the overarching essential questions being *Who are we?* and *Who are we in a diverse society?* These questions are asked in each unit, and we begin to

**Table 5.2** Overview of existing unit 'Who are the immigrants?'

| Unit title | Who are the immigrants? |
|---|---|
| Unit description | As part of the year-long study regarding immigration, students are first taught about the historical and cultural context of immigrants in the United States. After building on background knowledge, and students sharing information they have already learned, the teacher begins to look at perspectives of the immigrant experience in the United States.<br><br>This unit covers immigrant experiences from Puerto Rico, Cuba, Dominican Republic and Mexico. This topic digs deep into who are the Latinos in the United States and begins to look at how the experience of immigration is not equitable. |
| Enduring understandings | • Students will use essential key vocabulary to identify their opinions regarding immigration.<br>• Students will use both content and language skills developed in previous lessons to incorporate into writing and speaking for this unit. |
| Essential questions | Who are we? Who are we in a diverse society? |
| Outcomes | • When prompted, 'Who is an immigrant?' in the target language, students will be able to produce a response using complex language and vocabulary.<br>• Students will understand and reinforce language objective of present and past subjunctive use, and how to support opinions and understandings.<br>• Students will further develop content of historical knowledge about immigration, and relate it to current realities in society. |

discover that the development of understanding and a critical lens of answering these questions changes depending on the information. Table 5.2 summarizes the existing unit on which we built our project.

The critical elements in our project are the background knowledge students acquired and their understanding of the concept of immigration. Students began to understand that there are inequities in the groups that immigrate to the United States and not all immigrants are created equal. As students gained this knowledge, they began to understand how language and content are both woven into the lesson to create a deeper understanding of the immigrant experience.

## Analyzing Students' Existing Views

Students were assigned a scenario of an immigrant family just arrived in the United States and took on the role of interpreter for the family. Their task was to help the family settle, to make decisions and to act in the best interests of the family. The project began with a questionnaire, which students answered anonymously, on beliefs and values regarding immigrants in US society. Through this questionnaire we hoped to determine attitudes regarding immigrants, and track development in students over the course of the project. We hoped that the project would increase the cultural awareness of students, which is the precondition for engagement with societal issues. From an instructional standpoint, we cannot begin increasing IC unless we estimate where students are on their journey, and so we asked students whether they agree or disagree with certain widely held beliefs about Hispanic immigrants and used the results to describe their position on Bennett's (1993) Developmental Model of Intercultural Sensitivity (DMIS) scale. The statements and three-point scale in Table 5.3 charted students' views on the immigrant experience in the United States.

We found it surprising that so many students answered affirmatively to the first two statements: that *In the US if someone wants to work, they can find a job* (54.02%) and *You can become successful and wealthy in the US if you work hard enough* (64.77%). Many students also agreed that *There are issues in the US with illegal immigrants taking jobs from US citizens* (46.59%), which we hoped would change over the course of the project. In other areas, students showed that they knew quite a bit already. For example, the majority of students (76.14%) disagreed that *All Hispanic immigrants in the US are treated equally*.

**Table 5.3** Students' statements about immigrants

| Statement | Agree % (n) | Unsure % (n) | Disagree % (n) |
|---|---|---|---|
| In the US if someone wants to work, they can find a job. | 54.02 (47) | 21.84 (19) | 25.29 (22) |
| You can become successful and wealthy in the US if you work hard enough. | 64.77 (57) | 11.36 (10) | 26.14 (23) |
| If you are residing in the US you should be able to speak English. | 66.67 (58) | 13.79 (12) | 21.84 (19) |
| All immigrants in the US are treated equally. | 3.45 (3) | 11.49 (10) | 86.21 (75) |
| All Hispanic immigrants in the US are treated equally. | 7.95 (7) | 19.32 (17) | 76.14 (67) |
| There are issues in the US with illegal immigrants taking jobs from US citizens. | 46.59 (41) | 34.09 (30) | 19.39 (17) |
| It is the responsibility of each family to have healthcare for its members. | 55.68 (49) | 29.55 (26) | 14.77 (13) |
| The media accurately displays Latinos in society. | 9.09 (8) | 27.27 (24) | 63.64 (56) |
| Second and third generation Latinos are more assimilated than their parents. | 76.14 (67) | 23.86 (21) | 0 (0) |

This seemingly surprising statistic can be explained by a unit on different immigrant groups that had previously been introduced in class.

The questionnaire also included an open-ended response where students were asked to tell us about their views on immigration, and we used certain key concepts and terms to sort the responses. We then allocated responses to a stage on Bennett's (1993) DMIS model. Usually this is a measurement of response to difference and therefore we had to interpret the responses as indirect reactions to difference. We are also aware that the model is usually used with a quantitative measurement, the Intercultural Development Inventory (IDI) (Hammer *et al.*, 2003), but we decided it would be a helpful instrument to classify these qualitative data and help us get a sense of where our students started from.

The statements seemed to fall across the range of the DMIS spectrum, although most responses fell near the minimization stage. Denial and defense were relatively uncommon and there were no responses under the integration stage, as we expected, although some responses did not fit neatly into one single category:

## Denial

Some students reflected denial in their responses. At this level, people experience their own culture as the only 'real' one, and other cultures are either not noticed at all or are understood in an undifferentiated, simplistic manner. One student, when asked for their opinion, replied 'I don't know, I'm from Glastonbury.' The student used their place of living as a reason for not knowing about the issue of immigration in the US. We found that students at this level were extremely uncommon, but here is one other example:

I have no opinion. Since my parents have a job and I do too, I don't mind the illegal immigrants and others taking US jobs.

## Defense

At this level, own culture is experienced as the best way to live, and people often think in terms of opposites – us/them – and this is frequently accompanied by overt negative stereotyping. More students accepted that immigration was an issue within the United States, but had mostly negative opinions regarding immigrants. One student wrote that 'they need to go back to there [sic] country.' Another student accepted some immigrants, but 'While I think that immigrants add diversity to a population, there is such a thing as too many immigrants. I also think that if you live in America you must be able to speak English.' A different student stated that 'there are a lot of illegal immigrants and that there should be greater restrictions. Also i [sic] think that if you live in america [sic] you should be able to speak English.' Another student wrote that 'some of the stereotypes are true, and the immigrants need to work to get rid of the negative stigma'.

## Minimization

Many more students fell under the minimization category. People at this level recognize superficial differences such as food or customs, but believe that all human beings are essentially the same. However, commonalities are based on ethnocentric terms – that these other people are just like 'us', for example. Many of these students rely on the idea of welcoming immigrants into 'our' society and 'our' culture.

> I think that immigrants are treated unfairly as a whole in the United States. The media and stereotypes portray these people as dirty, unsophisticated, and poor aliens. I think that many immigrants who come to the US are there for family: to provide for, support, and make proud. Since family is such a heavy value in our culture, I believe that the US as a whole should accept immigrants more hospitably because they are just like us, wanting what is best for family.

Here we see that there is an implication that others are 'like us' in that both they and we have a family life and value it.

> I think immigrants are fine as long as they come here legally. Most of them do the jobs no Americans want to do. And if they work hard enough to be capable of attaining a good job I give them even more credit than a person who was born in the US because immigrants have to go through much more to be viewed on the same level.

> My overall opinion about immigrants in the United States is that they are brave. It is obviously hard to move your entire family to another country in order to have a better life. Many of them work hard and are able to achieve a better life, however if they do not try their life could remain the same. I believe that in some time in history, we were all immigrants and therefore, should all treat each other equally.

In the two preceding statements, there is minimization in the sense that everyone should be judged by the same criteria of being hard workers and there is even more credit to 'the others' because of their disadvantaged position. In the next quotation the initial statement shows explicit minimization:

> We're all humans. … There are only so many jobs available, and they should be given to those most qualified. If an immigrant is the most qualified, he/she should be given it. Also, if an immigrant wishes to move to America, so be it. What separates countries in my mind is not so much border, but culture.

And in the next statements we see in the phrase 'we are all immigrants of different times' a similar search for common humanity:

> Overall immigrants are important to our society. We are all immigrants of different times. There are issues with the law and immigrants illegally crossing the boarder [sic] but some laws are unreasonable and the process is quite difficult to become a citizen or get a visa. But I welcome immigrants who are seeking opportunity or a different lifestyle.

> I think that all of the immigrants should go through the process of becoming a citizen. It is never 'ok' to be an illegal immigrant in the US.

The sentiments are well summarized in the following quote describing values and work ethics as well as the notion of equal opportunity:

> In my opinion immigrants are very hardworking people. They are very passionate and determined. Most are in search of a better life for there [sic] family. They are very family oriented. They are dedicated as well as protective. Immigrant parents simply want a better life for there [sic] children. They are willing to work 3 jobs to support there [sic] families. I feel that if an immigrant comes to the US in search of a job, they should be given the equal opportunity to get a job. They should not be discriminated against or receive comments such as 'They are stealing american [sic] jobs.' Everyone should have the equal opportunity to attain a job. Immigrants have a bad reputations [sic]. They have worked hard to get where they are today, and aren't given credit for it. They are often associated with poor adjectives and are seen as unworthy.

> I think if the immigrants are legal it is fine.

## Acceptance

People at the acceptance level not only recognize but appreciate cultural differences. They can interpret events within context and they continue to elaborate their cultural categories. The views of students at this level are more complex than students at the minimization level, and they do not see the immigration issue as wholly bad or wholly good.

> They should be accepted more readily. They do take opportunities away from citizens but also help to create more/improve America internally.

> A always growing [sic] number of diverse people who are unaccuratly [sic] portrayed as similar but in reality couldn't be more different. From the ones, particularly kids, who easily get accustemed [sic], to the ones

who never get accustemed [sic] (particularly the older people) every immigrant gets a different experience.

I don't have a good opinion because I don't know a lot about them, but I think they don't have enough rights because they aren't citizens. I'm not sure how hard it is for them to become citizens, but maybe if it was a little easier there would be less problems.

This then was an analysis of the group which gave us some sense of their beliefs and attitudes before we began. By looking at where students stand at the beginning of the project, we may also tailor the project stages to increase their level of IC using the DMIS. We may also track the growth of students' IC and create a clear before and after picture of the students.

## Developing a Teaching Method

We based our work on the 'DIE method', one of the most common and important methods of teaching IC (Nam & Condon, 2010). DIE describes a process: students distinguish (D) objective observations from subjective or culturally biased assumptions, and the process of moving from objective to subjective relies on interpreting (I) these assumptions and observations, such as making inferences or speculations about stereotypes and beliefs; students then evaluate (E) these beliefs. Nam and Condon (2010) argue that this approach may be used at the minimization and acceptance stage in Bennett's model to awaken cultural awareness. In a development of this approach, Abrams (2002) suggests using stereotypes as a point of discussion in the classroom, so that, when combined with the DIE exercise, students can analyze stereotypes for their validity. Stereotypes should be directly addressed, and they can involve students in classroom discussion effectively (Abrams, 2002). It provides a good starting point for students to begin discussion, since stereotypes are often well known.

While using stereotypes to talk about an already heavily stereotyped group may seem counterproductive, Abrams (2002) argues that discussing stereotypes should not be avoided. Making stereotypes creates order in our social environment, and they are often well enough known for discussion in lower level language courses. Using stereotypes can involve students in cultural discussion and develop cross-cultural awareness by contrasting cultures, regardless of language level (Heusinkveld, 1985); Mantle-Bromley (1995) also points out that students learn about other cultures better if the students are first exposed to their own culture's belief systems, values and traditions (cited in Abrams, 2002). By debating commonly heard statements, students become aware of implicitly held cultural beliefs and that there are multiple sides to any one issue. This step also follows the recommendations for students at the minimization stage on the DMIS scale, which is to raise cultural self-awareness (Bennett, 1993). Students then interpret the validity of these beliefs by debating them, and begin to evaluate each one. As a result, the exercise encourages students to observe other cultural phenomena which they had not noticed previously, and to be more aware of other phenomena in their lives (Nam & Condon, 2010). Students are exposed to new interpretations and may learn to empathize with them, which lays the foundation for a cultural frame shift (Phillips, 2001).

Abrams (2002) also suggests emphasizing diversity within a culture, because differences can be very subtle, and discussing stereotypes mostly addresses differences between two cultures rather than within one single culture. It is for this reason that we had included a statement in the questionnaire about whether all Hispanic immigrants have the same experience in the United States. In the course of the unit we hoped that this would be disproved, and that the students would deepen their understanding of the complexity of immigrant experience in the United States. They would no longer view Hispanic immigrants as one homogeneous group, but as a group of many diverse, different cultures, whose experience in the United States varies widely.

Discussing stereotypes can also allow the introduction of issues of social justice, and we designed aspects of social justice and language rights into the curriculum. For example, with respect to language rights and the availability of documents in languages other than English, we expected that students would experience frustration with missing resources in English while describing the tasks that they carried out, and that finding a resource already in Spanish would be much easier for their immigrant families.

At the end of the project, students were to complete another questionnaire and we expected that their answer to the statement that all immigrants should speak English in the United States might change. While it is true that English is not the official language of the United States of America, secondary socialization requires English; if one wants to advance in schooling or a professional career, speaking English is crucial. According to Reagan, 'there is simply no credible social or education argument that children in the United States should not learn English ... the issue, rather, has to do with the role of the native language in the acquisition of English, in the learning of other content while English is being mastered, and in terms of the maintenance of the native language as a positive outcome of the educational experience' (Reagan, 2006: 9–10). Reagan points out that 'language awareness is critical when one is concerned with the social, political, economic, historical, and ideological contexts in which language is used' (Reagan, 2006: 3). By awakening students to linguistic rights violations and difficulties, we hoped that the students' experience would raise questions about the role of English as the dominant language and its apparent superiority to the language of the immigrants. The role of English and an immigrant's native language in

American society is not easy to resolve, and we do not expect to solve this issue; it has been fought over for decades. At the very least, however, we wanted to awaken students to this dilemma.

By completing the questionnaire, we hoped that students would demonstrate they had increased cultural awareness, which is the precondition for social engagement. Gagel (2000) states:

> the pre-condition for democratic engagement is that the citizen becomes aware of the relationship between individual destiny and social processes and structures. Political awareness is formed through the recognition of one's own interests and the experience of social conflicts and relationships of governance. The politically aware and informed person should not be a passive object of politics, but as a subject should participate in politics. (Gagel, 2000: 27, as cited in Byram, 2008: 164)

In this vein, it was our intention that the students would have – perhaps unknowingly – participated in the public, political sphere by the end of the unit, for by completing this project students would create a public portfolio as a part of the assignment, and making this portfolio available for potential immigrants already fulfills some aspects of political engagement. We hoped, too, that these exercises would lead to sympathy and a shift of frame reference so that students would understand the status of immigrants in society, which might lead the students to consciously undertake politically oriented action, in addition to assembling a guide for immigrants coming to the United States, the political significance of which might be less evident to them.

## In the Classroom

After the students had completed the questionnaire as homework, Jocelyn led a more in-depth DIE process in class. She created groups and assigned each group to debate for or against a stereotype, with the intention that this should create an atmosphere of respect (Deardorff, 2010).

The next step was to introduce students to the project for the Spanish class. The class was taught entirely in the target language, although the project handout itself was in English. Jocelyn herself used the target language the entire time, and reminded students to stay in Spanish during the project.

Originally, we intended that Jocelyn would assign groups of students to act as immigrants coming to the United States. We chose to change this role because we could not expect students to behave in culturally appropriate ways, and this would have also been problematic because changing the behavior of students might change their identity as a members of a certain social group (Scollon, 1995). We cannot, and perhaps should not, expect students to act in culturally appropriate ways, although we can help them to develop alternative interpretations of events – interpretations that a different sociolingual group might have. In this way, we can expose students to new concepts, beliefs, values and ideas and begin the process of 'tertiary socialization' by which Byram refers to:

> the idea that teachers and others can help learners to understand new concepts (beliefs, values and behaviours) through the acquisition of a new language, new concepts which, being juxtaposed with those of the learners' other language(s), challenge the taken-for-granted nature of their existing concepts. (Byram, 2008: 113–114)

Byram (2008) suggests that tertiary socialization may result in a new international identity and intercultural communicative competence. The student does not lose their existing identities, and may develop a new identification with an international perspective.

By changing the role to interpreters, students begin to act as 'intercultural speakers', a role which Byram defines as seeing how two or more cultures relate to each other, and mediating between people socialized into these cultures (Byram, 2008: 68). Mediation is the most important concept; it implies action through explaining and understanding relationships between cultures (Byram, 2008: 68). This practice brings in Byram's *interpreting and comparing*, as students must 'identify ethnocentric perspectives in a document or event and explain their origins', in addition to mediating 'between conflicting interpretations of phenomena' (Byram, 2008: 232). In the task we gave them, rather than interpreting a document from another culture, students interpreted events in their own culture for those from elsewhere. By changing the role to mediator, students became intercultural speakers, and their change of identity would happen gradually and organically as they progressed through the units. Their mediating role continued through every single unit, as they decoded the American system for their immigrant family.

This change from taking on the immigrant identity to becoming an intercultural speaker and mediator is also appropriate for the learner's current stage (Hammer *et al.*, 2003; Phillips, 2001). As we saw above, most of the students were between the minimization and acceptance stage. Mediation requires that students stand outside their culture and evaluate, interpret and explain its intricacies. As a result, students would develop self-awareness by focusing on their own culture (Phillips, 2001), as Bennett (1993) also suggests. At the minimization stage, Bennett suggests providing students with frameworks to understand their own culture with the use of authentic materials. To support the learners at minimization stage, we identified stereotypes and explored common American perceptions and world views concerning immigrants and the American Dream – that anyone can be successful with hard work. We structured opportunities for difference seeking by assigning students to debate against and for certain aspects, which may be contrary to their own beliefs. Cultural knowledge was required to complete all the activities, since students needed to navigate through cultural phenomena in their environment and make sense of its processes for immigrants. This process should lead students towards 'acceptance' of difference on the DMIS scale.

For those in the acceptance stage, the activities appeal to slightly different aspects. The main goal at this stage is to refine the analysis of different cultures. We sought to provide this by including the idea that Hispanic immigrants are treated in different ways, not uniformly, in the United States, thus showing diversity within a larger cultural construct. This idea focuses on cultural difference while relying on cultural knowledge, which is also a requirement at the minimization stage, to deepen analysis (Bennett, 1993). Students will need to know about other cultures at this stage, and requiring students to help immigrants of many different cultures will deepen and diversify their knowledge of immigrant culture. Eventually, as a student moves through these stages to integration/adaptation and completes the activities in the project, the tasks become oriented around empathy and pluralism.

## Overview of the Activities

Table 5.4 gives an overview of the activities on a day-by-day basis. However, the design of this unit is flexible, and the teacher can modify response questions to address the students' IC evolution. For example, a question in this unit which reflects acceptance or minimization can be changed to address and advance adaptation or integration in students.

The immigrant 'profiles' assigned to students were based on statistical data, because 'ignoring cultural variation promotes stereotyping' (Phillips, 2001: 1), and with their specific immigrant families in mind, students acted in the family's best interest. We based the order of problems on our personal experience, from what is the most important to what is the least important. Students experienced new situations as well, such as finding affordable housing and budgeting grocery shopping. By using these 'disorienting dilemmas', teachers enhance students' critical reflection and students will act independently, going through processes of trial and error (Göbel & Helmke, 2010: 1572). These dilemmas directly addressed the stereotypes used in the pre- and post-questionnaire, such as the stereotype that everyone can find a job, and promote new perspectives (Gliczinski, 2007, cited in Göbel & Helmke, 2010).

## Reflections on the Process

### Assessment

The project introduction within the classroom met with various reactions. We assigned students a set order of activities to complete in one week. These

**Table 5.4** Overview of the activities

| | |
|---|---|
| Day 1 | Teacher primes background knowledge regarding immigration. Students earlier in the year researched their own history and their family's past in immigrating to the United States. Teacher builds on language and content, through graphic organizers, and highlighting key vocabulary. |
| Day 2 | Peer-to-peer discourse. Students pair into groups to discuss immigration, and their family's experience. Students bring their own notes to organize thoughts, ideas and key vocabulary. Students organize trends in experiences and discuss differences and similarities in each other's experiences. Language: Preterite, imperfect. Content: Immigration and vocabulary regarding immigration. |
| Day 3 | Project is explained: Each group receives a scenario regarding an immigrant group in the United States. Teacher uses roll-die method to determine.<br>• Country of origin<br>• Family structure<br>• City and state of residence<br>• Economic status<br>• Language level<br>• Occupation<br>• Home status (do they rent a home, have a home etc.) |
| Days 4/5/6 | • Research days: since students have some background on the groups, they research regarding immigration status.<br>**(I) Students also research**<br>• Cost of food<br>• Where they will live<br>• Cost of healthcare<br>• Occupations that are available<br>• Cost of insurance<br>• Transportation<br>• Income for occupation they have<br>• Grocery shopping (students used Peapod to grocery shop) |
| Living the scenario | The teacher uses the platform EMODO to update and receive information regarding status of each family. Students continue to problem solve and have discussions around financial decisions and the impact these have on their families. Students begin having difficult conversations about choices they have to make for their families. Students continue these discussions in Spanish and elaborate on language and context. Students are problem solving on where they will live, what they will eat, occupation, and financial management. |

*(Continued)*

**Table 5.4** (*Continued*)

| Presentations (2 days) | Presentation of scenario includes:<br>(I) Overall scenario<br>(II) Challenges in the scenario: one group had to decide between health insurance or car insurance. They could not afford both.<br>(III) Lessons learned<br>(IV) What they would have done differently.<br>(V) Their connection to the immigrant experience. |
|---|---|
| Class debrief (30 mins) | Students provide teacher with feedback on project and areas of strengths and other feedback. |

scenarios required students to work outside the classroom without teacher supervision. Through these scenarios we sought to provide a mixture of independent and guided experiences; students exercised independence through making decisions for their immigrant families, and most scenarios, in particular the food budgeting activity, required a combination of fieldwork and unguided experience. The teacher then guided discussion about the activities in class.

Byram (2003) advocates the use of autobiographies, in which students analyze an encounter with 'otherness' within their society or in another society (Byram, 2008: 224). The use of the Council of Europe's *Autobiography of Intercultural Encounters* (AIE) (www.coe.int/lang-autobiography) allows students to critically reflect on their own experience and how others might have understood the same experience. The AIE might also be a reflection on their own experience or independent learning task.

In this project, the autobiographic writing or journal was split into a spoken and written section for each activity. The written section described their decision-making process in each unit, which was guided by questions, and the spoken section at the beginning and end of the project documented their own emotions and opinions about this process. For example, in the food budgeting unit, students had to visit a grocery store and 'buy' groceries on their budget. Their written task questions asked students to describe their budget and what they bought: Did it contain plenty of fruits and vegetables? Was it healthy? Did it go over budget? Where did they shop? The spoken task questions for the same unit asked students to analyze the stores where they would buy food. Students had to explain where they shopped and why, and also include any remarkable observations about where they shopped. A student might notice that Whole Foods is expensive, yet offers many foods for customers with dietary needs and organic foods. One might infer that customers at Whole Foods have higher disposable incomes and care about the environment, and that this customer profile does not suit the needs of all immigrant families.

The project also included a performance assessment, a form of direct assessment explored by Byram (1997) and Ruben (1976). Direct assessments are not as common as indirect assessments, since data collection and analysis take much longer, although they account for many problems in indirect assessments and self-reflection assignments (Sinicrope *et al.*, 2007). The data are far more detailed and nuanced, and account for the individual in the group.

Many studies show that combining indirect and direct assessments is the best way to measure IC. Fantini (2006), Pruegger and Rogers (1994) and Straffon (2003) have all used mixed methods to assess IC (Sinicrope *et al.*, 2007). Pruegger and Rogers (1994) argue that researchers should use a mixture of assessments, because IC and its development is a complex, nuanced concept: 'sensitive and complicated issues ... may contain inconsistencies, contradictions, or ambiguities ... not amenable to paper-and-pencil analysis' (Sinicrope *et al.*, 2007: 31, citing Pruegger & Rogers, 1994: 382). Unfortunately, there is often only one teacher for a classroom of 20 students, and it is not possible to collect all the data. However, by combining direct and indirect assessments, we hoped to document the development of IC in students as accurately as possible.

Examples of indirect assessments include self-reports and the questionnaire which focused on multiple dimensions of IC. In our project, the pre- and post-questionnaire tracked the beginning and end result. However, questionnaires focused on the group rather than individual development and, furthermore, students may have tried to answer to please the teacher, a phenomenon known as 'social desirability' (Sinicrope *et al.*, 2007: 27). This is a particular risk with a topic such as immigration where social attitudes are marked and sometimes extreme. By making the questionnaire anonymous, we hoped that students would be encouraged to be honest, although we cannot be sure.

Another form of direct assessment is the video blog entry at the beginning and end of the project. This blog entry, spoken in English, is based on the notion of portfolio assessment (Sinicrope *et al.*, 2007). Portfolios encourage students to reflect on their experiences, thus aiding learning and growth, and the final portfolio measures IC growth at the end of the project (Sinicrope *et al.*, 2007).

Students had various responses to the immigrant families assigned to them. Some found them easy, others incredibly difficult. The reactions to the project as a whole varied. Some students appeared overwhelmed by the project because it was unlike any previous unit. They seemed relieved that sections of the project would be in English, namely the video blogs at the beginning and end of the project. Students also had questions regarding the role of interpreter and mediator in the process.

One group stated that 'Case Four is super easy'. One group member who had received a different scenario seemed annoyed that his family had to provide for five children, because this made their situation fiscally difficult. He stated that 'We're going to be eating a lot of Ramen Noodles', in English,

to which the teacher replied in Spanish, 'Well, if you are going to be providing for a family, don't you want them to eat healthy? They will need more
than Ramen Noodles.' Another group found their scenario very easy. The
father of the family spoke English, and at one point a pair of students talked
about the scenario: 'The lawyer one sounds so easy!' 'That's actually her
family.' In other words, this scenario seemed to be the same situation as one
of the students' families.

One group in particular had many questions regarding the status of their
immigrant, a Puerto Rican living in Hartford/Miami. One student asked,
'Can they (Puerto Ricans) vote (in the United States)?' and another asked
'What is their transition?', showing lack of knowledge regarding the cultural
changes that the family might go through. Students seemed to be confused
about what it means to be Puerto Rican and living in the United States. The
relationship between the United States and Puerto Rico is not clear or well-
known to these students.

This trend was not limited to this group. Students did not generally
understand the status of immigrants within the United States, although
they understood many common topics and programs within the United
States: 'Do immigrants qualify for Medicaid?' 'How do we get a green card?'
Students also knew little about average incomes and financial issues for families in the United States. Most groups needed to research average salaries for
each immigrant family, and Jocelyn needed to remind them about paying
income taxes. Some groups displayed disbelief at the salaries for their immigrant families. This disbelief ranged from shock at realizing that people earn
so little, to dismissing a salary because it was too high. Other statements
were uncompromising such as 'They don't HAVE to get this kid into college,
he can just take a year off', when looking at college costs.

Students also directly addressed the needs of their family – and whether
they were able to meet those needs or not, as seen in the Ramen Noodles
example. They researched whether their family would rent or buy a house,
and indeed whether that would make sense for their budget. One group,
before deciding on an apartment, said that the family should 'look at their
salary'. In the case of permanent settlement, students wanted to buy a house
for an immigrant family settling in Miami. Students also adjusted bedrooms
and layout based on the needs of their family, and whether they would need
a car or not based on the available transportation. Despite initial shocks and
trepidation, the learning atmosphere was energetic, active and on task.
Although the students were allowed to speak English for the video blogs at
the beginning and end of the project, some groups wanted to make notes in
English of points they would cover.

One group helping a Dominican family found that they had many potential difficulties. The family spoke limited English, which meant limited communication with other people and difficulties with the tax forms, because
not all tax forms are available in another language. They expected that

finding a house that suited their needs would be difficult because the family had several children. Another problem would be finding childcare because not all their children were of school age. The large size of the family (six people) strained finances; the family could not even afford public transport. Food budgeting would be extremely important for this family.

For a Cuban family living in Hartford, the group seemed to think that money was the greatest concern. They expected that getting insurance and healthcare would be difficult because they didn't have experience of this. Money also determined where the family lived and whether they had a car, and the group had to make sure that the car and house were cheap. They also had to consider whether the restaurant the family would open would be high end or not, and how much money the restaurant would bring in. Lastly, the group had to decide what to do with the 18-year-old son, who was of college age. They were not sure whether he would go to college or stay behind to work in the restaurant.

One area of Byram's model that became particularly active was 'knowledge', specifically about the relations between the United States and the immigrants' countries of origin. Students did not know the nature of the relationship between the United States and Puerto Rico, for example. They also did not know about their own country, such as common programs like Medicaid. Specifically, students' knowledge was lacking in the following areas (using Byram's categories of knowledge needed for IC): knowledge of/about historical and contemporary relationships between one's own and one's interlocutor's country; the national definitions of geographical space in one's own country and how those are perceived from the perspective of other countries; and the national definitions of geographical space in one's interlocutor's country and the perspective on them from one's own (Byram, 2008: 231). Students were also confused about exactly how different Puerto Rican culture was from American culture, as mentioned earlier in the transition question for the Puerto Rican family. This hints at another section of 'knowledge': 'the processes and institutions of socialization in one's own and one's interlocutor's country' (Byram, 2008: 231). This confusion also overlaps with Byram's skills of 'discovery and interaction', because students could not 'identify contemporary and part relationships between one's own and the other culture and country' (Byram, 2008: 233).

## Final Reflections

In language teaching there are many views regarding authenticity of task, meaningfulness and contextualization into a student's daily life. In working in this project, students had authentic conversations about critical issues in the target language. The various scenarios presented students with opportunities to genuinely discuss real decisions of deciding whether to buy a car, choosing between health insurance and transportation, or the idea that eating at a chain restaurant is more economical. For Jocelyn, as a teacher, it was the realism of this project that was striking. There was clear evidence of student engagement, in the conversations, responses and growth of their statements. Students truly understood that there were decisions that adults and families have to make, that impact them for the rest of their lives. Students realized these aspects on a spectrum of scales, from 'you can't eat in a chain restaurant every day, even though it is economical', to the realization that 'individuals make difficult decisions about their welfare'. Students also developed empathy for the process of immigration and discussed the idea that not all immigrants are treated fairly, and that the country of origin does in fact determine what resources will be available.

For Jocelyn, as an experienced teacher, this project truly transcended her previous experience of students and how they use language. When students were having conversations in these scenarios, there was a language production level that made her rethink the usual standards. It made her reconsider teaching that just demands one more grammatical structure, and one set of vocabulary words. This project was truly contextualized and meaningful, not only because of the students' learning, but also because this was the project that challenged, and validated Jocelyn's own beliefs about language learning.

## References

Abrams, Z.I. (2002) Surfing to cross-cultural awareness: Using internet-mediated projects to explore cultural stereotypes. *Foreign Language Annals* 35 (2), 141–160.

Bennett, M.J. (1993) Towards a developmental model of intercultural sensitivity. In R.M. Paige (ed.) *Education for the Intercultural Experience*. Yarmouth, ME: Intercultural Press.

Byram, M. (2003) On being 'bicultural' and 'intercultural'. *Intercultural experience and education* 2, 50–66.

Byram, M. (2008) *From Foreign Language Education to Education for Intercultural Citizenship: Essays and Reflections*. Clevedon: Multilingual Matters.

Deardorff, D. (2010) Theory reflections: Intercultural competence framework/model. Prepared for NAFSA Conference. See www.nafsa.org/_/file/_/theory_connections_intercultural_competence.pdf.

Fantini, A.E. (2006) *Exploring and Assessing Intercultural Competence*. World Learning Publications 1. See http://digitalcollections.sit.edu/worldlearning_publications/1.

Gagel, W. (2000) Einführung in die Didaktik des politischen Unterrichts [Introduction to the didactics of civic education] (2nd edn). Opladen, Germany: Verlag Leske und Budrich.

Göbel, K. and Helmke, A. (2010) Intercultural learning in English as foreign language instruction: The importance of teachers. Intercultural experience and the usefulness of precise instructional directives. *Teaching and Teacher Education* 26, 1571–1582.

Hammer, M.R., Bennett, M.J. and Wiseman, R. (2003) Measuring intercultural sensitivity: The intercultural development inventory. *International Journal of Intercultural Relations* 27, 421–443.

Heusinkveld, P.R. (1985) The foreign language classroom: A forum for understanding cultural stereotypes. *Foreign Language Annals* 18 (4), 321–325.

Mantle-Bromley, C. (1995) Positive attitudes and realistic beliefs: Links to proficiency. *Modern Language Journal* 79 (3), 372–386.

Nam, K.-A. and Condon, J. (2010) The DIE is cast: The continuing evolution of intercultural communication's favorite classroom exercise. *International Journal of Intercultural Relations* 34 (1), 81–87.

Osborn, T. (2007) Teaching world languages for social justice. *Journal of Christianity and Foreign Languages* 9 (8), 11–23.

Phillips, E. (2001) IC? I see! Developing learners' intercultural competence. *LOTE CED Communiqué* 3, 1–6.

Pruegger, V.J. and Rogers, T.B. (1994) Cross-cultural sensitivity training: Methods and assessments. *International Journal of Intercultural Relations* 18 (3), 369–387.

Reagan, T. (2006) The explanatory power of critical language studies: Linguistics with an attitude. *Critical Inquiry in Language Studies* 3 (1), 1–22.

Scollon, R. (1995) *Intercultural Communication: A Discourse Approach.* Oxford: Blackwell.

Sinicrope, C., Norris, J.M. and Watanabe, Y. (2007) Understanding and assessing intercultural competence: A summary of theory, research, and practice. *Second Language Studies* 26 (1), 1–58.

Straffon, D.A. (2003) Assessing the intercultural sensitivity of high school students attending an international school. *International Journal of Intercultural Relations* 27, 487–501.

US Census Bureau (n.d.) *State and County Quickfacts: Connecticut.* See https://www.census.gov/quickfacts/ (accessed June 28, 2017).

# 6 Beauty and Aesthetics

## Chelsea Connery and Sarah Lindstrom

## Introduction

The context of this study was two Advanced Placement (AP), Early College Experience (ECE) Spanish classes at Glastonbury High School in Glastonbury. AP classes offer high school students a college-level curriculum, the knowledge and skills to help them succeed in a college or university, and scoring well on AP exams can also earn students college credit. Thus, ECE classes are high school classes that have been designed to reflect the rigor of college classes and give students credit at the University of Connecticut or other universities that accept these credits. ECE courses are one type of AP course which are taught by a high school instructor who has been certified by a university, in this case, the University of Connecticut, and a course through the University of Connecticut ECE is equivalent to the same course offered at the university. Table 6.1 gives an overview of the participants and their course.

## Who Are We?

Chelsea completed two undergraduate degrees from the University of Connecticut in Spanish literature and culture, and world language education. She then went on to immediately pursue a master's degree in curriculum and instruction at the University of Connecticut, where she became involved in this project. During the project she worked part time in the Hartford Public Schools district at the high school level.

Sarah is a Spanish teacher who has been working with Glastonbury Public Schools for nine years. She did her undergraduate work at the University of Connecticut in Spanish education and received a master's degree from the same institution in curriculum and instruction, and a master's degree in Spanish for certified teachers from Central Connecticut State University. At the time of this chapter she was working on her doctorate in education at Central Connecticut State University with a focus on multicultural education. During her time in Glastonbury, Sarah taught in four

**Table 6.1** Summary of the classroom and students

| Type of school | Grade level(s) | Average age of the students | Average number of students per class | Number of classes per week | Number of minutes per class | Number of previous years of language study |
|---|---|---|---|---|---|---|
| High school | 11th grade and 12th grade | 17 | 25 | 5 | 49 | 11 |

schools, from 4th grade through 12th grade, and this was her first year teaching the AP course.

## The Context

The 'essential question' from the Glastonbury curriculum for the AP Spanish course is: *How are we transformed by our study of language and culture?* This is the final essential question and encapsulates all previous questions by asking students to reflect on the effect that all they have learned and continue to learn has on their understanding of the world. The class is taught entirely in Spanish and all elements of assessment are in Spanish as well. Following these norms, the project described in this chapter was entirely in Spanish, with instructions, teacher feedback and student work all in the target language.

In our specific context we had one class containing 25 students and one with 27 students. These high school students were all between the ages of 16 and 18. Average proficiency level reported on the American Council on the Teaching of Foreign Languages (ACTFL) Guidelines rating scale from computerized oral proficiency interviews and writing proficiency tests administered in the year of the project was between Intermediate Low and Advanced Low. According to the ACTFL proficiency guidelines, speakers at the high end of this range, Advanced Low (a sub-level of Advanced), are able to handle a variety of communicative tasks. They can narrate and describe in the major time frames of past, present and future. Responses produced by Advanced Low speakers are typically not longer than a single paragraph. The speaker's dominant language may be evident in the use of false cognates, literal translations or the oral paragraph structure of that language. Advanced Low speech is typically marked by a certain grammatical roughness, and vocabulary may lack specificity. However, speakers are able to use communicative strategies such as rephrasing and circumlocution. Advanced Low speakers contribute to conversation with sufficient accuracy, clarity and precision to convey their intended message without misrepresentation or confusion. On the other end of our student spectrum, the ACTFL proficiency guidelines indicate that Intermediate Low speakers can handle successfully a limited number of uncomplicated communicative tasks. Conversation is restricted to some of the concrete exchanges and predictable topics necessary for survival in the target-language culture. Speakers are primarily reactive and struggle to answer direct questions or requests for information. Intermediate Low speakers express personal meaning by combining and recombining what they know and what they hear from their interlocutors into short statements and discrete sentences. Responses are often filled with hesitation and inaccuracies as they search for appropriate linguistic forms and vocabulary. Speech is characterized by frequent pauses, ineffective re-formations and self-corrections (ACTFL, 2012). All students from these classes served as the participants for this project. Approximately 10 students out of both classes were first- or second-generation immigrants with perspectives and values that demonstrate a mix of Glastonbury culture with a home culture. The native countries included India, Dominican Republic, China, and others.

## Implementation

The unit was implemented between mid-February and early March of 2014. In this 2013–2014 academic school year prior units had included: education, language and identity; government and personal and public identities; technology and government and control over the individual. The specific project discussed in this chapter served as a cumulative and summative performance task implemented at the end of a period of instruction covering the unit topic 'Beauty and aesthetics'.

Throughout the unit students read a variety of texts on cultural perceptions of beauty, with themes such as self-esteem, definitions of beauty, trends in beauty and brand names. They also watched videos on themes such as the social and emotional effects of Photoshop usage in advertisements, and biological impulses and beauty. During these lessons students engaged in many discussions about various aspects and perspectives of beauty around the world. The unit is summarized in Table 6.2. The task we set for the students, and which we concentrate on here, occurred as a cumulative and summative project implemented at the end of the unit of study, although there were also many formative assessments within the unit itself.

After this, the students were asked to create a project that presented an aspect of beauty that might or might not differ between cultures that had not been discussed in class. The instructions were purposefully open-ended, to encourage creativity in the development of work. Students were told to create presentations about beauty and its manifestations across cultures and through history, and to add to our understanding of the subject and widen our perceptions. They were told to form groups of two or three students and include: an investigation of one aspect of perceptions of beauty; a new

**Table 6.2** Summary of unit on 'Beauty and aesthetics'

| Unit title | Beauty and aesthetics |
|---|---|
| Unit description | As part of the year-long study of how we are transformed by our study of other languages and cultures, students will explore different perspectives of beauty around the world. Students will examine contemporary aspects of beauty as a class then in small groups investigate historical and cultural perceptions of other aspects of beauty. The unit includes opportunities for investigation, presentation and discussion in the target language. |
| Enduring understandings | • Students will recognize varying perceptions of beauty.<br>• Students will understand the need to consider the historical and cultural context of perceptions of beauty.<br>• Students will understand that perceptions of beauty can change over time and across cultures. |
| Essential questions | • What is beauty?<br>• What personal, cultural and historical perspectives influence perceptions of beauty?<br>• What are similarities and differences between our own perceptions of beauty and those of others? |
| Content | • Students read articles about beauty and discuss their own perceptions of beautiful physical attributes and personality traits.<br>• Students practice research skills by surveying peers in the target language to inquire about their perceptions of beauty.<br>• Students form small groups and investigate and present an aspect of beauty not discussed in class using authentic research from the internet and data collection of opinions of peers.<br>• Students will recognize differences in perceptions of beauty between historical periods and cultures.<br>• Students will discuss and note new understandings and vocabulary from presentations. |

understanding their group has about beauty; information from class and authentic target language websites; facts, examples and visuals to help the class comprehend their presentation; an interactive component with class-mates so they are provided with the opportunity to consider and apply the information presented to them; and a bibliography following MLA conventions. The detailed project outline is provided in Appendix A.

The project goal was to introduce something new to classmates and allowed other students in the class to demonstrate their new understanding based on the presentation. Students were told they had a presentation time of 15–20

minutes. Overall the objectives the teachers had in mind included specific dem-
onstrations by students of attitudes from Byram's (2008) model, knowledge
objectives, and the development of interpreting and relating skills, as well as a
heavy focus on discovery and interaction skills. There were also objectives of
fostering students' critical cultural awareness. Appendix B presents the specific
content and intercultural competence (IC) objectives of the project.

Students worked on these projects over a period of three weeks both
inside and outside the classroom. During in-class working time, about three
days of full class, approximately three hours, were dedicated to working in
the computer lab to create a presentation which also contained an activity to
share with the class. Aside from these three full-class days, only brief meeting time was given in class to facilitate group collaboration. The rest of the
work was completed outside of class time, mostly through online collaboration. Sarah worked with students – using the target language – at the beginning and end, specifically to help them focus their ideas into a project that
would truly work to develop a new understanding in the minds of their
classmates. Many students shared work with the teacher through Google
presentations or email throughout the process to continue conversations
about project focus and delivery. The teacher gave feedback, asking probing
questions to encourage students to think more deeply about their research
and create questions that would foster new learning in the class. She also
provided error correction of grammar and vocabulary.

During this period, some students participated in an exchange program
to Madrid, Spain, where they lived with a host family, travelled and experienced Madrid schools. Because of the timing, these students did their
research there, and then compiled and presented their research upon their
return. Many of the students abroad also worked with the teacher, using
Google presentations and email to ask questions, focus their research and
request error correction. Students who were in Spain presented last, allowing
them to obtain additional teacher feedback in class.

## The Process

There was no previous project or unit design in place for our specific
content, although materials (texts, videos, etc.) were available. Thus, the two
authors worked together to determine how best to integrate Byram's (2008)
IC model into the unit. The unit took many different perspectives, touching
on how beauty has changed through history and context, biology, mathematics (beauty and symmetry), societal pressures (media, etc.), technology
(how modern medicine has changed beauty expectations), economy (cost
and business surrounding a market of beauty), and more. We chose to focus
first on the final project, and then later construct the unit, using a backward
design process (Wiggins & McTighe, 2005).

First we established our unit objectives, which included students being able to use evidence and multiple perspectives to evaluate beauty and choices regarding what is beautiful in phenomena of different times and locations. Students would also compare different historical perspectives to one another, and to current perspectives. Students would be able to analyze definitions of beauty in biological and mathematical perspectives and evaluate factors influencing definitions, and social pressures regarding beauty within L1 and L2 societies. Students would be able to compare factors influencing definitions and social pressures between L1 society and others as well as compare the perceptions of beauty from a variety of vantage points between L1 society and others.

With those objectives in mind we created essential questions to serve as the project guidelines: *Where do different perspectives of beauty originate from in my cultures and others? How do different perspectives of beauty affect daily lives in my cultures and others? What within cultures influences or perpetuates attitudes about beauty? Can beauty perspectives change? If so, what can change them? When and how did I learn that something is 'beautiful'?* and *How do varying concepts of beauty affect perceptions between cultures? Does this have an effect on individuals' interactions?*

The creation of a presentation representing an element of beauty and aesthetics from another time or place associated with the Spanish language was to demonstrate their IC, while integrating and encouraging collaboration and creativity that will incorporate 21st century skills. Students were given full autonomy as to the cultural element chosen and how to present on it. This seemed ideal, as it created even more opportunity for students to develop IC within the classroom on a micro level through working collaboratively and learning to tolerate ambiguity. Due to their strong level of Spanish proficiency all activities took place in the target language.

As the students put themselves in groups of two or three, the teacher reminded them to choose strategically, meaning that the groups should allow individual students to foster their developmental areas and create the most learning potential. Due to the relatively diverse population of the classes, groups represented a strong level of cultural diversity. Each group then chose a topic from a list of themes within beauty that had been discussed during the unit of study. Themes included: beauty/biology, beauty/mathematics, beauty/societal (pressure and influences of media, family, friends, trends), beauty/historical, beauty/gender expectations (biosocial), beauty/technology, beauty/economy (cost). Students also had the option to pick any area of personal interest to investigate provided it was agreed upon with the teacher.

Groups then created their presentation to represent their chosen topic within the target culture, their own and others, as they saw fit. The format of the presentation was entirely up to their creative devices (video, Prezi, PowerPoint, etc.). How students approached the topic and presented their information was also in their own hands, but they were required to bear in mind and address the essential questions within their topic context. They also had to use information from class and authentic internet sources, use visual data and examples to aid comprehension, and include an interactive component so that classmates could apply what they learned from the presentation.

Before beginning their research, the class had a discussion about the need for us to be able to understand that all personal perspectives are shaped to some extent by a group's shared beliefs and values. The teacher also reviewed content objectives, which were 'to deepen our own perceptions of beauty and be more open minded about others'. Students began the project in class with the teacher presenting possible project ideas and aiding in finding appropriate materials. They were instructed to find a variety of sources such as articles, journals, videos, media representations, fiction works. Throughout their time of working in and out of class, students were able to share their work with the teacher and get comments and corrections. At the end of the project timeline, students presented their chosen topic to the class. Each group member was required to contribute orally.

## Student Projects

Projects included themes such as: *'Modificación corporal a través de las culturas'* (Body Modification across Cultures), *'Belleza y género'* (Beauty and Gender), *'Belleza en bailes culturales'* (Beauty in Cultural Dance) and *'El color de la piel en culturas diferentes'* (Skin Color in Different Cultures). Students followed the guidelines and shared data and insight into cultural perceptions of beauty that most of the class had not considered before. The projects had images that demonstrated differences and beliefs, while the presentations explained some reasons for the practices and the activities allowed students to inquire about aspects of the presentations or further develop their understanding. Students presented to their classmates over a two-week period. The expectation set by the teacher of 15–20 minutes minimum for presentations was far exceeded with each presentation lasting 30–40 minutes, including discussion, in Spanish, at the end.

All presentations included a visual component and most students chose PowerPoint as their mode of presentation. Some used Prezi.com and many groups showed videos from YouTube.com. Each presentation was done entirely in Spanish with all members of the group speaking about different aspects of beauty that were investigated as part of their chosen project theme. Activities were mostly done with all group members facilitating the participation of the other students in the class. Many students volunteered observations as their classmates presented. Throughout the presentations students did not fail to ask probing questions about what they were seeing.

The discussions that stemmed from the activities were often cut short because of the time constraints of a 44-minute class.

Below are some images from the presentations. These are screenshots of presentations and activities that were done in class.

The project depicted in Figure 6.1 discussed perceptions of beautiful women depending on race and culture. Women in the United States were likely to adapt to the dominant culture of long, straight hair, light skin and thin bodies. Among African American, Latina and Asian women, there was evidence of hair extensions, skin lightening and plastic surgery. The class showed surprise at pictures of women years before their now famous images and in the activity expressed concern over loss of identity and a need to fit into traditional images of beauty set by media standards in the United States.

The students who did the project in Figure 6.2 were especially interested in math and science. They decided to discuss the golden ratio as a scientific rationale for what we perceive as beautiful. They included examples of the golden ratio in human faces of various races, in architecture in a variety of countries all over the world, and in common elements of nature. Students in class were intrigued and surprised by the consistency of the formula's application throughout all the subjects presented. Through discussion, students demonstrated an understanding of how we are all similar, beyond culture's impact on perception of beauty.

Figure 6.3 shows a slide from a group that presented on products and measures taken to be considered beautiful in various cultures. One example was the idea that often Caucasian people desire to have dark skin and go tanning while some Asian people desire lighter skin color and use umbrellas

**Figure 6.1** Screenshot of *Beauty Across Cultures* project

# La máscara de proporción divina

- Hay una máscara de belleza que aplica a muchas razas y nacionalidades

  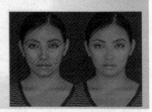

**Figure 6.2** Screenshot of *The Golden Ratio* Project

and creams to keep their skin light or lighten it. This project was impactful in its juxtaposition of ideas and opposite perceptions of beauty. The class discussed the desire to have what one does not have as a possible explanation for the differences shown.

In Figure 6.4 this group presented different cultural dances and included descriptions of the movements, costumes and music. They discussed the historical and cultural meanings of the dances and compared similarities and differences. This project showed formal representations of beauty through dance and the class was able to see wide-ranging differences in what was aesthetically pleasing on multiple levels.

In Figure 6.5, the group discussed skin color as a scientific phenomenon and explained differences in perception based on location and dominant traits of the region. They also explained historical changes in race as a result of immigration and conquest. This project explained the superficiality of

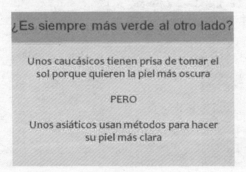

**Figure 6.3** Screenshot of *Body Modification Across Cultures* project

**Figure 6.4** Screenshot of *Beauty in Cultural Dance* project

color as a basic reaction of skin to the sun over time, and encouraged a discussion of the importance of perception and stereotyping based on unfamiliarity and ignorance.

The presentation in Figure 6.6 focused on the concept of masculinity and femininity in different cultures. It highlighted differences in the two genders and asked students to consider why some practices are acceptable for a gender in some cultures but not in others. The question of gender as an identification marker was discussed as well as how cultures assign values to gender that may be irrelevant.

**Figure 6.5** Screenshot of *Skin Color in Different Cultures* project

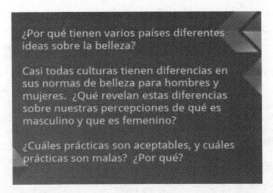

**Figure 6.6** Screenshot of *Femininity and Masculinity in Different Cultures* Project

Figure 6.7 is a screenshot of an activity done by a group that presented body modifications across different cultures. The presentation showed modifications that were extreme or dangerous and asked students to discuss the meanings of the modifications and the pressure from others to look a certain way. The survey was done with Polleverywhere.com, and students in the audience were asked to respond in real time with their cell phones to questions such as the example above: *Which modifications are acceptable and which are not? Why?* Students were shocked by this presentation's graphic images of extreme modifications, which the group compared to pressure to be thin or fit in the United States, leading to excess exercise and dieting. Students had the opportunity to see women in other countries overeating, stretching their necks, breaking their feet, men with plates in their lips, and more. The lasting effect of this project's imagery and message was obvious in the class's discussion of these modifications weeks later in and out of class.

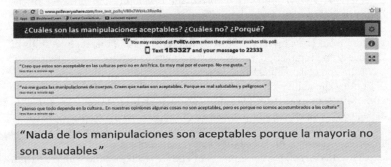

**Figure 6.7** Screenshot of class activity designed and presented by students

Chelsea had been involved in the planning but did not partake in the instruction. However, she visited and observed a sample of the student presentations. The outside perspective was extremely informative. The students were incredibly engaged in what their classmates had done; their curiosity and self-generated higher order questioning was inspiring. It appeared that they took their autonomous roles very seriously and thoroughly investigated their chosen theme, incorporating multiple perspectives and moving beyond stereotypes. It should be emphasized here that the students were also well versed in how to navigate these themes in the target language, a testament to how true interest in learning through an intercultural lens can assist in intrinsic motivation to learn the target language.

## Assessment

In the class 20 students participated in a self-assessment where they were asked to analyze their presentations using the checklist in Appendix C. This checklist aligns with the objectives of IC based on Byram's (2008) model. The teacher discussed the individual aspects with the students when it was handed out so that they had a working understanding of the concepts.

When asked about the presence of the factor 'attitudes of curiosity and openness' as well as 'readiness and willingness to suspend beliefs about other cultures', all 20 students reported that they believed these factors were reflected in their project. However, just 18 students reported that they believed the factor of readiness and willingness to suspend own belief about their own culture was present. Eighteen of the 20 students also reported that the factor of 'knowledge of social groups and their products and practices in the country/culture' being analyzed was present. Sixteen students reported the presence of 'knowledge of the general processes of societal and individual interaction'. Twelve students reported the developmental presence of the 'skills of interpreting and relating', specifically, the 'skills of interpreting a document or event from another culture, explaining it and relating it to documents from one's own'. All 20 students reported the presence of 'skills of discovery and interaction, reflecting the ability to acquire new knowledge of a culture and cultural practices'. In regard to the skills of discovery and interaction as 'the ability to operate knowledge, attitudes and skills under the constraints of real-time communication and interaction', 19 students reported this factor present. Finally, 19 of the 20 students reported the factor of 'critical cultural awareness' being present. In this instance, more students reported a presence of 'the ability to evaluate critically and on the basis of explicit criteria, perspectives, practices and products of other cultures' than the ability to do the same in one's own culture.

Both classes were asked what they thought about beauty after doing their research and watching the presentations and how their opinions had changed. Many students said they liked and enjoyed the presentations. Most students also said they gained new perspectives on beauty and their own perception of beauty changed. Some said that while they now know how other cultures perceive beauty, their own perceptions were not changed.

Students' projects were assessed for content mastery using rubrics that are used throughout the class and across classes. The rubrics assessed expression of ideas, grammar and vocabulary use, elaboration, clarity and presentational technique. The elements assigned in the project description were the focus of the ideas section and students had opportunities to work with the teacher prior to presenting on the presence of the necessary components of teaching new perceptions. Students were also assessed by the teacher for the IC objectives using the checklist during their presentations but also through teacher observation during discussions.

## Challenges and Opportunities

We had originally hoped to connect the two Glastonbury classes to an AP Spanish class in Hartford, CT, the state capital and Glastonbury's urban neighbor. Ideally there would have been interaction between the two classrooms via Skype, email or a shared class website. The goal of this interaction was that students would create a survey for the AP Spanish class in Hartford surrounding the topics of their presentations. Each student would also have administered this survey to two other people in their lives (family member, co-worker, friend, another teacher, etc.). However, for logistical reasons it was not possible to create the class connection, but many students were able to interview native speakers of Spanish from other countries and some gained new perspectives during their exchange in Madrid, Spain.

This was a fortunate and exciting opportunity that many students reflected on as providing new and worthwhile information that both surprised them and made them think differently. For example, one student reported, 'Before these conversations I thought America was the only country with beauty issues/obsessions.' Another reported, 'Interacting with native speakers gave me a new and interesting perspective. In some ways, the students and people I encountered were very similar to me, however, in others they were very different … when I interviewed many of the native speakers, their views intrigued me.' Another girl said of her interactions that, 'I interviewed several people while in Spain about their thoughts on voice and beauty. Just being immersed in the culture gave me a new perspective and understanding.'

## Analysis and Reflections on the Project

How did we implement Byram's (2008) IC model into a unit of study about beauty and aesthetics in an AP Spanish classroom? Our process in creating this project was not a linear one. We began highly ambitiously, although naively, wanting to take on the unit planning day by day, which eventually became an overwhelming task. We quickly realized time constraints would not allow this and while we may have been planning quality activities we lacked an end goal. Thus, we began looking at it from the other side, that is to say, backwards design (Wiggins & McTighe, 2005). On taking this approach, the process seemed much more manageable; we developed objectives and essential questions we wanted our students to be able to answer. From here the process is a blurred one. We were starting and stopping regularly, constantly revising in the hopes of maintaining the IC objectives and not accidentally stumbling into stereotypes. An added complication was the logistics of it all, because we were two busy people rarely in the same place. In the end the struggles and collaboration have made us both more competent, tolerant in the face of ambiguity, self-reflective and able to see things from the perspectives of others. We hope to encourage the same process with our students.

Table 6.3 demonstrates how IC components, including critical cultural awareness, were planned for the project.

Further dimensions of the theory we planned into the project are included in Table 6.4.

The components of the unit and the project were shaped by and contingent upon the direction in which the students themselves took the class, the topics they chose, the questions they came up with and where their perspectives took discussions.

To generate knowledge we put the students at the center. As they took charge of their learning in preparing their presentation they also took charge of their peers' learning. This project served as a learning opportunity but also as a cumulative task performed at the end of a unit. All topics were touched upon which had appeared throughout the unit via various sources and practiced through various activities. Thus, it was an assessment task that was structured so the students would be discovering and exploring culture using their prior knowledge rather than taking a pencil and paper exam, regurgitating 'facts' presented by the teacher.

This process itself also fostered students' autonomy and tolerance for ambiguity. Students were given very few guidelines and requirements and were encouraged to be creative. This could have caused discomfort in students, especially in a classroom setting where they are often accustomed to being given explicit instructions. There were many questions and subsequent frustrations when it was reiterated that they were to take control. Based on our prior experiences and on research, we hoped that students would

**Table 6.3** The ways in which IC components were incorporated into the student projects

| Knowledge | • Social distinctions of beauty in one's own and target culture.<br>• Processes and institutions of socialization within the theme of beauty and aesthetics within one's own and target culture.<br>• Concepts of beauty from various perspectives in own and target culture.<br>• Investigating how differing perspectives of beauty affect daily lives of people within one's own and target culture and how these can also affect the interactions of individuals from different cultures.<br>• Urban versus suburban community development from historical, political, societal and cultural viewpoints. |
|---|---|
| Skills of interpreting and relating | • Identifying ethnocentric perspectives of 'beauty', investigating the origins of these.<br>• Mediate conflicting interpretations within their group, within their culture and others and within their community.<br>• Relating perspectives within one's culture.<br>• Relating perspectives between one's own and target culture through interpreting media (advertisements, television, news, videos, pictures), statistics, scholarly articles, first-hand accounts, etc. |
| Skills of discovery and interaction | • Students discover unfamiliar perspectives on beauty through texts, pictures, videos, readings, research.<br>• Interaction with authentic materials.<br>• Mediation with each other via collaborative work and discussion.<br>• Urban versus suburban relationships within one's own culture.<br>• Effects of differing perspectives of beauty and aesthetics in contemporary and past relationships between one's own and other culture.<br>• Interaction among community members.<br>• Students will interact with native speakers through writing, possibly Skype or email or sharing an interactive webpage.<br>• Evaluation of survey results. |
| Attitudes | • Students' attitudes will be exposed through daily journal reflections.<br>• Students' attitudes will be exposed through their presentations and their ability to work creatively through the ambiguities of the project.<br>• Willingness to question the values and presuppositions in cultural practices in one's own environment will come through investigating their chosen topic within their own culture, using evidence and multiple perspectives.<br>• A readiness to engage with the conventions of verbal and nonverbal communication and interaction will be revealed through the group work process, presentation, interaction with Hartford class and surveying people in their lives.<br>• Attitudes will also be exposed in final guided reflection on the project and survey analysis. |

*(Continued)*

**Table 6.3** (*Continued*)

| Critical cultural awareness | • Students will question their own perspectives through discovery of unfamiliar perspectives.<br>• Students will question own society and reflect on societal impacts globally and individually.<br>• Students will question other cultures' perspectives from the same standpoint from which they question their own.<br>• Analyze documents, videos, observations based on evidence and multiple perspectives.<br>• Survey will oblige students to mediate an intercultural exchange in accordance with the explicit criteria of forming appropriate questions surrounding the topic – results will allow them to negotiate acceptance based on knowledge, skills and attitudes. |
|---|---|

eventually take ownership and thrive. Our hopes were met as the students were engaged and created final products that demonstrated impressive research and positively developing attitudes. However, for that to happen they had first to navigate and learn to tolerate ambiguity, a skill that served them well in all aspects of the project as an experience of university-type work, as well as developing as interculturally competent beings.

Curiosity in particular was demonstrated throughout the project, as students were observed asking questions of each other's project topic, especially during presentations. Building on this, students also demonstrated the willingness to suspend disbeliefs about other cultures and suspend their beliefs about their own culture (Byram, 2008). This was evident from their conversations during the project process, through their presentations as well as through the questions and discussions that developed during the

**Table 6.4** Other elements of Byram's (2008) IC model and the ways in which these were incorporated into the student projects

| Creating a community of practice and going beyond the walls of the classroom | • Group project; working collaboratively.<br>• Students take responsibility for their learning and learning of their peers.<br>• Connection with exchange students.<br>• Interviewing native speakers of all ages while in Madrid, Spain and sharing that information with classmates. |
|---|---|
| Cross-curricular | • Ideally we would have wanted to try to make connections with what students are doing in their other classes so they have more than one platform on which to think about and express their ideas regarding this topic. Cross-curricular options based on topics surrounding beauty include biology, math, social studies, English, art and photography. This was unfortunately not possible at this time.<br>• Skills of interviewing. |

presentations. These components were both represented within the IC objectives and thus it reflected positively on the students' development.

The process of collaboration even just within the classroom microcosm created a community of practice that fostered skills of interaction, relating and mediating. It also happened that within groups unexpected processes arose in regard to both content and IC. For example, there was increased vocabulary input and output while negotiating meaning and form as well as exposure to varying interpretations of the chosen topic that led to discovery and mediation.

The incorporation of the peer engagement and application of IC components presented in the presentations obliged students to pay attention to these aspects and reflect more on what they truly meant and how it could be shown. This also showed that the teacher was taking into consideration multiple perspectives during assessment, making it a shared learning experience.

We also incorporated an action component, an action in the community, by students interviewing host families and other people in Madrid. For those students who did not go to Spain we encouraged them to reach out to the accessible community in a different way. This aspect was not a requirement but some groups saw the value in this and created surveys based on their project topic. This opportunity of interaction was encouraged in an effort to make students see target culture interlocutors as dynamic individuals, and not stereotype figures. In doing so we hoped to minimize any 'us' versus 'them' interpretations and reflect the understanding that 'other' cultural perspectives do not just exist in 'other' places but that in every community there is diversity. By using Spanish (and products created in Spanish class) with people outside the school setting we made connections between the foreign language classroom and their contemporary world.

## Conclusion

We believe this project yielded data demonstrating that throughout the process students had progressed towards IC. However, this is a case study of only two classes within a state and nation-wide foreign language system. There needs to be a more collaborative approach to addressing language and culture as holistic and reciprocal. Language policymakers need to take up the IC issue in policy and curriculum to facilitate individual choices by the learner and teacher to support IC development (Liddicoat et al., 1999). This requires collaborative advocacy for IC, which will only manifest when teachers are knowledgeable about its purpose, importance and implementation. We hope that by describing this project and its success in fostering not only student progress toward IC but also their curiosity and intrinsic motivation, we can inspire other teachers to understand its importance and the vast possibilities of implementation.

Furthermore, IC is not something that should be confined to the foreign language classroom; it is integral to all branches of education with its roots deep in student-centered critical pedagogy. Critical pedagogy is a pedagogy of reflection, dissent, difference, dialogue, empowerment, action and hope, within which cultural knowledge is not a 'distant object to be acquired but [a] process of reciprocal identification and representation, accomplished mostly through interpersonal relations' (Guilherme, 2002: 89). This served as part of our reasoning behind making the project so open, and encouraging student autonomy. It also inspired us to encourage authentic interpersonal relations by having students not only work in groups together to experience differing perspectives but also by pushing them to interact with people outside of the classroom to expand even further their contact with varying interpretations of the content and application of their knowledge and skills. A principal dimension of the critical pedagogy process is also recognizing that discourse is negotiated between and among students and teachers (Reagan, 2006). This further inspired us to create a student-centered project and create a more reciprocal relationship between student and teacher, learning together, instead of the teacher 'imparting' knowledge to the students. There was more of a mutual learning process where the students took as much control as the teacher. The teacher merely served as a mediator, providing scaffolding and a sounding board for ideas.

## Appendix A: Project Guidelines

As given to the students in Spanish:

Proyecto Nombre: _____
Belleza
Español 6 AP Fecha de entrega: 4 de marzo de 2014

El 4 de marzo la clase tendrá presentaciones sobre la belleza y sus manifestaciones a través de culturas e historia. Pasamos varios días estudiando algunos aspectos de la belleza en clase y vamos a continuar estudiándola individualmente y en grupos para añadir a nuestro entendimiento del asunto y aumentar nuestras perspectivas.

La presentación va a ser en grupos de 2 o 3 y debe incluir:

a.  Una investigación de un aspecto de percepciones de belleza
b.  Un entendimiento nuevo de tu grupo en cuanto a la belleza
c.  Información de clase y de sitios auténticos en español de la red
d.  Datos, ejemplos, visuales para ayudar la comprensión de tu presentación
e.  Una parte interactiva con tus compañeros de clase para que consideren o apliquen la información que ustedes se presentaron
f.  Una bibliografía en el estilo MLA

English translation:

Project Name: _____
Beauty
Spanish 6 AP Due Date: March 4, 2014

March 4th class will have presentations about beauty and its manifestations through cultures and history. We have spent various days studying some aspects of beauty in class and we will continue studying it individually and in groups to add to our understanding of the subject and widen our perceptions.

The presentation should be in groups of 2 or 3 and include:

a. An investigation of one aspect of perceptions of beauty
b. A new understanding your group has about beauty
c. Information from class and authentic target language websites
d. Facts, examples, visuals to help the class comprehend your presentation
e. An interactive component with your classmates so they are provided the opportunity to consider and apply the information you have presented to them
f. An MLA bibliography

# Appendix B: Unit Objectives

## Content objectives

Students will be able to ...

- evaluate beauty – based on evidence and relativist perspectives (both emic and etic) – in terms of worldwide historical perspectives and choices regarding what is beautiful in different times and contexts;
- compare historical perspectives to each other and to current perspectives;
- analyze definitions of beauty in biological and mathematical perspectives;
- evaluate factors influencing definitions and pressures of beauty within L1 and L2 societies;
- compare factors influencing definitions and pressures of beauty between L1 society and others;
- compare the perceptions of beauty from a variety of vantage points between L1 society and others.

## Intercultural competence objectives (derived from Byram's [2008] model)

Attitudes: students will demonstrate ...

- curiosity and openness, readiness to suspend disbelief about other cultures and belief about one's own;

- a willingness to question the values and presuppositions in cultural practices and products in one's own environment;
- a readiness to engage with the conventions and rites of verbal and non-verbal communication and interaction.

Knowledge: students will know ...

- the processes and institutions of socialization in one's own and one's interlocutor's country;
- social distinctions and their principal markers, in one's own country and one's interlocutor's;
- institutions, and perceptions of them, which impinge on daily life within one's own and one's interlocutor's country and which conduct and influence relationships between them.

Skills of interpreting and relating: students will be able to ...

- identify ethnocentric perspectives in a document or event and explain origins;
- mediate between conflicting interpretations of phenomena.

Skills of discovery and interaction: students will be able to ...

- identify significant references within and across cultures and elicit their significance and connotations;
- identify similar and dissimilar processes of interaction, verbal and nonverbal, and negotiate an appropriate use of them in specific circumstances;
- use in real time knowledge, skills and attitudes for mediation between interlocutors of one's own and a foreign culture;
- identify contemporary and past relationships between one's own and the other culture and country;
- discovery of other perspectives on interpretation of familiar and unfamiliar phenomena both in one's own and in other cultures and cultural practices.

Critical cultural awareness/political education: students will be able to ...

- identify and interpret explicit or implicit values in documents and events in one's own and other cultures;
- make an evaluative analysis of the documents and events that refer to an explicit perspective and criteria;
- interact and mediate in intercultural exchanges in accordance with explicit criteria, negotiating where necessary a degree of acceptance of them by drawing upon one's knowledge, skills and attitudes.

# Appendix C: Intercultural Competence Checklist

Topic_____
Student(s) name(s)_____

| | | Present | Not Present | Not addressed |
|---|---|---|---|---|
| **Attitudes:** | A1: curious and open; receptive to cultural differences | | | |
| | A2: readiness/willingness to suspend belief(s) about other cultures | | | |
| | A3: readiness/willingness to suspend own belief about own culture | | | |
| **Knowledge:** | K1: of social groups and their products and practices in one's own culture | | | |
| | K2: of social groups and their products and practices in country culture being studied | | | |
| | K3: of the general processes of societal and individual interaction | | | |
| **Skills of interpreting and relating:** | IR1: ability to interpret a document or event from another culture, to explain it and relate it to documents from one's own. | | | |
| **Skills of discovery and interaction:** | DR1: ability to acquire new knowledge of a culture and cultural practices | | | |
| | DR2: ability to operate knowledge, attitudes and skills under the constraints of real-time communication and interaction | | | |
| **Critical cultural awareness/ political education:** | CA1: ability to evaluate critically and on the basis of explicit criteria perspectives, practices and products in one's own culture | | | |
| | CA2: ability to evaluate critically and on the basis of explicit criteria perspectives, practices and products of other cultures and countries | | | |

# Appendix D: List of Project Titles

The following titles have been translated by the teacher from Spanish into English:

- What is cute? Babies and beauty
- Body modifications across cultures
- Skin color in different cultures
- Beauty in cultural dance
- Voices and beauty
- Different perceptions of beauty
- Wealth and beauty
- Architecture
- Beauty and the golden ratio
- Beauty and gender
- Beauty: perceptions in Spain versus the United States

## References

ACTFL (2012) ACTFL *Proficiency Guidelines 2012* (pp. 6–8). Alexandria, VA: American Council on the Teaching of Foreign Languages.

Byram, M. (2008) *From Foreign Language Education to Education for Intercultural Citizenship: Essays and Reflections.* Clevedon: Multilingual Matters.

Guilherme, M. (2002) *Critical Citizens for an Intercultural World: Foreign Language Education as Cultural Politics.* Clevedon: Multilingual Matters.

Liddicoat, A.J., Crozet, C. and Lo Bianco, J.H. (1999) Striving for the third place: Consequences and implications. In J.H. Lo Bianco, A.J. Liddicoat and C. Crozet (eds) *Striving for Third Place: Intercultural Competence through Language Education* (pp. 181–187). Melbourne: Language Australia.

Reagan, T. (2006) Explanatory power of critical language studies: Linguistics with an attitude. *Critical Inquiry in Language Studies: An International Journal* 3 (1), 1–22.

Wiggins, G. and McTighe, J. (2005) *Understanding by Design* (2nd edn). Upper Saddle River, NJ: Pearson Education.

# 7 IC Online: Fostering the Development of Intercultural Competence in Virtual Language Classrooms

Manuela Wagner and Niko Tracksdorf

Proponents of online learning note that the number of higher education students taking online courses increased from the low thousands 10 years ago to almost 4 million in 2007. Skeptics continue to question the value of online learning and suggest that its impact will be limited. In the end, neither of these positions will matter, and the future of online learning will be driven by factors outside academia. Every faculty member who is not near retirement today is likely to teach online during his or her career. (Hislop, 2009: 94)

As more and more institutions offer online courses, there is also an increasing interest in teaching 'language and culture' courses online. As is also clear from the introductory quote, there are differing opinions about the efficacy of online education. A meta-analysis of online learning studies conducted for the US Department of Education revealed that students who learned the same content in online environments performed modestly better than those who learned it in a face-to-face classroom (Means *et al.*, 2009). For foreign or world language courses there is the additional consideration of language of instruction. This especially applies to beginner language courses, in which it is more difficult to give instructions in the target language at the beginning when students have limited or no linguistic skills in the target language. Another question might be how intercultural (communicative) competence (Byram, 1997) or intercultural citizenship (Byram, 2008) can be included in online language courses. In this chapter, we describe an attempt to include activities fostering intercultural (communicative) competence in a sequence of two online elementary German courses (Elementary German I and II) taught in an intensive summer program at a public university in the north-east of the United States. It would be beyond the scope of the current chapter to describe the details of the course design. However, we will offer background information when necessary in the context of intercultural competence (IC)/citizenship education.

## The Authors/Teachers

Manuela, Associate Professor of Foreign Language Education and Director of the German language and culture program in the Department of Literatures, Cultures and Languages at the University of Connecticut and Niko, graduate student of German studies in the same department, collaborated in this project. Manuela has a long-standing interest in intercultural communication in her research and teaching and has collaborated with colleagues in school and university settings. Niko has shared his expertise in implementing social networking and online tools into face-to-face language classrooms by offering workshops for secondary and postsecondary instructors.

## The Context

The two online courses were developed with the help of two grants from an online course development initiative at the university which provides help with online instructional design and also requires a specific design format. The courses needed to be developed during the first academic year, taught during the following summer, revised during the following academic year, taught again the following summer, revised again during the following academic year and taught the next summer. Elementary German I was developed during the academic year 2012/2013 when we received the first course development grant together with a colleague in the department. Niko taught the course for the first time in the summer of 2013. In 2013 Manuela and Niko received a grant to develop Elementary German II, and Niko and Manuela then co-taught Elementary German I, and Niko taught Elementary German II in the summer of 2014 (see Table 7.1).

In this chapter we report on the second implementation of Intensive Elementary German I and the first implementation of Intensive Elementary German II. For more information about the course see Table 7.2. We pay specific attention to the planning and implementation of intercultural (communicative) competence (Byram, 1997) in an online environment. We will point to specific opportunities as well as challenges from our experiences.

**Table 7.1** Schedule of course design and teaching

|  | Elementary German I | Elementary German II |
|---|---|---|
| Academic year 2012/2013 | Developing |  |
| Summer 2013 | TEACHING: Niko |  |
| Academic year 2013/2014 | Revising | Developing |
| Summer 2014 | TEACHING: Manuela and Niko | TEACHING: Niko |
| Academic year 2014/2015 | Revising | Revising |
| Summer 2015 | TEACHING | TEACHING |
| Academic year 2015/2016 | Revising | Revising |
| Summer 2016 | TEACHING | TEACHING |

**Table 7.2** Information about courses

| Type of school | Instructional modality | Pedagogical approach | Grade level(s) | Average age of the students | Average number of students per class | Number of synchronous meetings per week | Number of minutes per synchronous meeting |
|---|---|---|---|---|---|---|---|
| Post-secondary | Online | Flipped classroom | Elementary German I (6 weeks intense) | Adults | 15 | 3 | 120 |
|  |  |  | Elementary German II (6 weeks intense) |  | 11 | 2 | 120 |

# Course Design

We agreed that it was important to implement practices based on research and evidence in online education rather than merely transferring best practices from the face-to-face into the online learning environment. That approach resulted in a lengthy process of weekly or bi-weekly meetings over an extended period of time (a couple of semesters and a summer) for the planning of the courses. Manuela supervises all language and culture courses in the German program, and one of her concerns was the alignment of online course outcomes with those of courses taught during the regular academic year. Furthermore, she needed to consider that graduate students who were not involved in course planning and with varied prior teaching experiences should eventually be able to teach the course. Therefore, it was important to avoid certain practices that might be more difficult to implement with less experience.

In our theoretical framework for language education, we take the view that language is both embodied and dialogical (Hodges, 2009; van Lier, 2004). Therefore, we intended to create an environment in which students were able and encouraged to access information, collaborate and engage. We also believe in providing opportunities for learners to become part of a community in which learning takes place, resembling what Lave and Wenger call a 'community of practice' (Lave & Wenger, 1991). Finally, we favor 'authentic' (e.g. Van Lier, 2004) rather than simplified input. Research in online education confirms that participatory environments in which students who receive the instruction in an instructor-led or collaborative environment rather than in those where students work independently have better learning outcomes (Means et al., 2009). From our experience, we also agree with researchers and educators who point out that 'digital-age students want an active learning experience that is social, participatory and supported by rich media' (McLoughlin & Lee, 2010: 28).

Although we were aware that one of the most important advantages of online instruction is the flexibility of when to interact with the course materials, and despite the fact that the course was a six-week intensive language and culture course, we decided that in the case of elementary language online instruction we needed to insist on a rather high percentage of synchronous instruction, meaning that all students were asked to sign on at a certain time (29 hours of synchronous online interaction with instructor and students, compared to 45 hours spent in the face-to-face version during the regular academic semester).

Using the 'curriculum by design' or 'backward design' approach (Wiggins & McTighe, 2006), we aligned the objectives of each level with the face-to-face courses (German Elementary I and II) and then planned the assessments followed by the activities and materials used in the (online) classroom to achieve these objectives.

The flipped classroom model (Bergman & Sams, 2012) was used to structure the different components of the course. Instead of having the students learn new grammatical structures and having them explore cultural aspects during the synchronous meetings, we asked the students to study topics, vocabulary and grammar themselves. We divided each course (Elementary German I and Elementary German II) into six modules that corresponded with the chapters in the textbook we used (*Kontakte*, McGraw-Hill). Each of these textbook chapters contains a part written in English in which the structures that are used in the chapter are explained. We instructed our students to read that part before each online meeting. Students were also expected to study the vocabulary in order to come to class prepared to apply what they had studied. We assessed their vocabulary through an online tool called Quizlet (quizlet.com). In addition, students completed online activities offered in conjunction with the textbook (*Connect*, McGraw-Hill) which allowed them to practice the vocabulary and grammar in structured online activities. The synchronous time was then used to apply the knowledge by solving problems, interacting with each other, discussing and practicing.

## Conceptualization of Intercultural Competence

The main focus of this chapter is on our conceptualization, planning, implementation and evaluation of objectives and activities addressing intercultural (communicative) competence (Byram, 1997). Our main framework consisted of the 'savoirs' model and intercultural citizenship mentioned in the introduction to this book. Therefore, we used the model components (attitudes [of curiosity/suspending belief/disbelief], knowledge, skills of interpreting and relating, skills of discovery and interaction, critical cultural awareness) as our main planning and assessment tools to develop intercultural (communicative) competence in German I and the beginnings of intercultural citizenship in German II. We designed activities that foster a non-essential view of culture (Holliday et al., 2010) and encouraged initial reflections on issues of social justice (Osborn, 2005). Students' development of relevant sociolinguistic and pragmatic skills plays an important role in this context as well.

## Integration of Intercultural (Communicative) Competence in the Online Courses

Our intention was to integrate the various aspects of intercultural (communicative) competence from the start and in a variety of contexts. For example, we asked students to fill out a survey at the beginning of the course answering questions such as, 'Why did you decide to take German? What do you think of when you think about the German language? List some things you know about culture in German-speaking countries? How do you celebrate birthdays in your culture? If somebody asked you to describe "something typical" in your culture what example would you give? What would you like to know about German-speaking countries? What would you like to learn in this course? What would you like to be able to do at the end of this course?' The objectives behind this activity were to foster an environment in which students were asked to consider culture as well as language, to start the process of reflecting on one's own culture(s) as well as those of the target language and to inspire some curiosity about the course content, and then in German-speaking countries more widely. In addition, some of the answers provided a baseline for us teachers as to where our students were in terms of their reflections, and what their reasons for taking German were. Interestingly, a difference between students who were more interested in linguistic aspects and those who were also interested in cultural aspects could already be observed in the first few lessons as can be seen by some of the students' comments in their beginning journal entries: 'Originally, I had taken German as a way to sort of culturally get back in touch with the Yiddish speaking roots of my family'; 'I decided to study German because I knew that English is a Germanic language so I figured it should be both similar and interesting'; 'I decided to take German mainly for the credits. However, there are certain aspects of the culture that are interesting to me.' In the following we will describe contexts in which we implemented aspects of IC, each followed by a couple of examples.

## Activities in Synchronous Interactions

### Music

One opportunity to integrate IC was with activities and tasks during the synchronous online meetings. We began each class with a short video that we started to play before students entered the online platform (Blackboard Collaborate), and exposed students to music and culture from German-speaking artists primarily from DACHL (Germany, Austria, Switzerland and Liechtenstein) – a term often used in German as a foreign language to stress that German is not only spoken in one country and region, and that it includes more than just those four countries. Some students started to join before the official meeting time, partly to hear the music, and we tried to play music from different regions, periods and genres in order to show students some of the variety. Students had questions about the songs and often remarked on whether they liked or disliked the songs. Some were surprised by the popularity of German songs in the United States. They had heard songs without connecting them to a German-speaking artist. Our intention was to set the mood for the class as well as creating an awareness of the variety of German, Austrian and Swiss artists. We hoped to foster 'attitudes of curiosity' in our students and think that we succeeded when they asked us, often even after class, about the artists shown at the beginning of the class. Some students mentioned in the final reflection that they were now following German-speaking artists and discovered new favorite songs. Sometimes the music was also related to the content discussed in class. Students had then to interpret the songs and sometimes we feel that the students' analyses, linked with later reflections, led them to critically evaluate their preconceptions of certain topics. We will provide an example later that deals with the topic of gender and tolerance.

### Conchita Wurst activity

We also planned longer connected activities for the synchronous meetings, especially in the second half of Elementary German I and in Elementary German II. One example of a longer activity in an online synchronous meeting comes from Unit 2 in Elementary German II. Here, students had a higher level of competence in German, and had therefore more communicative tools to express their thoughts and opinions in the foreign language. The activity was planned around an event occurring shortly before the class was taught. The event was the Eurovision Song Contest – an annual competition viewed by almost 200 million people every year. In 2014 (at the time the course was taught), Conchita Wurst, an Austrian singer and drag persona who was born as Thomas Neuwirth, won the Eurovision Song Contest. During one of the synchronous meetings, the students were asked to describe the appearance and clothes of ordinary people and celebrities they saw in pictures, to practice newly acquired vocabulary like colors, clothes, body parts, and adjectives (Step 1). We then divided the students into pairs, and asked them to describe what they thought a typical DACHL woman and man looks like and wears (Step 2). They were allowed to use an online dictionary, and asked the instructor for unknown words. Some groups, for example, asked for 'Lederhosen' and 'Dirndl'. During this step, our intention was to activate some background knowledge (and if applicable, existing stereotypes) students had concerning clothes and gender.

One of the students in each group then received a picture of a celebrity from either DACHL or the United States. While the student described the appearance and clothes of the celebrity, the other student was asked to guess the gender and nationality of the person, and who the celebrity might be. The students switched roles after each picture, every team receiving a total of 12 pictures. The first six showed more 'traditional' images: DACHL women wearing Dirndl, DACHL men wearing Lederhosen, American women with long hair wearing dresses, and American men with casual jeans or suits (Step 2).

We then presented less traditional pictures of women with short hair and jeans, and pictures of the Afro-German model Sara Nuru (Step 3). Because the students were not allowed to use pronouns, and only say *'Ich sehe …'* (I see), it became harder for the students to guess the gender, and almost impossible to guess the nationality. Our learning goals here were 'knowledge' (including knowledge and analysis of stereotypes), 'skills of interpreting and relating', and 'skills of discovery and interaction', in this case with classmates and the teacher.

Finally, we shared a picture of Conchita Wurst (Step 4). Conchita Wurst, who chose the second name 'Wurst' in order to point to the German saying *'Das ist mir doch alles Wurst'* (It's all the same to me), is a female character who stands for tolerance, love and respect for those who do not fit the norm (Davies, 2014), and who is noted for her beard. Most students paused for a second, and described her as follows *'Ich sehe … lange Haare, braune Haare, ein Tattoo, ein Armband, ein Kleid, hohe Schuhe, … und einen Bart'* (I see … long hair, brown hair, a tattoo, a bracelet, a dress, high heels, … and a beard). The students who had to guess nationality and gender were now confused, hearing that this person was wearing a dress and high heels, but also had a beard.

In the English conversation at the end of the unit, we discussed what the drag persona Conchita Wurst could stand for, defined what stereotypes meant for the students, and revisited their description of a typical man or woman in a German-speaking country (Step 5).

Apart from practicing the relevant vocabulary and the accusative case, the students were challenged about their partly stereotypical images. In the beginning (Step 1), they learned about some traditional images of the target cultures ('knowledge'). When they noticed that the descriptions were partly stereotypes (Step 5), they started 'suspending beliefs' about gender, the other culture and their own culture, and challenged the norms ('attitude'). When we talked in English about stereotypes at the end of the units, and the way they influenced the perception of the students, they became aware of their own values and views, and how influential they were in creating their judgments ('critical cultural awareness'). In Appendix A we provide samples of students' reflection on Conchita as part of their journal entries.

## Five- to ten-minute period at the end of each meeting

As we were aware that it might be difficult to create a community in the classroom exclusively on the basis of the limited interactions in the online synchronous classroom at the beginning of Elementary German I, and because we wanted to help our students think deeply about issues from the beginning, we decided to use some time at the end of each synchronous meeting to have conversations in English. We checked how everyone felt, and also chose topics we considered could be interesting and/or thought-provoking for students. Sometimes the topics came from comments in the journal entries; sometimes we continued a conversation we started in one of the activities but could not explore further in the target language. Quite often these five to ten minutes offered the opportunity to discuss IC-related topics. We were able to ask questions and point to the complexity and/or ambiguity of a topic. For example, when we discussed when people eat the biggest meal of the day in America versus in German-speaking countries, it became clear that there is no easy answer. The complexity also showed variety in the US context as students compared their different opinions.

## Greetings and Partings activity I

As students were instructed to come to class prepared with some prior knowledge of the grammar and vocabulary we were going to use in each online meeting, our intention was to provide opportunities for students to use the language they learned with each other in meaningful and, if possible, authentic contexts. One question we asked ourselves was whether students might encounter a similar task in real-life interactions.

For example, when dealing with greetings and partings in the German language, we included variations of greetings, for example from different regions, age groups and across social statuses, in order to introduce varieties in language and culture. We also asked students to interpret videos showing different greetings with regard to formality, familiarity of interlocutors and setting, and to compare them with a similar situation in their own cultural context in order to reflect on possible differences.

## Activities in Asynchronous Interaction

In addition to fostering IC in real-time interactions, we also integrated activities relating to the 'savoirs' in the asynchronous time of the online class.

### Greetings and Partings activity II

Some of the goals of the synchronous Greetings and Partings activity were achieved through homework in the form of a journal entry and reflections in English. Students were also asked how they think they would feel if they were greeted in the same way the person in the videos was greeted. That resulted in some students' admissions that some greetings seemed 'weird' to them. They then explained what seemed 'weird'. We intended to help students understand that we often make judgments without realizing it. We therefore tried to expose them to more situations and to information from a variety of perspectives so that they could contextualize the greetings and perhaps come to a more informed opinion of why certain greetings happen the way they do in other cultural contexts.

### Roommate activity

After looking at roommate ads from different DACHL regions on websites like wg-gesucht.de and easywg.de (Step 1: interpretational reading), the students themselves took the role of exchange students who were looking for a roommate in a German-speaking country. We were interested in what students would do with the cultural differences they encountered. For example, the ads often mentioned the age of the person looking for roommates, information about smoking, and some details that the students thought would only be shared on dating platforms (e.g. personal life goals). In addition, they were surprised at the low costs of internet and cable TV and the proportion of apartments with wooden floors. Many ads came with pictures of the apartments, which added an additional element of discovery, and an insight into a real person's home.

Now it was time for the students to create their own advertisement. We instructed them to collect information about the apartment they had in mind, to describe themselves, and to identify what they were looking for in a roommate. They then were asked to create an ad that would be posted online (Step 2: presentational writing). After all the ads were published online, students browsed through the ads that the others had created and replied to the ones that caught their attention (Step 3: interpersonal writing). Every student created a table with the information they had received from students interested in living with them, compared the possible roommates, and decided which students to invite for an interview (Step 4: interpretational writing). Finally, the students interviewed each other synchronously in an online videoconferencing environment (Step 5: interpersonal speaking). In addition to writing/speaking about themselves, their daily schedules, likes, dislikes and talents in German (Steps 2, 5: 'discovery and interaction'), and interpreting simple written and spoken German (Steps 1, 3, 5: 'interpreting and relating'), the students also learned about conventions of communication and interaction in the foreign country, and noticed language varieties of different regions while analyzing the provided ads ('knowledge'). In an English discussion at the end of the unit, they talked about the different values of renting versus buying living space in German-speaking countries and the United States, and attributed part of it to the role of mobility in each culture ('skills of interpreting and relating').

This activity led to beginning critical cultural awareness. After making assumptions at the start of the activity, the students began to evaluate the underlying values in the roommate ads, and reflected on their own values, looking back at their own roommate ads in comparison to the German ones. They started making judgments based on evidence, and critically reflected on their own culture.

## Journal entries

In addition to the class activities, students were asked to write about three journal entries per module. The journal entries were a tool for the students to reflect in the moment and also to observe their own reflections over time. They were not shared with other students but with teachers. In Elementary German I we started our reflections with some questions students could answer in German. However, they were allowed to write large parts of their reflections in English. Soon we asked them to write whatever they could in German and what they could not express in German they could still write in English. Some students took the opportunity to write quite a bit in German from early on, while others felt more comfortable using more English in the journal entries. Some of those who used both languages in one entry used one language per paragraph; others were code-mixing. We replied to journal entries online at fairly regular intervals. We intended to show that we read the entries and sometimes felt that we could encourage further thought about a topic. Due to time constraints we were not able to engage in an extended conversation about their journals with each student. However, we were able to observe students' reflections, which were especially interesting concerning their thoughts about culture.

In addition to encouraging students to think about their learning experience, we also challenged them to reflect on more complex issues, such as language and identity. We included several questions about 'German culture', letting students hypothesize about what German-speaking people do in certain situations. For example, in the beginning we asked what students knew about German culture in order to understand how much experience they had and to also see whether they would find it easy to make assumptions.

Depending on the chapter topic we then asked students about clothes/celebrations/housing, etc., in their country and in German-speaking countries. For example, one of the current topics was the football World Cup occurring in Brazil during the time of the course. Because in Elementary German II we felt we could move away from the focus on themselves and encourage students to take a closer look at topics in German-speaking countries, the topic of the football World Cup offered various opportunities to look into important subjects such as nationalism and patriotism in the context of the target cultures. Students reflected in their journals on the following quotes (translated here) from a German newspaper article:

'This victory will be pure prestige for Germany, and it could also affect other areas beyond sports, like politics and the economy.'

'For millions of Germans, it made the World Cup victory not only pure pleasure, but an exercise in soul searching.'

'Even into the 1990s, flagpoles at schools were bare of the national flag and children weren't taught the national anthem.'

'Only in 2006, when Germany hosted the World Cup, were black, red and yellow tentatively draped from windows and attached to car antennas.'

Students' responses to the journal entry prompts varied greatly in length, number and what we label as 'depth of reflection'. Some students seemed to enjoy their reflections and wrote long entries while for others the journal entries were not an important part of the course. This variance might be due to the fact that the journal was not a big part of the grade (10% in German I, 12% in German II). In addition, journal entries made it clear that some students focused more on 'learning the language' and they were more concerned with the process of learning the formal aspects of the language while other students seemed to gravitate more towards the open questions about culture.

In general, students seemed to find it easier at the beginning of the course and in Elementary German I to generalize what people in German-speaking countries might do in certain situations. While some students in their early reflections tended to say something like 'I think it is pretty much the same in Germany' or 'I imagine they (German culture and customs) are very different from American culture and customs', they would be more careful later, making statements such as 'I honestly do not know' or 'I just don't know the details'. Students also stated opinions they had changed. For example, one commented that he found that 'While not exactly a Romance language, German is not as harsh as it is sometimes portrayed'. Some students made explicit connections with facts which they learned in their 'research' for the journal entries and by which they were surprised, and we surmise that this might have caused them to be more cautious in their assumptions.

It is important to note that not every student underwent such a development during Elementary German I. However, we feel that students engaged in all components of the *savoirs* model in their journal entries and that the entries were useful for us in that we were able to observe their development to some degree and foster more reflection when we felt it was needed.

## Projects

In Elementary German II we asked students to investigate a topic of their choice for the duration of the semester. We encouraged them to choose a topic that we did not cover in the course, but about which they wanted to learn more. Students chose diverse topics including patriotism, feminism, WWII, beer culture, German music, film, football and Konrad Zuse (a German civil engineer [1910–1995] and inventor of the 'first working programmable computer') (see Schmidhuber [n.d.] for more information). Some students were quite engaged in their projects and wrote long reflections about them in their journals. Based on the classroom conversations and their prior knowledge and research, we asked them to create a questionnaire with a program called Surveymonkey (www.surveymonkey.com). The task was to create the survey in German and in English and to each invite at least four students in the course to complete the German survey and at least ten friends in English to complete the English survey. We teachers also elicited responses to the German surveys from our circles of German-speaking friends and colleagues. Finally, we asked students to interpret the results on their webpage and then to present and discuss the results in class.

Our goal with this activity was to help students: (a) to gain knowledge (in class, through research on the internet, by interacting with others); (b) to develop skills of discovery and interaction (in discussions, emails, and with the survey); and (c) to learn how to interpret and relate (first by interpreting the information obtained in class and through their research to create the questions, followed by their interpretations of the answers to their surveys in relationship to the gained knowledge). Although the stimulus for the activity came from us, we hoped that the opportunity to choose their own topic would pique their curiosity, which in turn would contribute to their being open to new experiences and learning new information. In particular, students would not only learn from each other, but also from the extended communities of their peers and teachers.

Finally, by helping students deconstruct the questionnaire responses and by discussing some issues in more depth, we hoped students would develop critical cultural awareness. In some cases, we confirmed that students indeed developed such critical awareness. In their journal entries they described how some surprising answers and results caused them to reconsider a previously held opinion and, more importantly, helped them understand just how complex issues can be and how important context is in such complex topics.

## Websites

In addition to researching a topic of their choice, the students each had a website on which they published their findings while investigating a selected town or region from different perspectives throughout the semester. For example, students were asked to research on the various course topics in the chosen town/city (e.g. spare-time activities, restaurants, directions, means of transportation, landmarks, food, vacation). Students chose towns/cities in Germany, Austria and Switzerland. We also brought up topics such as social justice (e.g. in transportation, education, gender, environmental protection). By publishing their findings on the website, their products or research and reflection became available to a wide audience, and allowed for further discussions.

## Additional planned activities

In addition, we had planned to ask students to note open questions that arose from the various topics in the course and that they would be interested in pursuing further. The plan was either to invite German-speaking colleagues and friends who would volunteer to chat with students or to create a survey to send to colleagues and friends. We hoped to receive multiple answers to each question which would further encourage students to evaluate with evidence and from different perspectives.

## Assessments

One of our design objectives was to include as many 'authentic' assessments as possible, i.e. we test what we want the students to be able to do (Wiggins, 1990). Our aim therefore was to conduct (integrated) performance assessments (CARLA, 2009; Glisan et al., 2003; Wiggins, 1998, 2006) rather than assessing separate skills, but that does not mean that we did not focus on form. While we assessed our students' communicative skills we provided numerous activities in their homework and in synchronous meetings to make them become familiar with and learn to apply the formal aspects of language (vocabulary, grammatical structures, pronunciation, etc.) required to develop proficiency in the language. Our assessments then consisted of communicative tasks and activities that students needed to complete each of the six modules. Part of completing a communicative task consisted of correctly applying knowledge of formal aspects of language. We made sure that students were asked to perform in each of the three modes of communication (interpersonal, interpretive, presentational) (Swender & Duncan, 1998) and in the four corresponding skills (listening, speaking, reading and writing). In all our assessments we tried to be mindful of integrating opportunities for students to develop the necessary attitudes and skills and gain the knowledge to develop their IC as described in the *savoirs* model.

While we included assessment of the knowledge part of IC by including guided questions in the journals and during the synchronous meetings, we also made an effort to integrate the other *savoirs* into our performance assessment, which was often included in our regular instruction. For example, in the asynchronous and synchronous Greetings and Partings activity (see above), in which students watched a video in which people greet each other in different ways, including an adjustment to different levels of formality depending on the situation, students showed that they were able to identify areas of misunderstanding or conflict, and offered suggestions for mediation in their accompanying journal entry (skills of interpreting and relating).

We also asked the students to call us on our cell phone or on Skype to interview us about certain topics. We paid attention to interacting naturally. For example, when students spoke with Manuela, they used the more formal version of the second person pronoun as she had also used this with the students. When they spoke with Niko they used the informal version. We also deliberately used some vocabulary students had not encountered yet, so that they had to negotiate meaning in context (skill of discovery and interaction in real-time communication). This was an example of one of our authentic assessments in which students also had the opportunity to learn while being assessed.

## Challenges

As we expected, most of the challenges we experienced were related to time constraints because the courses we report on were two six-week intensive summer courses. It might be important to note that regular summer courses at our university last five weeks, but the instructor can decide to choose six weeks if the course content requires that (e.g. in writing courses). We decided to choose six weeks to allow some more time for students to process and practice the material. We also felt that the online format posed some challenges and here we provide suggestions for how to deal with them.

## Creating a community

Due to our approach to education (learning and teaching) as a dialogical and community-based activity and because of our methodological concept of a communicative approach, we wanted to create a community among the students from the very beginning. In addition, we thought that if the students felt they were part of a learning community they would be more encouraged to discuss topics with each other in and outside the meetings. We also knew from experience when we taught Elementary German I the first time the summer before, that students can become anxious when they do not know how to use the required technology and when they are then asked to follow the teacher's instruction in a language they do not know yet. The students' limited linguistic ability, especially at the beginning of the language learning experience, problems with technology, and the almost unavoidable 'confusion' one experiences in any foreign language classroom can be daunting in an online classroom, especially at the beginning.

In addition, students did not always see each other or the teacher because not all students could have their cameras or microphones turned on at the same time due to restrictions in the online software we used. Sometimes we even decided to do activities without cameras altogether in order to avoid bandwidth problems. Consequently, the teachers could not always see all the students either. That could potentially lead to students being lost or to being less attentive on purpose.

## Time, time, time

As is probably true in education in many contexts, time was our biggest challenge. In our case, students registered for a summer course hoping that they would be highly flexible as to when they would study for their German course. However, we had decided to ask students to spend a considerable amount of time in synchronous online meetings with each other and us, as we felt they would need our support to practice what they learned in scaffolded activities. Consequently, we asked them in our six-week course to spend about 70% of the time they would spend in a 13-week face-to-face classroom in synchronous meetings. For some students that was nearly impossible, as they came from various different backgrounds, had different schedules, and lived in different time zones.

The already somewhat limited time in synchronous meetings was further used more for linguistic explanations than was desirable, as the teachers needed to ensure that everyone had the tools to complete the communicative tasks. Therefore, the activities could not always include as much of an IC component in class as we had wished.

Time also played an important role in the teachers' workload. The two courses were prepared with the help of online course development grants and with the help of online course designers. Nevertheless, the time spent on designing the course, preparing the course materials, teaching the sessions and grading and reviewing the students' work (assessments, journals, online exercises, emails, etc.) by far exceeded any amount of time we had spent on very time-intensive face-to-face courses. We estimated the amount spent for the course to be about three times as high compared to our face-to-face courses.

The above-mentioned time constraints sometimes prevented us from including more IC in synchronous meetings. While we had more ideas about activities, we needed most of the available time left for core course design, including setting up the learning platform. At times we also felt over-whelmed and might not have focused on IC as much as we would have liked. For example, there were opportunities to work more with what students explored in their journals, but we did not have more time or space in our curriculum to investigate a topic further. We also wanted to include an extended community more, but the semester went by so fast and was con-sumed with so many other requirements that we felt we could not push this aspect beyond what happened organically and naturally.

Our suggestions to deal with issues of time:

- *Collaborate with experts in online education.* Finding appropriate educational technology to support online language education and then learning how to use it can be extremely time consuming. Our collaboration with experts in online education design was very helpful.
- *Be creative as to how and when to include IC in activities.* We saw that our limited time in the online synchronous meetings might not always be the best time to include IC. We planned additional activities, such as journal entries, online assessments, and projects in which students were encouraged to reflect on issues of IC. We also allotted a small portion at the end of each synchronous meeting to chat in English. We often used this time to discuss IC-related issues, hoping that students' interest would be piqued and that they would continue to reflect about questions they found intriguing.
- *Revise activities for the following year.* Whenever we felt we missed an oppor-tunity in the current course we planned to integrate it more thoughtfully the next time.
- *Try to find topics that students find interesting.* We clearly saw in our stu-dents' work that they thought most deeply about IC-related topics when they were able to choose the topic themselves. That caused us to think more about how we can give students even more control as to what they investigate and talk about. Adding questions for reflection and helping them develop the necessary skills is certainly easier when they are already interested and engaged in the topic.

Our analysis of student products (e.g. journal entries, webpages, project reports) also led us to reflect on what we felt were the benefits of the online format for our students' development of IC.

# Affordances

One of the most obvious benefits of our online courses were the journal entries we asked students to complete for each module. We felt that they thought quite deeply about IC-related topics from the beginning of their German-learning experience. That led to an understanding that they were not only learning a language but also a way of interacting with people who are part of cultures that are in some ways different from their own. As we encouraged students to compare what they learned to their own context, we feel that they also reflected more on their own contexts.

Although we usually use only German in our German classes, we decided to use the last five to ten minutes in each class to discuss issues in English in our online courses. Although that was a compromise in terms of pedagogy, we felt that these occasions helped us deconstruct certain issues in IC as well as foster an environment of curiosity about cultural issues.

Another positive effect of our focus on facilitating communities in and outside the classroom was the students' understanding that they could use German to gain information from the very beginning in their own environment and not just from German-speaking sources and German-speaking countries.

Our inclusion of more authentic assessments, mostly in the form of integrated performance assessments (IPAs), helped students be more active in deciding the course content. Students, for example, often asked for specific vocabulary that they were interested in using in the given contexts. Therefore, we decided to replace or add to some of the, in our opinion, irrelevant vocabulary in the textbook, and provided vocabulary that the students requested.

The projects in which students could choose their own topic revealed another affordance that we want to explore more in the future. Students were clearly very engaged in that aspect of the course and spent much time researching and analyzing their findings. That opens up a variety of opportunities to implement IC in a more organized and systematic way.

# Future Perspectives

Overall, we came to the conclusion that students in our online courses might have generally gained more insight into IC than in our comparable face-to-face courses, as we provided more guided opportunities for them to reflect on IC from the very beginning. Using the *savoirs* model (Byram, 1997) as the main framework for implementation, and formative assessment of our students' IC development, while drawing from our additional related experience, enabled us to add a variety of opportunities for students to explore IC while learning the language. We thought that the clear time constraint combined with the online format might have caused us to think more deeply about how we can systematically implement IC. We also emphasized the concept of 'community' more, and overall tried to include more authentic language, partly asked for by students. We found that there are many opportunities to help students explore IC in online language and culture courses. However, we will have to continue to revise our activities and assessments in our online as well as face-to-face courses in order to ensure that all students benefit from the curriculum, as we agree with Perry and Pilati (2011) that online teaching can help teachers reflect more deeply on their teaching in order to provide more opportunities for students to interact with the material and, as we would add, with one another.

## Appendix: Samples of Students' Journal Entries

### Sample 1: Eurovision Song Contest

*'Guten Tag,*

According to the contest's website, the Eurovision Song Contest is a televised European singing competition that has run since 1956. Anyone from the European Broadcasting Union can participate in the contest. The competition is supposed to be free from politics but contestants from certain countries occasionally still receive 'boos' from the audience when they take the stage. The winner of the 2014 competition was Conchita Wurst, a contestant aus Österreich who sparked some controversy for the competition when she won as she is transgendered. She delivered a televised message to notably anti-gay Russian President Vladimir Putin after she won, saying, 'I don't know if he is watching this now, but if so, I'll say it: We're unstoppable.' Frau Wurst is the second transgendered winner of the Eurovision Song Contest, the first being Dana International from Israel in 1998.

I feel that it is wonderful that she won and that both the judges and the audience fully accepted her for her talent. I feel that the United States is still years away from something similar happening on an American singing competition such as 'American Idol'. I simply cannot imagine a bearded woman being treated with the same level of respect and acceptance here on a national level. I also feel it was very brave and admirable that Frau Wurst sent that message to Putin. Whether or not he watched the competition, I am sure he received that message one way or another.

Sources: http://www.eurovision.tv/page/history; http://www.huffington-post.com/2014/05/10/beareded-drag-queen-eurovision_n_5302731.html

## Sample 2: Eurovision Song Contest

*'Guten Tag!*

The Eurovision Song Contest or the ESC is an annual song competition that is held among the members of the European Broadcasting Union (EBU) since 1956. The winner of the Eurovision Song Contest of 2014 that held place in Copenhagen, Denmark was 'Conchita Wurst'. Born as a 'he' but now as a 'Sie' geboren aus Gmunden, Österreich. Sie ist 25 Jahre alt. She sang the song 'Rise like a Phoenix' in the finals of this competition making her the only winner among the many European competitors from different countries. My reaction to this is that people should not judge by the appearances, as Conchita Wurst, I believe each person, each single one of us has a 'virtue' that we must take into account and show it to the world if it's necessary. Like Frau Wurst, I want to be a person who can be recognized by the society not only because of what I have/possess but because of the person I am.

## References

Bergmann, J. and Sams, A. (2012) *Flip your Classroom: Reach Every Student in Every Class Every Day.* Eugene, OR: International Society for Technology in Education.

Byram, M. (1997) *Teaching and Assessing Intercultural Communicative Competence.* Clevedon: Multilingual Matters.

Byram, M. (2008) *From Foreign Language Education to Education for Intercultural Citizenship: Essays and Reflections.* Clevedon: Multilingual Matters.

CARLA (2009) Integrated performance assessment (IPA). Minneapolis, MN: Center for Advanced Research on Language Acquisition, University of Minnesota. See www. carla.umn.edu/assessment/vac/CreateUnit/p_2.html (accessed 31 December 2014).

Davies, C. (2014) Conchita Wurst pledges to promote tolerance after jubilant welcome home. *Guardian Online,* 11 May. See www.theguardian.com/tv-and-radio/2014/may/11/conchita-wurst-pledges-to-promote-tolerance (accessed 31 December 2014).

Glisan, E., Adair-Hauck, B., Koda, K., Sandrock, S. and Swender, E. (2003) *ACTFL Integrated Performance Assessment.* Yonkers, NY: American Council on the Teaching of Foreign Languages.

Hislop, G.W. (2009) The inevitability of teaching online. *Computer* 42 (12), 94–96.

Hodges, B. (2009) Ecological pragmatics: Values, dialogical arrays, complexity, and caring. *Pragmatics & Cognition* 17 (3), 628–652.

Holliday, A., Hyde, M. and Kullman, J. (2010) *Intercultural Communication: An Advanced Resource Book for Students.* London: Routledge.

Lave, J. and Wenger, E. (1991) *Situated Learning: Legitimate Peripheral Participation.* Cambridge University Press.

McLoughlin, C. and Lee, M.J. (2010) Personalised and self-regulated learning in the Web 2.0 era: International exemplars of innovative pedagogy using social software. *Australasian Journal of Educational Technology* 26 (1), 28–43.

Means, B., Toyama, Y., Murphy, R., Bakia, M. and Jones, K. (2009) *Evaluation of Evidence-Based Practices in Online Learning: A Meta-Analysis and Review of Online Learning Studies.* Washington, DC: US Department of Education.

Osborn, T.A. (2005) *Teaching World Languages for Social Justice: A Sourcebook of Principles and Practices.* New York: Routledge.

Perry, E.H. and Pilati, M.L. (2011) Online learning. *New Directions for Teaching and Learning* 128, 95–104.

Schmidhuber, J. (n.d.) *Konrad Zuse (1919–1995)*. See http://people.idsia.ch/~juergen/zuse.html (accessed 31 December 2014).

Swender, E. and Duncan, G. (1998) ACTFL performance guidelines for K-12 learners. *Foreign Language Annals* 31 (4), 479–491.

van Lier, L. (2004) *The Ecology and Semiotics of Language Learning: A Sociocultural Perspective.* Amsterdam: Springer.

Wiggins, G. (1990) *The Case for Authentic Assessment.* ERIC Digest No. ED328611. See www.ericdigests.org/pre-9218/case.htm (accessed June 28, 2017).

Wiggins, G.P. (1998) *Educative Assessment: Designing Assessments to Inform and Improve Student Performance.* San Francisco, CA: Jossey-Bass.

Wiggins, G. (2006) Healthier testing made easy: The idea of authentic assessment. *Edutopia*, 3 April. See www.edutopia.org/authentic-assessment-grant-wiggins (accessed September 3, 2006).

Wiggins, G. and McTighe, J. (2006) *Understanding by Design.* Pearson: Merrill Prentice Hall.

# 8 Becoming Interculturally Competent Through Study and Experience Abroad

## Lauren Rommal and Michael Byram

Earlier chapters in this book have focused on 'learners' rather than 'teachers' but teachers too have been and remain learners, continuing to develop their linguistic and cultural competences. In particular, teachers are conscious that in order to develop the intercultural competence (IC) of their learners, they themselves need more than knowledge and skills in and about language. Sometimes they question whether they can teach IC adequately unless they have themselves have had experience in a country where the language they teach is spoken. This is an important issue we cannot enter into here, although responses to this and other 'frequently asked questions' are available in Byram *et al.* (2002).

On the other hand, we should not assume that mere experience of another country equips teachers to teach IC without further ado, and so in this chapter we focus on different modes of experience and what research tells us about them. We shall begin with 'Study Abroad', whereby university students of any subject may spend part of their required period of study in another country at another university. Secondly, we shall turn to the more particular experience of students of languages – many of whom will become teachers – who are encouraged and sometimes required to study or work abroad as a means of developing their linguistic and other relevant competences. Thirdly, this chapter includes the small amount of research on the experience of those who are already language teachers and are given the opportunity of experience in a country where their language is spoken.

The main conclusion of this review will show that there is a need for thorough preparation and follow-up to residence abroad for all types of sojourners and we will address this issue in more depth by considering approaches through workshops and similar activities. Ultimately, all those involved – whether the sojourners themselves, those who finance and administer sojourns or those responsible for language-teaching curricula – need to know how effective residence abroad might be in the development of IC, how change in IC can be measured and how increased IC impacts on how language teachers teach both linguistic competence and IC and the relation between them.

## Study Abroad

Study Abroad is, in the United States as elsewhere, on the increase. More students are taking part each year and, during the last decade, the number of Study Abroad programs has increased more than two-fold, with approximately 223,000 US students abroad in 2009 (Clark *et al.*, 2009: 173). The time spent abroad allows students to continue their studies while experiencing life in another country. They have in principle the support system of their home university and Study Abroad program to help them through the difficulties of culture shock, and this support probably helps to ease the transition into this new experience. Many students describe the experience as life changing, and studying abroad can lead to an increase in students' self-perception of how proficient, approachable and open to intercultural communication they are (Clark *et al.*, 2009: 173). However, while Study Abroad looks impressive on a résumé or curriculum vitae and gives the student a chance to travel and see the world, we have to ask whether it offers more for the developmental growth of the young adult or is not much more than a glorified 'party year' or 'grand tour' in a modern form.

If we take as a starting point the views of those who organize Study Abroad, it is clear from Deardorff's (2004, 2006) work that many but not all university administrators who make considerable efforts to facilitate Study Abroad hope and expect that the outcome will include the development of IC. However, Deardorff found a wide range of definitions and understandings of the concept, and to consider the precise nature of the experience of Study Abroad we need to turn to the work of other researchers.

Stepanovienė (2011) analyzed how frequently exchange students and students from the host country interact and the difficulties present in these interactions. Such difficulties include cultural differences, trouble communicating due to stereotypes, culture shock and politeness differences, and non-verbal communication. Stepanovienė (2011: 60) also noticed that students elect to 'mix with people from their own community rather than interact or communicate with students from other cultural backgrounds'. For although studying abroad offers the chance to immerse oneself in a new culture and language, some students are not quite ready to take the plunge, and have a tendency to create a circle of friends from their own background in the new country (Stepanovienė, 2011: 60). While this may help ease the transition into the new country, it ultimately reduces the benefits of studying abroad

(Geeraert *et al.*, 2014). If American students mostly or only spend time with other American students, their language abilities will not develop as much as they would if they were to spend time with students from the host country, and the same applies *mutatis mutandis* to other nationalities. Spending time with people from a similar cultural background does not give students an opportunity to experience new cultural phenomena and therefore become more interculturally competent, as they work through becoming accustomed to living in a new country. Engle and Engle (2004: 221) state, 'it has become increasingly easy for young American sojourners in foreign countries to live in a comfortably superficial and ultimately unchallenging relationship with their host cultures'.

Engle and Engle (2004) suggest an alternative vision, one which focuses on the effects of a program offering one to two semester Study Abroad experiences with 'complete immersion'. Students take courses exclusively in the target language and sign pledges to state that they will use the target language exclusively during their stay. They are also required to take a course 'designed to aid the cultural integration process' as well as taking part in weekly community service and tandem meetings, and all students are housed with non-English speaking families. These authors use Hammer *et al.*'s (2003) Intercultural Development Inventory (IDI) to define intercultural sensitivity in terms of six stages of developmental evolution which range from an ethnocentric to an ethnorelative world view. They conclude that 'full-year program participants make significantly more progress than others in areas of cultural understanding and cross-cultural communication and that their rate of progress increases significantly in the second term' (Engle & Engle, 2004: 235).

A more recent study of students on a one-year program also used Bennett's Developmental Model of Intercultural Sensitivity (DMIS) and the IDI (Pedersen, 2010). The findings suggest that mere exposure to experience of another country in Study Abroad does not lead to change. Indeed the indications were that there was no significant difference from those who stayed at home:

> Students participating in the year-long study abroad program in this sample did not move along the DMIS, as measured by the IDI, by mere participation in the program (Group 2). In fact, their pre/post change paralleled that of the control group of similar students (those signed up for the same program the following year) who studied at home. (Pedersen, 2010: 76)

As Pedersen points out, these results conflict with previous studies, and he calls therefore for more research. The call has been answered by research in Britain in a study using both quantitative and qualitative data to analyze the change in UK students and non-UK students in a British university psychology department (Lantz, 2014). Also using the IDI and Bennett's DMIS model, Lantz's conclusions support Pedersen from a different perspective:

> The quantitative analysis found that UK and non-UK students in this study started their first year at university at the same developmental stage with most in lower minimisation (91.83). Although generally students reported high levels of intercultural contact over their first two terms at university, there was no significant change in the mean score for either group (90.48) with only about 14% of all students moving up a developmental stage and about one-quarter regressing one or more stages. (Lantz, 2014: 263 – scores here refer to the use of the IDI)

Interestingly, Lantz's data also suggest that intercultural contact can inhibit rather than promote IC. For, despite the 'high levels of contact' noted in the previous quotation, Lantz reports that students referred to 'cultural challenges' which may have led some students to cluster by culture and thus have limited contact. There may be a differentiation by experience but even students with previous intercultural experience had difficulties:

> Cultural challenges (…) may have negatively impacted development particularly for lower scoring students with less experience of cultural diversity although even students with extensive experience with diversity could experience cultural challenges. (Lantz, 2014: 263)

In the light of such research, Vande Berg (2009) argues that the existing 'master narrative', i.e. the underlying and unquestioned assumption that Study Abroad in some sense inevitably leads to change and IC development, is gradually changing and becoming more nuanced:

> Exposure to the new and different is thus a necessary, but not a sufficient, condition for learning: students learn in the new culture through actively engaging, reflecting on, and trying out new hypotheses. Thus the primary goal of learning abroad is not only to learn about, but to have an experience of, another culture. Intercultural learning is developmental, not transformational. (Vande Berg, 2009: S25)

In Europe, the phrase which is often used for 'Study Abroad' is 'the ERASMUS year', alluding to the policy of the European Union over many years to encourage student mobility by providing financial support; the acronym refers of course to the famous scholar, and means European Region Action Scheme for the Mobility of University Students. There has been considerable research on this phenomenon but there is none we can find that deals directly with the development of IC during, or as a consequence of, the ERASMUS experience. Neither do the purposes of the program explicitly include IC, although one of the purposes – to develop a sense of European identity – might be expected to be related to IC.

Research on the ERASMUS experience has often shown that, as with Study Abroad programs, participants have little interaction with host-country students (e.g. Budke, 2008; Papatsiba, 2003), but rather live in their own social group with members from many European countries, the 'ERASMUS cocoon' (Papatsiba, 2003). As an indication of this work we can cite an ethnographic study by Tsoukalas (2008) located in Greece and Sweden, which found a change in identification, but perhaps not the one expected in the ERASMUS program policy:

> While abroad their intensive social life secludes them effectively from the surrounding environment and gives free rein to their internal identity formation process. The resultant sense of belonging is particularistic and exclusive in character. Most ERASMUS students see themselves as special and feel proud of their common status. (Tsoukalas, 2008: 144)

The longer term effect of the experience, whether the identification is sustainable after the end of the ERASMUS experience, remains unclear.

Finally, one recent study has taken up again the issue of the impact of keeping in close contact with people of one's own country. A study of students aged about 17 and spending a year in an exchange program examined the impact of close contact with host-country people and with co-nationals (Geeraert et al., 2014). The authors say that there may be difficulty in transferring findings to different kinds of groups such as university students but their conclusion is nonetheless worth quoting:

> Over time, too much close contact with co-nationals can hinder cultural adjustment and increase stress, implying that having more close contact with host nationals and perhaps other internationals would allow the sojourner to profit more readily from the novel cultural environment. (Geeraert et al., 2014: 94)

## Students of Languages Abroad

Students of languages constitute a particular sub-group of those who have experience abroad. In Britain, there has for many decades been a requirement that such students spend a year in a country of their language, commonly called the 'Year Abroad'. In other European countries this is not a requirement but is nonetheless a widespread phenomenon. Often students become teaching assistants, or 'language assistants', in secondary and sometimes elementary schools, although they may also use the ERASMUS system to study abroad like any other student. Unlike other students, however, a

prime if not the major purpose of their Year Abroad is to develop their linguistic and, though less frequently mentioned, their cultural competence and
knowledge about the language and country.

Some early research on changes in attitudes of such students towards the
people of a country where they spent their Year Abroad demonstrated results
which were 'counter-intuitive' (Coleman, 1996). Where it might be expected
that students of languages would be motivated to interact with speakers of
the language they are studying and become as a consequence more positively
engaged, Coleman's study concluded that 'whatever the target language, the
experience of residence abroad for language students will not necessarily
enhance their view of the target culture, and may well diminish it' (Coleman,
1998: 55). As a consequence of this kind of research, there were attempts to
prepare students more thoroughly for the Year Abroad, *inter alia* by introducing them to principles and methods in ethnography, as we shall see below
(Roberts *et al.*, 2001).

Despite the growing interest in the Year Abroad, research on the development of IC during the Year Abroad has remained limited, although a recent
study addresses the relationship between friendship circles and intercultural
learning (Mitchell, forthcoming). Alred and Byram (2002) discuss the degree
of IC gained by students after the Year Abroad. This study uses Jensen *et al.*'s
(1995: 41) definition of intercultural communication: 'the ability to behave
appropriately in intercultural situations, the affective and cognitive capacity
to establish and maintain intercultural relationships and the ability to stabi-
lise one's self-identity while mediating between cultures.' Similar to
Stepanovienė's (2011) research, Alred and Byram (2002: 342) find that when
students are engulfed in the new reality of the host country and are 'under
pressure to accept their (the host country's) reality', they tend to find a way
to recreate a safe haven of their own, familiar society by socializing with
people from their common cultural background, not unlike the ERASMUS
students mentioned above living in their 'cocoon'. Students who appeared to
have gained the most from their Year Abroad experience had prior experience
with other cultures and languages. The two experiences are 'complementary
and (the) "time abroad" is an opportunity for developing not just attitudes,
but also the social action of the mediator' (Alred & Byram, 2002: 346).

## Teachers of Languages Abroad

In many parts of the world, teachers of languages do not have the opportunity to reside in, or even visit on a short-term basis, a country whose language they teach, before they begin their teaching career. One case study of
a program for teachers of various subjects suggests, however, that such an
opportunity can be very positive, provided there is sufficient preparation and
support for the sojourner (Marx & Moss, 2011).

Sometimes teachers have an opportunity during their career to catch up on what they might have missed, through in-service development workshops, conferences and the like. There is, however, no research that addresses the specific question of if and to what extent such experience has an impact on teachers' own IC, let alone how it might influence their teaching of IC during their career. Such opportunities are usually of brief duration and it might be expected that any impact may be difficult to evaluate.

On the other hand, in one major study, teachers of languages in New Zealand who were given the opportunity to spend a substantial period abroad were studied with respect to their change in language proficiency and IC. They were also asked about their understanding of the concept of IC – a requirement for their ability to teach IC to their own students – and were observed teaching after their sojourn. The evaluation report (Harvey *et al.*, 2011) used Byram's (1997, 2008) model of intercultural communicative competence (ICC) – the model also used in earlier chapters of this book – and found, from questionnaires and interviews that teachers gave, examples of how they were able to improve their knowledge about a country during their sojourn. The authors conclude from analysis of open-ended questions and interviews that:

> The high number of comments identifying the importance of being able to interact and engage in various ways with the local community as much as possible (homestays, socialising, taking part in local activities) would indicate that many of the participants were demonstrating objectives within the subcompetencies (in Byram's model) of 'attitudes' and 'skills of discovery and interaction'. Specifically these objectives are 'willingness to seek out or take up opportunities to engage with otherness … [r]eadiness to experience the different stages of adaptation to and interaction with another culture during a period of residence … [u]se in real-time an appropriate combination of knowledge, skills and attitudes to interact with interlocutors from a different country and culture' (Byram, 2008: 230–232). (Harvey *et al.*, 2011: 68)

Unfortunately and, as the authors say, surprisingly, the impact of the sojourn and teachers' increased IC and understanding of this concept does not correlate with teaching competence, and indeed seemed to show a negative correlation:

> correlation of data showed less understanding of *teaching* IC as *understanding* of IC increased, indicating that teachers were not yet confident in intercultural communicative language teaching (iCLT). Observations confirmed that teachers did not appear to be aware of the various instructional strategies to foster IC. (Harvey *et al.*, 2011, emphasis added)

Although teachers said they felt more confident about 'teaching culture', they continued to treat it as a matter of 'background', and 'focused primarily on the "four Fs": food, fairs, festivities and facts' (Harvey *et al.*, 2011: 92). In order for teachers to make better overall use of their sojourn and in particular see how it might help them in teaching IC, the evaluators recommend more effective preparation and follow-up, and this is an issue of more general concern to which we turn next.

## Preparation and Follow-up, and the Development of Intercultural Competence

Given the major investment of time, money and personal energy and commitment involved in Study Abroad, the Year Abroad and other types of experience, it is somewhat surprising that the notion of preparation, and especially follow-up activities after return to the home environment, has developed only in recent times. Students may have serious difficulties which prevent them from learning from their experience, as Henze (2007), for example, shows. She analyzes the difficulties faced by American students in Germany in regard to the different communication styles, culture and language barriers, and she discusses the training which they can receive in advance. She underlines that adjustment is not 'brainwashing' but rather openness in understanding the new culture, and describes the training as becoming 'aware of one's own culture and understanding the foreign culture' (Henze, 2007: 153). Intercultural training is defined as 'the efforts and methods designed for preparing the participants to interact and communicate successfully and to build interpersonal relationships with people from a different culture by being aware of one's own culture and understanding the foreign culture' (Henze, 2007: 153).

Henze then describes a pre-Study Abroad workshop that can be utilized to give students background knowledge about the culture and offer Study Abroad participants prior knowledge of intercultural communication in order to ease their transition to living abroad. This type of workshop aims to give students the tools to reduce the stress of culture shock and move through Oberg's (1960) stages (honeymoon, crisis, recovery and adjustment) more quickly in order to spend more time as an integrated member of the new culture (Henze, 2007: 154). The workshop assists students in understanding the impact cultural norms have on daily life and offers information about cultural differences which exist between American and German culture. This would lessen the degree of culture shock shown as being one of the major impeding factors in conversing with people in the host country as argued in Stepanoviené's (2011) study. A workshop such as this would also be able to address students' prior conceptions and stereotypes about the host country's people and culture, and allow them to work through these notions before arriving in the host country. However, students would need to possess an open attitude about other cultures and a willingness to work through cultural differences.

To evaluate the efficacy of such preparatory work, Henze (2007) compared questionnaires from 30 students who had attended the pre-Study Abroad workshop and 16 students who had not attended the workshop. The results showed that 17 students in the experimental group felt that they were at present in Oberg's period of 'recovery', and 13 regarded themselves as having already reached the stage of 'adjustment'. In contrast, in the control group, five students felt they were in the period of 'adjustment' and eight students were still in the 'crisis', the actual culture shock. None of them described themselves as having reached the final stage. These are very small numbers and are at best indicative of the effects of such workshops, and the implementation of a pre-Study Abroad workshop would not necessarily be enough to completely eliminate the effects of culture shock on students. Nonetheless, the results from this questionnaire show the workshop would aid students in working through the stages of culture shock more quickly and in reaching a stage where they are better able to understand the new culture and be more interculturally competent. Their attitude towards other cultures would be more accepting, as the workshop leads to an examination of their own culture. The workshop could also include students who had studied abroad in the host country previously, who could act as mentors to answer questions students might have, in addition to acting as living examples of what went 'wrong' during their stays and how future students could avoid the same pitfalls.

Similarly to Henze's idea of a pre-Study Abroad workshop, Lee (2011, 2012) discusses the role of blogging as a method of reducing stereotypes about the host country and as an 'exchange space where students shared and negotiated their understanding of cultural issues through responses with comments' (Lee, 2012: 11). Blogging allows them to 'reflect critically on the content' (Lee, 2012: 8). If the students' blogging is monitored and guided by an instructor, the cultural exchange between students becomes more efficient, as the instructor has the ability to ask questions to encourage reflective thinking and therefore develop a deeper cultural exchange (Lee, 2012: 9). Lee too used Byram's (1997) IC model as well as Bennett's (1993) approach of non-judgmental attitudes and respect to understand cross-cultural perspectives (Lee, 2011: 90, 2012: 8).

In a more substantial preparation specifically for language students, Roberts et al. (2001) trained them for their Year Abroad using elements of ethnography and anthropology. Students were taking a four-year course in French, German or Spanish and were required in their third year to work or study in a country of their language. In fact they went to France, Germany and Spain. In the second year, students were taught – by their language teachers under the guidance of an anthropologist – a course in which they studied both concepts and principles of ethnography and also ethnographic methods, in particular for fieldwork. There were 19 units of work, one per week, with alternative weeks of focus on concepts and principles on the one hand and methods on the other. During their Year Abroad, students wrote an ethnographic report on a social group or event in their environment. Examples included: The Pétanque Club of Aubervilliers; The Nice Carnaval: Who Wants to Become a Carnavalier?; 'Ellbogenschaft': A Study of Assertiveness in Germany; Prostitutes and Identity in Cadiz; ONCE – An Organisation for the Blind (in Spain). Students wrote their reports in their foreign language, which in itself created a complex relationship with their topic and, as they put it, during the Year Abroad they 'lived the ethnographic life'. The materials developed from this course were then made available to all British universities.

## Overcoming obstacles during the development of intercultural competence

In addition to measures which may be taken prior to experience abroad, some researchers have investigated the experience itself and the obstacles which might undermine successful and enjoyable experiences.

Stepanovienė reviews the topics of conversations exchange students had with students from their host country. Overwhelmingly, they chose to talk about basic subject matters which required little cultural knowledge – topics such as their studies, daily greetings and the weather, and cooking. Topics such as families, news and current affairs and sports ranked lowest on the list, as they required a higher level of cultural knowledge in conversation. Language competence did not influence the students' subject matter choices, as 'all the participants had studied English or German for at least 8 years, and before they came to study abroad, had passed the foreign language test that indicated sufficient proficiency in English and German to enable them to deal with the topics listed' (Stepanovienė, 2011: 62). The communication problems stemmed rather from stereotypes and culture shock, both of which need to be overcome before the students are able to move forward in becoming interculturally competent. Byram's (1997) preconditions for successful intercultural interaction include attitudes that value others and put oneself in relation to others, and the willingness to suspend beliefs in both one's own behaviors as well as others' behaviors (Byram, 1997: 34). They also include a knowledge of one's own behaviors as well as those of others and how one group views the other and vice versa. These preconditions need to be met in order for the student to move on to the necessary skills needed for successful intercultural interaction.

Since, as we have seen above, students have a tendency to remain with people from similar cultural backgrounds while abroad, instructors could use this inevitable occurrence in a more positive manner to encourage learning.

Students could be asked to keep blog entries similar to those discussed in Lee's (2012) article. Although Lee's work involved students who remained in their native country and discussed IC and differences in other cultures without actually entering the country themselves, with all contact coming from a partner school in the foreign country, the approach could be applied to students studying abroad. The blogs could be used for students to work through the cultural differences they experience while abroad and help each other understand what is happening and why. By writing down what they are experiencing, students would have the chance to better reflect on the differences they encounter and better make sense of them. Instructors or Study Abroad advisors at the home university would also have the chance to read these entries and give feedback as to why certain events are occurring.

One could go even further and adapt the Study Abroad program shown in Engle and Engle (2004), mentioned above, where students are asked to sign a statement that all communication will be in the target language. In addition to this statement, students are enrolled on a course which has a goal of helping students overcome cultural misunderstandings and live with host families. The course, which lasts for several weeks, is similar to the idea of a pre-Study Abroad workshop, but is more intense and has the ability to address more of the problems which could occur while abroad, and can be altered to better fit the individual students' experiences. Rigorous Study Abroad programs of this kind appear to increase the intercultural communication gained by students, as they are forced to become part of the new culture and cannot rely on their native language and friends or roommates from a similar background.

## Measuring the Effects

We began this chapter with our main question about whether study and other experience abroad leads to increased IC. In this book, the interest in this topic is related to how teachers become interculturally competent as part of feeling that they are equipped to provide for the development of IC in their learners. There is, however, a wider issue as to how study and experience abroad is a valuable and valid source of IC for anyone who has such experience as part of their education. For, after all, there is a major commitment of time and money for individuals and for the education authorities involved. Yet it is surprising, as Deardorff points out with respect to Study Abroad, that 'few (...) institutions have designated methods for specifically documenting and measuring intercultural competence' (Deardorff, 2006: 232).

Deardorff therefore investigates the possible measurement of IC as an outcome from Study Abroad by inviting administrators in 73 post-secondary institutions in the United States to complete an 11-item questionnaire with both closed and open-ended questions to determine how 'that institution addressed intercultural competence as a student outcome' (Deardorff, 2006: 235). Of the 73 invited, 24 institutions responded, ranging from two-year public community colleges to large research universities. They were almost evenly split between public (54%) and private (46%). Of the institutions responding, 38% already measured IC through differing methods including 'student interviews, papers/presentations, student portfolios, observation of students by others/host culture, professor evaluations (in courses), and pre/post tests' (Deardorff, 2006: 240). Deardorff also discussed this with intercultural experts, who agreed that the best way to measure is by utilizing a combination of qualitative and quantitative assessments (Deardorff, 2006: 241).

More recently, Stepanoviené (2011) also sought to measure progress in students' IC. He created a definition of IC which is a hybrid of Knapp's (2001), Damen's (1987), Lustig and Koester's (2003) and Jandt's (2004) definitions: 'intercultural communication describes the interaction between individual and groups with different perceptions of communicative behaviour and differences in interpretations' (Stepanoviené, 2011: 61), and he measured progress with a mixture of closed and open response questions in a questionnaire, together with interviews to obtain more information than the questionnaires could provide.

Researchers have also measured the possible benefits of a short-term Study Abroad, of less than one semester (Gullekson et al., 2011; Jackson, 2011). In Jackson's study, for example, IC was defined using Bennett's DMIS model (Jackson, 2011: 167). She found that there is some increase in the level of IC in Study Abroad experiences as short as two weeks, but the students tended to overrate their increase compared to the degree to which they had really progressed. Jackson believes the presence of pre-Study Abroad preparation can help students gain the most from their Study Abroad experience and inadequate preparation could have negative consequences such as enduring culture shock and negative stereotypes (Jackson, 2011: 183). Gullekson et al. (2011) agree that a short-term Study Abroad program is beneficial in increasing intercultural interaction and attitudes towards 'global awareness' when compared to students who did not study abroad. Global awareness is defined as 'intercultural awareness, personal growth and development, awareness of global interdependence, and functional geography and language' (Gullekson et al., 2011: 94). However, the benefit is not as pronounced as in studies of students who completed a semester or a year Study Abroad.

As a recent example of a different approach to measurement, we can mention the Impact of Living Abroad project (Demes & Geeraert, 2014) which does not refer to IC but to measures of 'adaptation', 'perceived cultural distance' and 'acculturation orientation'. This represents a different tradition and disciplinary approach which seeks to measure psychological change. It contrasts therefore with work that is based on the notion of 'competence', the latter being used as a basis not only for conceptualizing change as a consequence of experience abroad, but also as a link to the field of education and the possibility of teaching IC.

# Conclusion

Language teachers who have had first-hand experience of a country where the language they teach is spoken have undoubtedly a rich fund of knowledge on which they can base their teaching. They can at the very least talk to learners about their experience and provide that personal link to another country which brings it into the learners' own world. Anecdotes are powerful. In a research project which explored over a one-year period how teachers of French in England brought a cultural dimension into their teaching, learners could often repeat anecdotes from teachers they had had two or three years previously. 'What Teacher says' is influential and long-lasting (Byram *et al.*, 1991). On the other hand, that same research demonstrated that, without systematic planning of a cultural dimension in lesson-planning – rather than the inspiration of the moment sparked by some chance reference – there was no measurable impact on learners' understanding of another country and culture. We hope that the systematic teaching presented in earlier chapters of this book will lead to more positive outcomes if adopted over longer periods of time.

The significance of planning, of preparation and follow-up, for making the most of experience abroad in the development of one's own IC has become evident in this chapter. It has become equally clear that teachers need to be aware of their own IC as a basis for their pedagogical work with learners, but that this is not enough, as was shown above by the study in New Zealand (Harvey *et al.*, 2011).

The pedagogical basis for teaching and facilitating the development of IC in language learners is just as important, and just as complex, as the pedagogy of teaching language competence. Experience abroad is crucial but in itself is not enough. There needs to be self-analysis, extension of reflection as to how that experience can be turned into good pedagogy, and a sound training for teachers in how they can draw on their experience for the benefit of their learners. What is most prominent by its absence in the literature we have presented is precisely the training in intercultural experience to enhance intercultural pedagogy. The project on which this book is based is an initial step in filling this gap by bringing together in-service teachers and university students, who draw on whatever sources are available to them, including their own study abroad. It needs to be complemented by language teacher training for pre-service teachers which is grounded in their study abroad, perhaps even taking place in parallel during their sojourn.

# References

Alred, G. and Byram, M. (2002) Becoming an intercultural mediator: A longitudinal study of residence abroad. *Journal of Multilingual and Multicultural Development* 23 (5), 339–352.

Bennett, M. (1993) Towards a developmental model of intercultural sensitivity. In R.M. Paige (ed.) *Education for the Intercultural Experience.* Yarmouth, ME: Intercultural Press.

Budke, A. (2008) Contacts culturels et identités ethniques des étudiants ERASMUS en Allemagne. In F. Dervin and M. Byram (eds) *Échanges et mobilités académiques. Quel bilan?* (pp. 43–64). Paris: L'Harmattan.

Byram, M. (1997) *Teaching and Assessing Intercultural Communicative Competence.* Clevedon: Multilingual Matters.

Byram, M. (2008) *From Foreign Language Education to Education for Intercultural Citizenship: Essays and Reflections.* Clevedon: Multilingual Matters.

Byram, M., Esarte-Sarries, V. and Taylor, S. (1991) *Cultural Studies and Language Learning: A Research Report.* Clevedon: Multilingual Matters.

Byram, M., Gribkova, B. and Starkey, H. (2002) *Developing the Intercultural Dimension in Language Teaching. A Practical Introduction for Teachers.* Strasbourg: Council of Europe. See www.coe.int/t/dg4/linguistic/source/guide_dimintercult_en.pdf (accessed June 28, 2017).

Clarke, I., Flaherty, T.B., Wright, N.D. and McMillen, R.M. (2009) Student intercultural proficiency from Study Abroad programs. *Journal of Marketing Education* 31 (2), 173–181.

Coleman, J.A. (1996) *Studying Language: A Survey. The Proficiency, Background, Attitudes and Motivations of Students of Foreign Languages in the United Kingdom and Europe.* London: Centre for Information on Language Teaching.

Coleman, J.A. (1998) Evolving intercultural perceptions among university language learners in Europe. In M. Byram and M. Fleming (eds) *Language Learning in Intercultural Perspective. Approaches through Drama and Ethnography* (pp. 45–75). Cambridge: Cambridge University Press.

Damen, L. (1987) *Culture Learning: The Fifth Dimension in the Language Classroom.* Reading: Addition-Wesley Publishing Company.

Deardorff, D.K. (2004) The identification and assessment of intercultural competence as a student outcome of internationalization at institutions of higher education in the United States. Unpublished dissertation, North Carolina State University, Raleigh, NC.

Deardorff, D.K. (2006) Assessing intercultural competence in Study Abroad students. In M. Byram and A. Feng (eds) *Living and Studying Abroad: Research and Practice* (pp. 232–256). Clevedon: Multilingual Matters.

Demes, K.A. and Geeraert, N. (2014) Measures matter: Scales for adaptation, cultural distance and acculturation orientation revisited. *Journal of Cross-Cultural Psychology* 45 (1), 91–109.

Engle, L. and Engle, J. (2004) Assessing language acquisition and intercultural sensitivity development in relation to Study Abroad program design. *Frontiers: The Interdisciplinary Journal of Study Abroad* 10, 219–236.

Geeraert, N. and Demes, K. (2012) The impact of living abroad: Research Report. Colchester: University of Essex.

Geereart, N., Demoulin, S. and Demes, K.A. (2014) Choose your (international) contacts wisely: A multilevel analysis on the impact of intergroup contact while living abroad. *International Journal of Intercultural Relations* 38, 86–96.

Gullekson, N.L., Tucker, M.L., Coombs, G.R. and Wright, S.B. (2011) Examining intercultural growth for business students in short-term Study Abroad programs: Too good to be true? *Journal of Teaching in International Business* 22 (2) 91–106.

Harvey, S., Roskvist, A., Corder, D. and Stacey, K. (2011) *An Evaluation of the Language and Culture Immersion Experiences (LCIE) for Teachers Programmes: Their Impact on Teachers and Their Contribution to Effective Second Language Learning.* Wellington: Ministry of Education. See www.educationcounts.govt.nz/publications/ (accessed July 2014).

Henze, Y.A. (2007) A model for intercultural training for Study Abroad in Germany. *Unterrichtspraxis/Teaching German* 40 (2), 153–163.

Jackson, J. (2011) Host language proficiency, intercultural sensitivity, and Study Abroad. *Frontiers: The Interdisciplinary Journal of Study Abroad* 21, 167–188.

Jandt, F.E. (2004) *An Introduction to Intercultural Communication: Identities in a Global Community.* London: Sage.

Jensen, A.A., Jaeger, K. and Lorentsen, A. (eds) (1995) *Intercultural Competence: A New Challenge for Language Teachers and Trainers in Europe.* Aalborg: Aalborg University Press.

Knapp, K. (2001) *Conceptual Issues in Analyzing Intercultural Communication.* Oxford.

Lantz, C.C. (2014) Exploring the intercultural development of first year UK and non-UK psychology students. Unpublished PhD thesis, University of York.

Lee, L. (2011) Blogging: Promoting learner autonomy and intercultural competence through Study Abroad. *Language Learning and Technology* 15 (3), 87–109.

Lee, L. (2012) Engaging Study Abroad students in intercultural learning through blogging and ethnographic interviews. *Foreign Language Annals* 45 (1), 7–21.

Lustig, M.W. and Koester, J. (2003) *Intercultural Competence: Interpersonal Communication Across Cultures.* Boston.

Marx, H. and Moss, D.M. (2011) Please mind the culture gap: Intercultural development during a teacher education study abroad program. *Journal of Teacher Education* 62 (1), 35–47.

Mitchell, R. (forthcoming) 'The real France': Friendship and intercultural learning during residence abroad.

Oberg, K. (1960) 'Culture shock: adjustment to new cultural environments.' *Practical Anthropology* 7, 177–182.

Papatsiba, V. (2003) *Des étudiants européens. Erasmus et l'aventure de l'altérité.* Bern: Peter Lang.

Pedersen, P.J. (2010) Assessing intercultural effectiveness outcomes in a year-long Study Abroad program. *International Journal of Intercultural Relations* 34 (1), 70–80.

Roberts, C., Barro, A., Byram, M., Jordan, S. and Street, B. (2001) *Language Learners as Ethnographers. Introducing Cultural Processes into Advanced Language Learning.* Clevedon: Multilingual Matters.

Stepanovienė, A. (2011) Exchange students' experiences in intercultural communication. *Kalbų Studijos/Studies about Languages* 18, 61–65.

Tsoukalas, I. (2008) The double life of Erasmus students. In M. Byram and F. Dervin (eds) *Students, Staff and Academic Mobility in Higher Education* (pp. 131–145). Newcastle: Cambridge Scholars.

Vande Berg, M. (2009) Intervening in student learning abroad: A research-based inquiry. *Intercultural Education* 20 (supp. 1), S15–S27.

# Conclusion

## Rita Oleksak, Manuela Wagner, Dorie Conlon Perugini and Michael Byram

In the past eight chapters, we hope we have taken you on a trip showing how a group of language educators collaborated in order to integrate intercultural competence (IC) in language education in a meaningful and systematic way. Throughout the book we reported on our activities as a group in order to: (1) learn about IC; (2) collaborate to modify units to integrate IC in a systematic way; (3) implement the units in the classrooms; and (4) reflect on the implementation. We would like to emphasize that we intentionally added sections in each chapter in which we described challenges that arose in any of the phases. We do not only consider challenges unavoidable in a collaborative project, but we welcome them as opportunities to learn more about ourselves, processes of collaboration and the subject matters involved.

We would be remiss if we did not mention that in our project, as in any human endeavor, there were some combinations of participants' personal and professional situations which worked well and others which worked less well. We had discussed possible causes for concern at the outset and decided that we would like to foster an open environment in which everyone could voice their concerns. For example, different expectations of what students can do at various levels and how the project should therefore be planned and implemented, conflicting schedules and availabilities during different times of the project, and resulting perceived asymmetries of time spent on the project, as well as lack of experience in one context or another can potentially lead to misunderstandings. We were also aware that there could be issues of perceived differences of 'power'. For example, graduate students might feel as though they could not contribute as much with regard to the practical aspects of teaching younger students due to lack of experience, while teachers might feel that their opinion did not carry as much weight in discussions of theories. Our goal was to create a democratic community in which everyone's contribution was taken seriously and in which we willingly learned with and from each other. We hoped and mostly confirmed that if all participants were committed to communicating with each other, any challenge could become an opportunity to grow as individuals and/or as a community. We feel that we (meaning the whole community of practice) were successful in creating a community, in that in most cases participants were well able to work through any issues that arose themselves or with some mediation on the part of another member of the community. As a result, even participants with perceived and reported misunderstandings were able to conclude the project, leading to the development and implementation of new ideas described in the preceding chapters.

In summary, our lesson learned is that it is crucial to know that conflicts can arise in any situation in which colleagues collaborate. However, in our opinion, it is not possible nor desirable to try to make recommendations about how to resolve problems because they occur in a specific contexts and require customized attention and solutions. We consider ourselves fortunate to have worked with such a competent and committed group of colleagues.

The next and last section of this book is written by Rita Oleksak, Director of Foreign Language and English Language Learning in the Glastonbury Public School District, without whose support and encouragement this project would not have been possible. We feel that her perspective will be helpful for administrators who intend to implement a similar project in their own context.

# Glastonbury Public Schools' Intercultural Competence Definition

> Intercultural competence is not about knowing everything about another culture but rather recognizing cultural nuances and being able to adapt/ understand without judgment. It is understanding that culture is a very complex and changing concept and you cannot look at it just from the surface. It is not about answers, but rather the questions that are generated by curiosity and observation. (Comenale & Campbell, 2013)

Who would have thought this is where we would have ended up? What an amazing journey it has been since 29 April 2009 when Glastonbury was notified that we had been awarded a five-year Foreign Language Assistant Program (FLAP) grant. Christine L. Brown (former Glastonbury Public Schools' Assistant Superintendent for curriculum and instruction) and I immediately began to create a list of potential 'Glasport' task force members who would counsel, advise and think outside the box as we moved forward on our ambitious journey to aid in the development of national assessment tools that would help to improve the articulation of curriculum and instruction over time from elementary to high school to higher education.

Glastonbury Public Schools has had a longstanding partnership with the University of Connecticut's (UConn) Department of Literatures, Cultures and Languages, in particular with Dr Manuela Wagner (Associate Professor of foreign language education) and Barbara Lindsey (then Director of the Multimedia Language Center). The Glasport task force convened twice a year as a think tank, dealing with some very theoretical issues around meta-cognition, IC and reflective judgment. From the beginning, Manuela always tried to steer the task force in the direction of taking a closer look at Dr Michael (Mike) Byram's accumulated works on IC. Mike is a noted educator from the UK and author of *From Foreign Language Education to Education for Intercultural Citizenship*. Manuela patiently, and consistently, reminded us of the different factors pertaining to IC and encouraged task force members to read Mike's work. As language educators know, a student needs far more than linguistic skills to maneuver appropriately in the target culture. Before the end of our time together, Mike came to UConn and Glastonbury where we were guided by his expertise and, with his permission, the task force developed the rubric needed to guide future development for our 'Glasport' prompt.

The task force was keenly aware that the study of a foreign language has 'collateral benefits' and this concept was discussed/addressed many times during our task force meetings. What are students gaining from the study of another language besides the ability to communicate? What kinds of adjustments is the brain making when a student studies multiple foreign languages? Does the study of another language affect a student's ability to think critically? How does learning a second language make the student a global citizen? These questions provided many hours of meaningful and thoughtful dialog among task force members. In turn, this enabled the Glastonbury Public Schools' task force committee to consider three constructs that we could possibly assess and perhaps, with a thoughtfully crafted rubric, measure as well: metacognitive awareness, reflective judgment and IC.

## Why Should Something Like This Happen?

Opportunities for teachers to gather around a topic of professional interest have great possibilities for spearheading new thinking and future initiatives within a languages department. Bringing teachers together within a progressive school district which has a strong exchange program, while working alongside a diverse group of UConn students on a topic of mutual interest, was the seed to develop a garden of new thinking. As part of our professional partnership, the opportunity to offer a course on IC for a cohort group of Glastonbury teachers in town was very exciting. Each teacher came to the course from a different place in their educational thinking but left the class having grown tremendously from their first in-depth exposure to IC and Mike Byram's work. They were self-motivated people who worked together in an effort to bridge theory and practice.

Well-established teachers often look for ways to continue to improve their teaching by expanding their learning. Glastonbury's teachers fully embrace an embedded model of teaching language in culturally appropriate contexts and the IC course was the next natural step for teachers who wanted to revise and expand their curriculum, looking for ways to make it more authentic. As Foreign Language Director, I have always encouraged teachers to be innovative and to take risks with their teaching and learning. I was able to provide these teachers with the opportunity to revisit units/ lessons and work specifically to make them more interculturally competent by speaking to components of Mike Byram's rubric where attitudes and beliefs became an integral part of the lessons. As a result, teachers now think about their teaching differently.

## What Needs to Be in Place?

Glastonbury is fortunate in having a large foreign/world language staff and many of them are in the group that I would call ten-percenters. They are the ones who love to think outside the box. They are always taking risks to improve their teaching and learning while engaging and empowering students to fully develop themselves in order to become college- and career-ready global citizens. The Glastonbury Public Schools has had a long history of accepting the challenge, when invited, to pilot new opportunities in areas of curriculum, instruction and assessment. The semester-long Intercultural Competence Course whetted the teachers' appetite for more learning. When I sent an inquiry email to the teachers who had participated in the course, in order to discern who might be interested in continuing along this learning journey and partnering with UConn students to look at a specific unit of study in order to make it more interculturally competent, I had several volunteers come forward immediately, dispersed throughout the K-12 curriculum.

## Lessons Learned for Colleagues?

There is much to be said for intrinsic motivation! Teachers came together around a topic of mutual interest. They represented the K-12 spectrum and were motivated by a genuine interest to move forward in their understanding and knowledge of what motivates people and how people think and reflect. Working alongside UConn graduate students, teachers and students needed a lot of give and take in their conversations and thinking. Everyone in the project was busy – busy professional lives; busy educational lives; busy personal lives. The ebb and flow of the time and tasks to be completed was often challenging. Each group set up times to meet, either in person or virtually. Each group had different issues to work through. A Glastonbury foreign language teacher and 'Glasport' task force member, Dorie Conlon Perugini, worked with Manuela and Mike to encourage and support the class members as the coursework unfolded into the heart of the teachers' classrooms and then as the transformation was captured on paper. This was not a project for the faint of heart! And nothing has been said yet about the deep thinking that took place. Project participants had to wrap their heads around some very deep ideas around knowledge, attitudes, skills and ways of interpreting in Byram's model.

## Outcomes and Advantages for the Program?

The outcomes have been amazing! The teachers and UConn students have come together to produce a significant collection of stories to share with colleagues. What great examples for a 'train the trainer model'! To think that this all happened in such a short time is truly amazing. IC continues to be one of Glastonbury's optional student learning objectives that foreign language teachers might choose to work on as they set out to help students see the world with a different pair of lenses. Seeds of opportunity exist throughout our foreign language curriculum and teachers embrace the professional time and support to take risks as they review their units and ponder what it really means to become more interculturally competent.

K-16 partnerships are invaluable in an effort to build college- and career-ready students who embrace a global perspective. This is so important in a program like Glastonbury's where culture is an integral part of each and every unit and lesson. Manuela, Dorie and Mike, as editors, worked closely with the authors (teachers and UConn students) throughout the entire process. They were not micromanagers and respected each person as a professional, providing a safety net and lots of encouragement to ensure that each story was shared as the authors envisioned. This kind of supported model is what we want for all of our students, allowing extended opportunities for lifelong learning.

## Reference

Comenale, R. and Campbell, L. (2013) Unpublished official Glastonbury Public Schools Foreign Language Department Position Statement on Intercultural Competence, developed during ICC Workshop with Manuela Wagner.

# Glossary of Terms

**ACTFL (American Council on the Teaching of Foreign Languages)** is an individual membership organization of more than 12,500 language educators and administrators from elementary through graduate education, as well as government and industry. Its mission is to provide vision, leadership and support for quality teaching and learning of languages (from ACTFL's website).

**Community of practice** consists of 'groups of people who share a concern or a passion for something they do and learn how to do it better as they interact regularly'. See Wenger, E. (2011) Communities of practice: A brief introduction. Available at: https://www.vpit.ualberta.ca/cop/doc/wenger.doc.

**DMIS (Developmental Model of Intercultural Sensitivity)** is a framework developed by Milton J. Bennett designed to explain how people at different stages perceive cultural difference. See **Ethnocentric** and **Ethnorelative**.

**Enduring understandings** are statements that summarize what was learned in a unit that have lasting value beyond the immediate classroom use.

**ERASMUS Year** is a phrase often used in Europe for 'Study Abroad', alluding to the policy of the European Union over many years to encourage student mobility by providing financial support; the acronym refers of course to the famous scholar, and refers to the European Region Action Scheme for the Mobility of University Students (see p. 158).

**Essential questions** are 'questions that are not answerable with finality in a brief sentence ... Their aim is to stimulate thought, to provoke inquiry, and to spark more questions – including thoughtful student questions – not just pat answers'. See Wiggins, G. and McTighe, J. (2005) *Understanding by Design* (expanded 2nd edn). Alexandria, VA: Association for Supervision and Curriculum Development.

**Ethnocentric** is a view which assumes that 'the worldview of one's own culture is central to all reality'. See Bennett, M.J. (1993) Towards ethnorelativism: A developmental model of intercultural sensitivity. In R.M. Paige (ed.) *Education for the Intercultural Experience* (2nd edn) (p. 30). Yarmouth, ME: Intercultural Press.

**Ethnorelative** is the idea that 'cultures can only be understood relative to one another, and that particular behavior can only be understood within a cultural context'. See Bennett, M.J. (1993) Towards ethnorelativism: A developmental model of intercultural sensitivity. In R.M. Paige (ed.) *Education for the Intercultural Experience* (2nd edn) (p. 46). Yarmouth, ME: Intercultural Press.

**FLES (Foreign Language in the Elementary School)** is a term used to describe K-5, or up to K-8, foreign language programs in the United States.

**Glasport** is a task force assembled by the Glastonbury Public Schools Foreign Language Department in 2011 with the objective of developing alternative assessments for world language instruction.

**IC (Intercultural competence)** (see p. 1).

**ICC (Intercultural communicative competence)** (see p. 161).

**Intercultural Mediation** is the process of intercultural speakers acting as mediators between people of different cultures.

**IPA (Integrated Performance Assessment)** is a cluster assessment featuring three tasks, each of which reflects one of the three modes of communication: Interpretive, Interpersonal and Presentational. The three tasks are aligned within a single theme or content area, reflecting the manner in which students naturally acquire and use the language in the real world or the classroom. Each task provides the information and elicits the linguistic interaction that is necessary for students to complete the subsequent task. Definition from Center for Advanced Research on Language Acquisition (http://carla.umn.edu/assessment/vac/CreateUnit/p_2.html, accessed June 22, 2017).

**Model, e.g. Byram's model,** is a means of identifying the principal elements of intercultural competence as they might be useful for foreign language teachers. It explicitly focuses on elements which were considered at the time – and still are today – as feasible teaching objectives for language teachers who had already accepted the principles of 'communicative language teaching'. It deliberately excluded elements of non-verbal communication, not because they are unimportant – for they are very important – but because they would be, and probably still are, beyond what foreign language teachers can envisage within the constraints of ordinary classrooms (see p. 6).

**Social justice** is '… a philosophy, an approach, and actions that embody treating all people with fairness, respect, dignity and generosity'. See Nieto, S. and Bode, P. (2008) *Affirming Diversity: The Sociopolitical Context of Multicultural Education* (5th edn) (p. 11). Boston, MA: Pearson Education.

**Systematic implementation** is the idea that IC must be intentionally included and carefully planned into the foreign language curriculum. This is in contrast to the belief that IC is inherent to the foreign language curriculum and IC will be developed regardless of the teachers' intentions.

**Target language** is the language a course is designed to teach (e.g. Spanish is the target language of a Spanish class).

# Index